Chaucer's Ovidian Arts of Love

haucer's Ovidian Arts of Love

Michael A. Calabrese

University Press of Florida
Gainesville Tallahassee Tampa
Boca Raton Pensacola Orlando
Miami Jacksonville

Library of Congress Cataloging-in-Publication Data

Calabrese, Michael A.
Chaucer's Ovidian arts of love / by Michael A. Calabrese
    p.   cm.
Includes bibliographical references and index.
ISBN 0-8130-1301-1 (acid-free paper)
1. Chaucer, Geoffrey, d. 1400—Criticism and interpretation
2. Love poetry, English (Middle)—History and criticism.
3. Chaucer, Geoffrey, d. 1400. Troilus and Criseyde. 4.
Chaucer, Geoffrey, d. 1400—Knowledge—Literature. 5.
Troilus (Legendary character) in literature. 6. Ovid, 43
B.C.–17 or 18 A.D.—Influence. 7. English poetry—Roman
influences. 8. Trojan War in literature. 9. Love in literature.
I. Title.
PR1933.L6C35   1994
821'.1—dc20   94-8387

The University Press of Florida is the scholarly
publishing agency for the State University System of
Florida, comprised of Florida A & M University,
Florida Atlantic University, Florida International
University, Florida State University, University of
Central Florida, University of Florida, University of
North Florida, University of South Florida, and
University of West Florida.

University Press of Florida
15 Northwest 15th Street
Gainesville, FL 32611

For my sister Mary Ann, a *bon vivant*,
my brother Joe, and for our parents,
Orlando and Beatrice Calabrese

Contents

Acknowledgments

OR GUIDANCE and for detailed help in the preparation of this book, I have many people to thank. At the University of Virginia Mark Morford worked with me on much of the trickier Latin. A. C. Spearing read many drafts of the chapters and provided much-appreciated suggestions and valued support. Barbara Nolan, my teacher and mentor for the past ten years and one of the finest Ovidian scholars in the world, has guided me with care and with wisdom. Hoyt Duggan, my own Dr. Johnson, taught me much about craft and low cunning. This great and generous man has never failed me as a friend and model. I also thank my brilliant friends and colleagues, James Berger, James Hurley, Tom Helscher, Greg Roper, Michael Uebel, and Dennis Swaim, who supported me with faith and created an inspiring and impassioned critical environment during our time as graduate students. While a student at Columbia University I lived with a host of great men, and all are still my brothers: Darius Sollohub, David Rosenberg Korish, Lou Tilmont, Paul Pesce, Gideon Besson, and Simon Black.

At the University of West Florida, where I completed this book, several colleagues read chapters and looked over material. I offer my thanks to Allen Josephs, Gregory Lanier, Cynthia Smith, and Philip Momberger, my great friend and noble chairman, who guided me in all matters of thought and life. My friend Eric Eliason of Gustavus Adolphus College read the manuscript and has always been my closest colleague and loyal brother. I must also thank Pat Salem, for carefully preparing the manuscript for publication, and the editors at the University Press of Florida, Barbara O'Neil Phillips and Michael Senecal, for their expert and kind help. I offer deep thanks to editor-in-chief Walda Metcalf for her wise guidance and support. Marilyn Sparks at Whitman College provided invaluable checks while I proofread the final proofs. Errors of any kind that remain are my responsibility.

Several scholars in the Ovidian and Chaucerian communities have likewise offered reactions, commentary, and encouragement on parts of the book, and I thank Peter Allen, Carolyn Dinshaw, and Ralph Hexter, whose book on Ovid was inspirational and indispensable to me. My final note of professional gratitude must go to my great teacher and friend at Columbia University, Robert W. Hanning, who made me a medievalist and has closely followed and sustained my education and development.

This book is humbly dedicated to my family, and I must also mention with reverence my grandfather Angelo Michael LoRusso, who emigrated from Avigliano, Italy, to the United States in 1906 at the age of nineteen and died in 1970. He could neither read nor write English or Italian, until my father taught him to write his name when he was sixty-one.

A note on translations: Sources for translations used are indicated in the text and notes. Where no citations are given the translations are mine. I have translated all the Latin.

Introduction
Chaucer's Ovidian Arts of Love

 EARLY six hundred years ago the French court poet
Deschamps hailed Chaucer in a poem of praise as
"Ovides grans en ta poëterie" [a great Ovid in {his}
poetry].[1] Perhaps Deschamps saw that Chaucer read
Ovid by day, studied him by night, and rewrote him
in between. Ovid is Chaucer's favorite poet, the one
to whom he is closest in spirit and to whom he refers
by name more than any other literary authority.
Chaucer is, in many ways, the "medieval Ovid."

That formulation may sound stark, and I assure
the reader that evidence is on the way. The conjunc-
tion of Ovid with a medieval poet, however, should
come as no surprise. No other classical author ex-
erted so great an influence on medieval literature,
and he is evoked in medieval works of all kinds from
all periods. Ovid takes his place in a spectrum of
medieval texts in any number of guises: noble *auctor*
of history, doctor of love, father of antifeminist lore,
advocate of female power, prophet of mutability, and,
at times, dreaded corrupter of youth and peer of Satan.[2] The Roman poet provides medieval authors
with literary models, mythic characters, and all sorts
of wit, wisdom, and doctrine. Because of his vast and
complex medieval identity, Ovid becomes for the
medieval poet much more than just a source for history, myth, and bawdy seduction. He becomes a philosopher and scholar, someone to imitate, cite, or

1

combat, depending on the ethical demands of the medieval poet's text.

Were we to survey the world of medieval European authors, particularly those writing of love, we would find that they all must at some point confront Ovid: vernacular authors such as Chrétien, Marie, Boccaccio, Jean de Meun, Gower, and Christine de Pizan; scholastics such as Andreas Capellanus; theologians such as William of St. Thierry; logician-lovers such as Abelard; and abbesses such as Heloise, to say nothing of the many nameless schoolmasters glossing texts for daily study. Often we can read not only the poetic artistry of a medieval work but also its moral universe by "reading its Ovid." If we can find how the author treats Ovid, we have found how he or she treats love. Ovid was that popular, that prominent, that complex, and is, therefore, that important for the modern reader seeking to understand what is at stake in a medieval love text.[3]

Accordingly, Ovid appears—and will continue to appear—ubiquitously in modern scholarship. Contemporary critics in various branches of medieval studies have, especially in the past few years, developed our apprehension of Ovid's many roles in a host of texts and contexts, trying to assess his immeasurable influence upon Western literature and thought. We see him in studies not only of love poetry but also of rhetoric, critical theory, lovesickness, witchcraft, and homosexuality. Never before has it been so clear that Ovid indispensably aids almost any critical attempt to understand the complexity and diversity of medieval reactions to history, to literature, and to human expressions of desire.[4] In particular, I think it will become increasingly clear that we will have to turn again and again to Ovid as we study the gender/power relations that underlie love doctrine in medieval texts. Ovid is the father of medieval "sexual poetics," and to understand those poetics, we have to know him.[5]

Fortunately, we have seen a powerful effort in recent years to make fresh and well-wrought translations of Ovid's poems available to modern readers. Two translations of the *Heroides* appeared in 1991, one by poet David Hine, the other, in the Penguin Classics series, by Harold Isbells. Peter Green and A. D. Melville have offered new translations of Ovid's *Erotic Poems*, and David Slavitt has made some of the most neglected works of Ovid available in his translation of the poems of exile. In those poems Ovid appears not as the doctor of love or the prophet of change, but as the man of many sorrows, singing the woes of his banishment. As we contemplate Ovid's modern popularity we see that he was right when he boasted in the final line of his great epic poem on mutability: "vivam" [I will live].[6]

The demand and the need for Ovid are clear. However, his role in medieval literature and culture needs clarification, for the identity and function of classical authors in the Middle Ages differ dramatically from modern conceptions of literature and authorship. When I say "Ovid" I do mean the same, the classical poet available to modern readers in the parallel pages of the Loeb Classical Library and in the lively modern translations I have mentioned. However, when approaching Ovid as an influence on medieval authors, in our case a vernacular English poet, we must be aware of what "Ovid" meant in the Middle Ages. "Ovid" was not only the poet's own primary texts, which were schoolbooks in Chaucer's time, but also the copious glosses, categorizations, moralizations, and allegorizations that introduce or literally surround the words of any medieval text by an *auctor.* John Fyler, author of *Chaucer and Ovid,* writes that "Chaucer took his Ovid straight." In this fine phrase Fyler helps us to see that Chaucer was not drearily bound to inherited Christian allegorizations of Ovid's poems. So much is true. Yet we must not dismiss medieval commentary so quickly, for to do so can lead us to misrepresent Chaucer's reception of Ovid's texts.[7] Chaucer did not take—and could not have taken—Ovid "straight." Granted, the tradition of school commentary is not known for its artistry or liveliness, and so we can see why critics have sometimes neglected it. But this tradition does give us some of the vocabulary with which Chaucer read his Ovid, a vocabulary that helps us understand "Ovid" in the late fourteenth century.

Chaucer's interest in rhetoric and love is rooted, therefore, not only in the actual texts of Ovid but also in the commentaries on them.[8] The invaluable editorial work of (among others) Alton, Ghisalberti, Huygens, Stroh, Coulson, and most recently Hexter has made it possible for us to reconstruct how Ovid appeared in the medieval schoolroom and how the presentation of Ovidian texts developed over the centuries of the Middle Ages.[9] For instance, in tracing the evolution of medieval "biographies" of Ovid, Ghisalberti tells us how the work and life of Ovid appeared in the late fourteenth century. By emphasizing these medieval Latin *vitae,* I do not mean, however, to exclude the other most important filter for Chaucer's reception of Ovid—other Ovidian poems written by vernacular poets. We know that Jean de Meun's encyclopedic art of love, the *Roman de la Rose,* so often directly derived from Ovid, mediates Chaucer's relationship with the classical doctor, and the Ovidian Boccaccio too is never far in the background.[10] Chaucer's Ovid, then, is this "medieval Ovid," this extending web of scholastic and poetic texts, treatments, and testimonies. As we study Chaucer's sources we must try to recreate, albeit imperfectly, Chaucer's elusive, protean Ovid.

Mine is not the first book to connect Chaucer with Ovid. Ever since Dryden compared the two, Ovid has been recognized as a major influence on his medieval counterpart.[11] Perceiving such a comparison to be apt and fruitful, modern critics, including such noted medievalists as Fyler and Winthrop Wetherbee, have been sensitive to Chaucer's use of Ovid in individual passages and as part of his skeptical poetic sensibility in general. We have learned that Chaucer was, like Ovid, a poet of "flux" and metamorphosis.

Both, too, are poets of rhetoric, studying ways in which language invents reality.[12] Ovid weaves story and game, and he eschews the prophetic, Virgilian strains of authority. Chaucer exercises this same disinterestedness as he creates rhetorician-characters and his own narrative personae. As Richard Lanham puts the matter in his seminal study of the two poets, "Chaucer conceived the self in rhetorical rather than serious terms."[13] Steeped in Ovidian rhetoricity, Chaucer and his creations enjoy and often profit from its power. Ultimately, however, they must also face its limitations; they must learn what words can and cannot do.

Concerning love, Chaucer's apprehension of Ovid was broad and deep. One need only look as far as the Wife of Bath's *Prologue* to see the rich presence of Ovid in Chaucer's poetry. The Wife adopts and shapes explicitly Ovidian love doctrine in her martial marital arts. She tells a story from the *Metamorphoses*, and her fifth husband, Jankyn, has a copy of the *Art of Love* in his antifeminist anthology. Put another way, the Wife uses Ovid as both model and source, and her husband reads Ovid as an *auctor*. Certainly, something catalytic is going on here between Ovid and Chaucer. Any reader of the two poets "feels" this. But when we look closely, we not only feel their shared spirit; more important, we see Chaucer's specific and sustained effort to confront Ovid and to study human desire and Christian doctrine in relation to Ovid's arts of love.

How else does Chaucer actualize his fascination with Ovid? Perhaps no other classical poet had given voice to gender as Ovid had in the *Heroides*—letters by scorned women recounting their own stories, as opposed to the traditional truths of classical, mythic *his*tory. This achievement alone would have had a powerful impact on medieval literature, as it did on the *Legend of Good Women* and on Heloise in her letters to Abelard and Criseyde in her discourse with Troilus. Ovid gave voice to those women silenced by tradition, gave expression to their desires that had been crushed by the ever-turning wheel of fate and history. We can say, in fact, that the gendering of power is one of Ovid's greatest themes in the *Heroides*, in the arts of love, and also in the *Metamorphoses*. Ovid provided Chaucer, then, with a series of studies of gendered discourse and identity. Chaucer turns to Ovid as he creates his own voices of gendered power and shapes his own, medieval Christian "arts of love." As Chaucerians continue to try to come to terms with Chaucer's "ethical" and "sexual poetics," a consideration of Ovid, both in his original texts and in his various medieval scholastic and poetic manifestations, will help us understand how Chaucer himself saw these issues and conflicts.

Ovid's contribution to the history of sexuality is enormous and profound for Chaucer and for all of Western literature. But Ovid supplied even more to his progeny. He offers voices of desire and psychological studies of seduction, sex, and lovesickness, but he also tells his own life story, the thrilling drama of a love poet thrust into exile by the oppressive censorship of an unyielding emperor. It is the stuff of fiction—for Ovid himself, for Chaucer, and for us.[14]

These poems of exile, by far the most neglected part of Ovid's corpus today, constitute not an end to Ovid's imaginative faculty but a focusing of his art into what some scholars have called the poetics of exile. Chaucer knew these poems because medieval schoolmasters and authors read and glossed them in the context of Ovid's entire biography, the medieval vita, the forerunner of the *Norton Anthology* headnote. Medieval readers all committed what we might now call an intentional fallacy when reading classical authors, for they sought to understand the specific personal circumstances that had produced the given work.

It is the entire corpus of Ovid, then, that Chaucer embraces as he studies love and defines his own role as a love poet. The overall shape of Ovid's tragic career, from the playful games of the *Ars Amatoria* to the bitter exile of the *Tristia* and the *Ex Ponto,* has not yet been brought to bear upon Chaucer's poems or upon his views of his own life as a poet. We have not thoroughly exploited the varied relations between the two poets because we have never fully examined how Chaucer's characters, and Chaucer himself, explore the power and limitations of Ovidian imagination in their artistic and moral lives. Chaucer knew Ovid's poetry and knew his struggles with art, audience, and exile. Studying the two poets teaches us something about Chaucer's relations to his readers, to fiction, to his God, and, ultimately, to his own death. Chaucer, like Ovid, saw himself as vulnerable to the misunderstanding and woe that can befall a maker of fictions. In the context of Chaucer's comprehensive knowledge and use of Ovidian material, Deschamps's vision of him as "a great Ovid" may be a clue to the way Chaucer himself understood his poetic career. Like Ovid, Chaucer explores both the delights and the dangers of being a "servant of the servants of love."

In the chapters that follow, my approach is for the most part threefold: first, to look at Chaucer's uses of Ovid in individual passages and throughout a given poem to see how he plays one Ovidian text against another;

second, to evaluate how Chaucer may have received and perceived these texts of Ovid through medieval scholastic or poetic works; third, to trace Ovid's civic perils—as told in the *Tristia* and discussed in medieval commentary—when they can provide a context for Chaucer's own explorations of the relations between art and life. These strategies are by no means mutually exclusive, and a brief outline will show how the chapters relate to one another.

Chapter 1 is an attempt to recreate "Chaucer's Ovid" by recounting medieval biographical data on Ovid and indicating the depth of the medieval reader's knowledge of and interest in Ovid's life and work. Chapters 2 and 3 trace the role of Ovidian art and the play of Ovidian texts in the *Troilus*.[15] Chaucer's Greek and Trojan characters did not, of course, read Ovid, who was not to be born for a thousand years. Nor do they magically conceive themselves to be reading Ovid. Rather, they act with the "wisdom" of an Ovidian perspective. They trap themselves and each other in a literal reading of Ovid's love poems, which constitutes a naive, destructive misreading of experience. As we see at the end of the poem, Chaucer dramatizes in the *Troilus* a struggle that ultimately is seen in light of the "Word" beyond rhetoricity and beyond Ovidianism, which had been up to that point the driving force of discourse and identity in the poem.

Chaucer's use of the later, darker poems of Ovid, the *Metamorphoses* and the poems of exile, serves as a prelude to this Christian palinode. To illustrate this progression, I study the relations between the *Troilus*, particularly the final two books, and the *Tristia*. I compare the literary career of Ovid and the romantic life of Troilus, both of whom face, in ways that Boccaccio's Troilo does not, types of "exile" because of their involvement with the *Ars Amatoria*. The clash of Ovidian texts and perspectives against one another and against the divine generates the drama in this grand, stately Chaucerian art of love.

Chapter 4 is a study of the *Wife of Bath's Prologue and Tale*, in which Chaucer creates a character who is, like Ovid, a master of "experience."[16] As the Wife and her husband, Jankyn the clerk, do marital battle, they turn, like many characters in the *Troilus*, to Ovidian texts for power and authority. When we sort out all these various "Ovids" we uncover a profound struggle in which the combatants vie for supremacy by appropriating and shaping Ovidian texts and doctrines. The Wife revives and reclaims *Ars Amatoria* III as a woman's text, extending and shaping Ovidian strategy according to her own ambitions. She is Ovid's "armed Amazon," and she has modernized Ovid's ancient armor in the new war against almost fourteen hundred years of male texts.[17] As part of this "modernization," the

Wife's *Prologue* allows Chaucer to reexamine the function of the Ovidian rhetoric he had studied in the *Troilus*. We are no longer in the stately world of ancient Troy, but in gritty, fourteenth-century England. Ovidian art serves not a noble couple, but a gat-toothed weaver, a wife five times over.

In this new context we also have to pay attention to the Wife and the medieval reception of Ovid. Since the *Ars Amatoria* figures so prominently in her monologue, knowing how it was read by a medieval audience helps us see how the Wife has shaped her own "art of love." The fourteenth century was aware that Ovid was banished in part for "corrupting wives" and leading them to adultery—an observation central to our understanding of antifeminist ideology and of the Wife's role as a corrupted and corrupting wife.[18]

I have called both the *Troilus* and the Wife's *Prologue and Tale* "arts of love" even though we usually do not classify them as such. Both the novelistic romance of the *Troilus* and the personal monologue of the Wife seem quite removed from the plotless, epigrammatic Ovidian handbooks. Neither work, furthermore, mimics the *De Amore* of Andreas Capellanus, a three-part scholastic handbook based explicitly on the *Ars Amatoria* and the *Remedia Amoris*. However, we can see Chaucer's two works as "arts" because in each poem love counselors teach Ovidian strategies and engage the audience in the intricacies of the games of love between men and women. The teachers in these poems thus bring Ovid's arts into a dramatic context, just as a host of counselors do in the *Roman de la Rose*, a free-form medieval art of love that Chaucer knew well.[19]

Together, the *Troilus* and the Wife's *Prologue and Tale* display Chaucer's evolving treatment of Ovidian art over the course of his career. These poems isolate two distinct but deeply related "Ovidian moments" for Chaucer. In Pandarus and Criseyde we see wit and we hear voices that we will see and hear again in the Wife's monologue. Both poems ask the same Ovidian question: What can language and game do for lovers? But Chaucer's answer to this question changes over time, for the Wife masters Ovidian art as no other Chaucerian character had before, and she uses it in ways unimagined by either of her Ovidian-Chaucerian predecessors, Pandarus and Criseyde. The skepticism surrounding Ovidian art in the *Troilus* now becomes celebration.

In the context of these two arts of love, chapter 5 is a discussion of the relationship between Chaucer's Ovidianism and his conception of himself as a poet. Chaucer's career-long interest in Ovid persists as he turns to evaluate what it has meant for him to have been a servant of the servants of love. Chaucer was not one of those scholars (some of whom were burned at the stake for the comparison) who claimed that "God has spoken in Ovid, even as he has in Augustine."[20] Chaucer may have regarded Ovid as his literary father and favorite poet, but he did not regard him as his sole authority. Chaucer's Ovidianism, as expressed in both the *Troilus* and the Wife's *Prologue and Tale*, shows how he allows the dramas of *homo rhetoricus* and *femina rhetorica* to unfold with little or no direct criticism. Both Ovid and Chaucer simply wind up the world of language and let it run. But ultimately, for Chaucer, where would this lead?

Chaucer's distance from overt moralization has been celebrated by modern scholars as a distinct virtue, and perhaps that is why Matthew Arnold complained that Chaucer lacked "high seriousness." In Arnold's famous evaluation we see the same type of criticism that Petrarch levels against the Ovid of exile. If Ovid had not had a lascivious spirit, says Petrarch, he would have earned a "greater reputation among serious men."[21] Ovid's suffering in his banishment to the Black Sea is well known, but what price did Chaucer pay for his own lack of high seriousness and his addiction to amatory literature?

To try to answer these questions, chapter 5 considers the two poets' views of art, death, and immortality, examining their comments on their own struggles to secure a place for themselves in their respective worlds. In discussing the history of authorship before the eighteenth century, Michel Foucault says that discourse "was essentially an act placed in the bipolar field of the sacred and profane, the licit and the illicit, the religious and the blasphemous. Historically it was a gesture fraught with risks."[22] We do not normally see vernacular authors as "subject to punishment," and Chaucer never exhibits any fear of imprisonment or exile. But his *Retraction* indicates that he and Ovid share this identity as "author" and confront dangers that arise when they do not *explicitly* express or respect the sacred, religious, and licit. The bipolar fields themselves are quite different for each poet, but each had to reconcile himself to divine authority, Ovid to his "god" Augustus, and Chaucer to the Christian "God" and to Christ the Word. The connections here go beyond source and analogue criticism and into the heart of what it means to be a servant of the servants of love and a maker of fictions. In his *Retraction*, Chaucer finally confronts the issue that devastated Ovid: an author's relation to his works. Through the characters he created in his arts of love, Chaucer studied both the power and the failings of Ovidian words and Ovidian game. Now he must consider the personal, spiritual implications of being a verbal artist and a love poet. From exile Ovid defended his amatory works by calling them *falsus*, mere games that no one could ever believe or be harmed by. Chaucer finally has to *retract* his poetic works that "sownen into synne" because they too are false, lacking the direct relations to reality, the one-to-one correspondence with authority that his translations, saints' lives, and other books of "moralitee . . . and devocioun" have. Ultimately, Chaucer found no defense for his "fained," fictive voices, only prayer—and here ends the drama of one medieval poet's encounter with the life and work of the great classical *magister amoris*.

1

Clerks of Venus
Chaucer's Life of Ovid

EFORE undertaking a study of Chaucer's two great arts of love, the *Troilus* and the *Wife of Bath's Prologue and Tale,* we have to try to determine who and what "Ovid" was to a medieval vernacular poet. The answer lies partly in medieval scholastic commentaries, the critical apparatus with which teachers annotated texts. These commentaries provide neither an answer-key nor an allegorical correspondence chart for Chaucer's poetry, but they do guide our view of Chaucer's understanding of Ovid's works and career. From commentaries, particularly from the biographical "headnotes" or the *accessus ad auctores,* we learn that medieval poets regarded Ovid's life and work as all part of one meta-narrative of "Ovid," embracing his poetry itself, its reception by Ovid's own audience, its relation to Ovid's personal and political fortunes, and its ethical utility to the current reader. Everything Ovid wrote is subject, then, to a basic set of questions: What does this work teach? What was its practical, historical function or goal during the poet's life? Was it successful? Of what value is the text to us now? In the medieval schoolroom, secular poetry like Ovid's taught not only rhetoric but history and ethics as well.

Ethics, audience reception, biography, personal and political fortunes—any of these areas alone inspires a score of questions about Chaucer as a student of Ovid and as a love poet in his own right. Did Chaucer believe that Ovid was a moral philosopher? Did Chaucer worry about the effect of his own poetry on his audience? Was he in any way engaged by the story of Ovid's life? Did he relate his own experiences to those of the classical poet he read? Was he burdened by the model of Ovid's life or by the ethical dictates he saw imposed on Ovid's poetry? To approach these questions and to provide a brief survey of medieval critical material, I divide the following discussion into two parts, isolating the main elements of the commentaries: biography and ethics. Examining these dimensions of the medieval reception of Ovid will give us some insight into Chaucer's perception of Ovid when the English poet created his own arts of love.

Vita Ovidii

What exactly would Chaucer have known about Ovid? First of all, Chaucer would have known—as the commentaries knew—the history of Ovid's chaotic career, from his early love poetry, which won him vast renown, to his later works, composed in exile following Augustus's condemnation of the *Ars Amatoria*. Chaucer would have seen Ovid's poems in a context at once historical and biographical.[1] The schoolmasters' method of discussing the poet's life as an introduction to his poems formed a standard part of the commentaries on pagan authors throughout the Middle Ages, beginning with Servius's commentary on the *Aeneid*.[2]

Surveying such medieval "biographies" of Ovid, Fausto Ghisalberti traces the growing interest in bringing together the wealth of factual and theoretical information about Ovid in the later Middle Ages.[3] Most commonly, Ghisalberti tells us, the introduction to the *Metamorphoses* was made "into an introduction to the life and work of the poet as a whole."[4] Arnulf of Orleans, writing in the twelfth century, very clearly states, "When we have in hand Ovid's greatest work, then we will trace his life." By Chaucer's century, Ghisalberti says, "literary and biographical notices developed from the rudimentary medieval *accessus* . . . into the more complex form of the humanistic life" (17). Discussing one fourteenth-century *accessus* to the *Metamorphoses*, Ghisalberti shows that "the author embraced the whole life and work of the poet, discussing even the exile and its causes" (24). Giovanni del Virgilio, for instance, while introducing the *Metamorphoses*, traces the poet's life and discusses all his works in the context of the life, pointing out (erroneously) that the *Remedia* was written as part of a vain attempt to be recalled from exile.[5] One commentary on the *Metamorphoses* begins by stressing the importance of biography: "Concerning the greater authors, we ought to draw evidence of their lives out of their most important work."[6] Fourteenth-century biographies in particular, says Ghisalberti, provide a vita as introduction to both the *Metamorphoses* and the minor works of Ovid. Throughout the later Middle Ages and particularly in the fourteenth century, then, it was apparently impossible for a reader to pick up any text of Ovid and not become acquainted with Ovid's "life" and the occasion of each of his works.[7]

Medieval commentators who wrote these vitae knew Ovid's tragic story because Ovid himself composed his later works with his own biography in mind. He tells his story as that of a poet, a love poet who suffers sorrow and exile because of what he has written. In the *Metamorphoses* and the *Tristia* he summons images and scenes from his earlier love poems and "metamorphizes" them into dark, sorrowful conceits that reflect his downfall and woe. By mining his earlier works for the images that best express his new, sudden sorrow, Ovid consciously tells a dramatic, unified story. The highly rhetorical poems of exile form part of a poetic, political, and moral drama in which Ovid looks back on his career and discusses its trials. He describes how game has become earnest, singing of his own tragic transformation from the carefree love poet into a man of sorrows.[8] In exile and disgrace, but ever aware of his own oeuvre, he tells Rome that he is finally fit to be part of that "book of bodies changed" (the *Metamorphoses*) because "things are not now as they were before."[9]

The medieval vitae show fidelity (for the most part) to Ovid's self-conscious narrative. Although scholastic commentary often simply makes up stories about Ovid and the emperor's wife, the general outline it offers of Ovid's career is far from fantastical. Ovid sang something dangerous in the *Ars Amatoria* (his *carmen*), saw something scandalous (his *error*), and the emperor punished him for it. No one knew what the *error* was, but everyone knew the song.[10] As Chaucer's contemporary Petrarch starkly states: "[The *Ars Amatoria* is] a foul work and, unless I am deceived, the cause of [Ovid's] exile."[11]

Ovid's misspent youth and the high price he paid for it in his weary old age seem to draw particular attention from the biographers. For example, they see the love poems as works from a "lascivious youth," when Ovid, "struck by Cupid's sharp dart . . . led others into error."[12] Virtually all discussions of the exile in the "lives" and in the *accessus* to the poems of exile cite the *Ars Amatoria* as one of the causes of Ovid's banishment.[13] One commentary on the *Tristia* reports that Ovid was exiled because the *Ars Amatoria* "taught things that ought not be taught."[14]

As Ralph Hexter points out, even by the middle of the twelfth century "an increasing number of readers have a sense of the entire Ovidian corpus, and references to Ovid's exile elegies tend to place them within that larger corpus."[15] It became firmly recognized, then, that the *Tristia* and the *Ex Ponto,* those appeals to Rome for comfort and mercy, result logically from the *Ars Amatoria.* Schoolmasters saw these poems, quite accurately, as records of Ovid's regret for his love poetry and as attempts to win pardon from Augustus. Some commentators, with no evidence to support their claims, even saw the *Remedia,* the *Metamorphoses,* and the *Heroides* as acts of reparation in the hope of pardon.[16] These exaggerations testify that the scholastic tradition paid constant attention to poetry as personal history, tying all Ovid's works together as a logically developed literary and moral history.

Another set of documents, *La Querelle de la Rose,* composed at the beginning of the fifteenth century, shortly after Chaucer's death, also recounts in part the life of Ovid. The participants on both sides of the debate over the moral worth of the *Roman de la Rose* refer freely to Ovid's love poetry and his exile, treating Ovid's life as literary history and as moral exemplum. In his attack on Jean de Meun, Jean Gerson as Theological Eloquence argues that the work is a danger to readers, even though it may contain some virtuous material mixed in with the vicious doctrine. Such a balance of the healthful and harmful is no saving grace, writes Gerson, who offers the example of the crime and punishment of Ovid, who, Gerson implies, was justly exiled for writing scabrous poetry:

> Believe not me, but St. Paul the Apostle, Seneca,
> and experience, that evil speaking and writings
> corrupt good morals leading to immodest conduct
> and destroying all sense of shame. . . . Why was
> Ovid, a learned man and a most ingenious poet,
> sent into perpetual exile? He himself is a witness,
> that this happened to him on account of his
> wretched *Art of Loving,* which he wrote in the time
> of the Emperor Augustus. And he was exiled,
> despite the fact that he had sent out another
> book—*Of the Remedy of Love*—in refutation.[17]

Gerson continues his attack, saying Jean de Meun's poem contains "things even worse than anything in Ovid" (Baird and Kane, trans., *La Querelle,* 83).

In another context, Pierre Col, Gerson's and Christine de Pizan's opponent, clearly states that the *Ars Amatoria* caused Ovid's exile, though he maintains that Ovid was a victim of the Roman husbands who feared that

Ovid's work would lead their wives into scandalous adultery. Pierre explains:

> When Ovid wrote the *Art of Love*, he wrote in
> Latin, which women did not understand. There-
> fore he gave it only to the assailants [male lovers]
> to teach them how to capture the castle. . . . On
> account of this he was exiled, because of the very
> great jealousy of the Roman husbands. In fact, this
> motive was the beginning, middle, and end of the
> reason for his exile. . . . In fact, Ovid also recanted
> by making the book on the *Remedy of Love*. Truly, I
> do not understand at all how this exile can be
> justified by Reason. [Baird and Kane, trans., *La
> Querelle*, 108]

Like the authors of school vitae, these literary scholars battling over the *Roman de la Rose* matter-of-factly refer to the drama of Ovid's life and the definitive connections between his "art of love," the political and social reaction to his work, his failed refutation, and his punishing exile.

Since Ovid's life was part of a drama that involves all of Ovid's work, medieval readers could not have seen Ovid's "life" as separate from his "art." For in all these vitae, the *Ars Amatoria* poet *creates* the poet of the *Tristia* and the *Ex Ponto*, and the ethical, social, and poetic implications of the *Ars Amatoria* reveal themselves in these later laments. The exile elegies helped medieval students understand Ovid's art and life, the moral and poetic issues inherent in the work of the author they were about to study.[18] Chaucer the vernacular poet could not have seen Ovid as the poet of love without seeing him as the poet of exile.

Did an awareness of Ovid's "biography," of this story of a love poet exiled for his "song," influence Chaucer and other vernacular poets either in individual poems or in their views of their own status as love poets? How did they translate their knowledge of Ovid and the appeal of his story into their own lives and fiction? Robert Hollander studies how one very prominent vernacular poet responded. Giovanni Boccaccio, Hollander argues, "constructed details of his own 'vita' in accord with what he found in Ovid's."[19] Boccaccio, who wrote a life of Ovid while commenting on Ovid's appearance in the fourth canto of the *Inferno*, saw himself as a poet of love and as a carnal lover—in short, a "new Ovid."

Most important, Hollander discusses how both Ovid and Boccaccio address the issue of what it means to be a love poet:

> Each author has a complicated relationship to the
> guilty activity he owns as his own. He both
> celebrates the passions and condemns them. While
> in Ovid the distinction is neat (*Ars Amatoria* vs.
> *Remedia Amoris*), in Boccaccio it only seems to be
> so (early works vs. late works). . . . The tradition of
> the *Remedia* operates in Boccaccio simultaneously
> with that of the *Ars* as a continual correction to the
> bad doctrines of love. In short, Boccaccio, from the
> very first of his poems, regards himself as "the new
> Ovid" in a positive sense only. When he represents
> love in the tradition of the *Ars*, he does so in order
> to condemn it. [*Boccaccio's Two Venuses*, 115]

As he tries to put this neo-Ovidianism into perspective, Hollander raises the issue of the medieval Ovid's complexity, noting that some saw the *Ars Amatoria* not as a poem of lust but as a mock of carnal love. Our evaluation of what Boccaccio is doing "depends," Hollander says, "on the way in which one reads the [Ovidian] text. . . . Still, the best evidence would seem to indicate that Boccaccio, whatever his own methods of being the 'new Ovid,' looked upon the amatory verses of the original Ovid as indeed lascivious and culpable" (ibid.).

Some of this best evidence lies in Boccaccio's mention of Ovid in his commentary on the virtuous pagans in the *Inferno*. While discussing the fate of Ovid—one of the heathen who are damned because of their ignorance of Christ—Boccaccio accomplishes much. First, he gives the life of Ovid and also, later in the discussion, points out that Dante must be contradicting himself when he says that all those damned in this circle did not sin (non peccaro), for many here were in fact sinners. He then explains the crimes of Caesar, Aeneas, and Lucan, but he begins with Ovid, who composed some good and useful things, but also wrote love poems that show him to be "more than any other, an effeminate and lascivious man" [più che alcun altro effeminato e lascivo uomo]. Furthermore, Boccaccio says, in his *De arte amandi* (the *Ars Amatoria*) Ovid "gives the worst and dishonest doctrines" [pessima e disonesta dottrina] to his readers.[20] For Boccaccio, the details of Ovid's life and the ethical, practical function of his poems form a unified moral paradigm. Boccaccio's commentary shows us that when a fourteenth-century poet set out to explore the implications of being a servant of the servants of love, he set out, in poetry, to analyze the doctrines of the *Ars Amatoria*.

Another vernacular poet of no small consequence to Chaucer, Jean de Meun, also makes a series of self-reflexive comments as he portrays himself as Love's minion in the *Roman de la Rose.* The God of Love, telling the story of the composition of the *Roman,* promises that he will see that Jean Chapanell has a painless birth and is raised so that he will tend to the disciples of Love. Readers, says the god, will call his book a "mirror for lovers." Jean certainly sees himself, or at least sees the persona guiding the poem, as the new Ovid, Venus's favorite clerk and a *magister amoris.* The Ovidian love doctrine and love counselors, such as Ami and La Vieille, throughout the *Roman* bear out Jean's ambition, for indeed he offers many "arts of love," many mirrors for lovers in his completion of Guillaume's poem. Jean, like Chaucer, refers to his own life and work in terms of his calling as a love poet, a servant of the servants of love.

We should also consider the twelfth-century Ovidian poet Baudry, who wrote a version of the Paris and Helen letters in the *Heroides,* as well as an imagined pair of letters between the exiled Ovid and a sympathetic friend who is appalled at the poet's misfortunes.[21] He also wrote homosexual love poetry and used Ovid as his model. As L. P. Wilkinson points out, Baudry in his later poetry has to defend himself against a charge of frivolity, and he labors to dissociate his morals from his verse, as Ovid himself had to do in his own defense in the *Tristia.* Baudry's plea displays how Ovid's life provides a model for the playful poet who fears that his game may be taken for earnest and who thus must provide an apology or palinode for his youthful, libertine verses.[22]

Both the ambitions and the worries of these several *personae amatoriae* show us that these poets knew Ovid's life and work as part of their standard literary historical heritage. As they address love they address Ovid. Like Boccaccio, Jean, and Baudry, Chaucer inherits this Ovidian identity and lives out a bit of Ovidian biography. We see a striking display of this in the *Prologue* to the *Legend of Good Women* when Chaucer attempts to draw a parallel between his own literary vita and that of the medieval Ovid. We are fortunate that occasionally Chaucer provides a pseudo-biographical detail that, if not historically "true," still indicates how he chose to present himself as a love poet.

One of the major sources and models for the *Legend* is, of course, Ovid's *Heroides.* According to medieval commentaries, the love letters of mythic heroines and heroes serve to "exalt pure love" and "show the evil consequences of illegitimate forms of sexual intercourse."[23] As for the biographical "occasion" for these poems, some commentaries explain that Roman matrons offended by his *Ars Amatoria* prompted Ovid to offer the letters as correctives to his dangerous, scabrous arts of love. Other commentaries claim that Ovid wrote the *Heroides* from exile as part of his comprehensive attempt to win reinstatement.[24]

Chaucer may have written his *Legend* because of similar "political" pressure, that is, Queen Anne's dislike of the depiction of women in the *Troilus*. The story is not confirmable, but the God of Love does order that the poem be given to her, and critics have argued for this political, occasional reading. Chaucer's contemporary Lydgate reports that Chaucer composed the work "at request of the queen."[25] The alleged historical events notwithstanding, in the *Prologue* to the work Chaucer does simulate just such a dramatic occasion for writing the women's narratives.

The God of Love chastises Chaucer for leading lovers away from him by translating the *Roman de la Rose* and for "shewinge how that wemen han don mis" in the *Troilus*. In this rhetorical context the legends constitute Chaucer's attempt to use a new type of poetry to compensate for his past poetic offenses. Ovid brought on the wrath of the Roman matrons for leading them and others *into* love, but Chaucer, according to the God of love, made "wise folk" to "with drawe" from love—a seemingly parodic reversal of Ovid's situation. But in both scenarios, the poem is palinode, a public, political event in the poet's career. And indeed the *Troilus*, which caused Chaucer this trouble, is itself his own "art of love," fully saturated with Ovidian lore. Evidently the God of Love and the Queen of England approved of Chaucer's "art" as much as the Roman *matronae* and Emperor Augustus approved of Ovid's. Their backs to the wall, both clerks of Venus had to respond with correctives.

The drama that Chaucer constructs about the occasion for the *Legend of Good Women* shows that he could see his poems in the context of his career as a love poet and could poeticize the compulsions and pressures that he faced. As it happens, the pressures on Chaucer to write the *Legend* here comically reflect those on Ovid to compose the *Heroides*, the *Legend*'s source text. We should not be surprised if Chaucer actually based his decision to write stories of noble heroines on Ovid's similar circumstances. The *Heroides*, as the commentaries perceive it, was an instructive, ethical work, and therefore an appropriate model for repairing a tarnished poetic reputation and mending relationships with female audiences.[26]

It seems that every time Chaucer makes self-reflexive comments, he involves himself in some sort of palinode. In addition to this scenario in the *Prologue* to the *Legend*, we have the Man of Law's catalog of Chaucer's works and of course, finally, the *Retraction*. The Man of Law's list offers a vision of

Chaucer's career as a whole, in the way a scholastic *vita* would. The Man of Law may have recently been reading the *Metamorphoses* or the *Heroides*, both of which he names and in which he would have found a similar catalog of Ovid's works. Alfred David argues that the catalog and the subsequent tale indicate that the Man of Law "regards the function of all poetry, including love poetry, as didactic." By contrast, "for the Man of Law Chaucer is a follower of Ovid, especially the Ovid of the *Ars Amatoria* and the *Heroides*." At this point in the poem, furthermore, Fragment I (A), in its degeneration to the baseness of the Cook's fragment, has "compounded [Chaucer's] poetic felonies."[27] In light of Chaucer's reputation and in light of the low state of the tale-telling contest, the *Man of Law's Tale* serves as a palinode, "a return to the abandoned theme of the *Legends*, the praise of constant women" ("Man of Law," 222).

V. A. Kolve agrees, seeing the tale as inspired by the need to "demonstrate, for the first time within the opening sequence of the tales, what poetry can do at its maximum dignity, in the service of historical fact and Christian truth." Kolve calls the catalog a "mock palinode," a parody of the *Retraction*. "The Man of Law's summary catalogue offers a partial and prejudicial version of Chaucer's works prior to the *Canterbury Tales* as a means of reminding us that if indeed that were all Chaucer had undertaken or accomplished, his oeuvre would offer a partial and prejudicial view of poetry's potential dignity and use."[28]

Whether or not David and Kolve are right to see the tale as a palinode, they are right to see the catalog in the *Prologue* as a display of Chaucer's awareness of a "conflict of interest" concerning poetry and moral doctrine (see David, "Man of Law," 225). Chaucer, by having his works named and having himself depicted as a love poet, draws attention to his role as a servant of the servants of love, a great Ovid, or at least a new Ovid, who has surpassed the master by telling more stories of lovers "up and doun" than Ovid ever did (*Man of Law's Introduction*, ll. 53ff.). Like Jean de Meun and Boccaccio, Chaucer plays with his poetic identity, and Ovid stands close by as a point of comparison. Chaucer knew that he was an Ovidian poet and that his own vita at times fell into Ovidian patterns. This means that he saw the need for some sort of reckoning, which we find in the *Retraction*, to which finally, in David's well-borrowed phrase, he "does not wish to turn again."

These literary and biographical parallels provide an interesting context in which to read Venus's address to Chaucer toward the end of the *Confessio Amantis*, an allegorical pilgrimage from youth to old age written by Chaucer's friend John Gower. While banishing from her court the aging Amans, now identified as John Gower, and sending him where "moral vertu duelleth," the Goddess of Love tells Gower to greet Chaucer, her "disciple" and her "poete," who "in the floures of his youth" made many songs for her sake. She then calls him, exactly as Chaucer himself refers to Ovid in the *House of Fame*, her "owne clerk." Later, Venus says, in Chaucer's "daies olde" when he must "sette an ende of alle his werk," he must also "make his testament of love" and be shriven as Amans now is.[29] In this inside joke between Ricardian poets, Gower predicts that Chaucer will be summoned one day to account for his youthful love poems and will have to confess just as Amans/Gower has.

Did Gower base his statements on personal knowledge of Chaucer's career at the time? Was Gower upset by the direction Chaucer had taken in his poetry, away from the *Legend of Good Women* to the *Canterbury Tales*?[30] We do not know. But Gower does apply to Chaucer's life a paradigm that is central to the medieval vitae of Ovid: part of the standard evaluation of the amatory poems is, as we have seen, that Ovid produced them in his frivolous youth. Ovid himself makes this clear, telling a friend in the *Tristia:* "You know that this old song of mine is a game from my youth. These verses ought not to be praised, but should, rather, be seen as jests."[31] For Ovid, exile will serve as the final reckoning for his frivolity—he could never come to the type of shriving that the God of Love demands for Chaucer in Gower's poem. This pagan/Christian opposition notwithstanding, Gower was still capable of reading Chaucer's life as a medieval schoolmaster would read Ovid's.

Furthermore, despite Ovid's distinctly pre-Christian predicament, we must not forget the legends about Ovid's conversion to Christianity. As Quain summarizes: "Popular tradition had, on one side, made of him a teacher of morals, a Christian preacher, and they even 'found' a form of *retractatio* in which, having seen the light of Faith, Ovid changed the opening lines of the *Metamorphoses* so that it began with an invocation of the Holy Trinity." The "high point" of this tradition, says Quain, comes in the preface to the spurious *De Vetula*, said to have been found in Ovid's tomb: "Ad ultimum ponit fidem suam tractans egregissime de incarnatione ihesu christi, et de passione, de resurrectione et de ascention et de vita beate marie virginis et de assumptione in caelum" [At the end he placed his faith {in God}, drawing passionately on Christ's incarnation, the passion and the resurrection and the blessed life of the Virgin Mary and her assumption into heaven].[32] Whether Gower knew or believed such speculation is not important. Whether Ovid's life ended in miserable exile or in miraculous retraction,

Gower offers the life of a love poet, his own and Chaucer's, that reflects the paradigm we find both in the *Tristia* and in medieval evaluations of Ovid's life. His medieval readers saw Ovid as a frivolous poet in youth, and they knew that he had to be called to account, in punishment, conversion, or confession.

Scholastic commentary and the Ovidian paradigms played out by vernacular poets portray for Chaucer the burdens and dangers a love poet must face. Chaucer, as a willing clerk of Venus, could not escape confronting this paradigm as he took his place in the great host of medieval Ovids. But not all medieval love poets become Ovids in the same way. As Hexter sees well, Ovid's story "has the appeal of fiction" and has engaged posterity. This engagement can take many forms. Chaucer likely assimilated the details of Ovid's biography as part of his literary inheritance, but he also, of course, simply loved a good story.

In his autobiographical poems Ovid offers confession, monologue, self-reflexive discussions of craft, literature, virtue, and the connections between fiction and its maker. Ovid is aware of his audience and of the power of his voice. In odd ways his discourse in the *Tristia* has much in common with the Pardoner's *Prologue*, studying "intention" and the effect of texts on both author and audience. Indeed, in much of the *Troilus* and in the *Canterbury Tales*, Chaucer makes literature as Ovid does, creating a voice that reveals its history and desires, its virtues and vices, its relations to fortune, justice, and its own craft. Ovid's biography, as told by scholastic commentary, offered Chaucer a model of the life of a lascivious poet who had to answer for his crimes. Ovid's poems themselves gave him the dramatic, literary material that he could mold in his own way as he became the most prominent new Ovid in English. It is finally both classical text and medieval gloss that constitute Chaucer's "life of Ovid" and allow him to shape his own neo-Ovidian amatory fiction.

Ethice Supponitur

We have seen the central importance of Ovid's "life" in medieval commentary and the various ways Ovid's story could manifest itself in a vernacular poet's career. The other major facet of the medieval reception of Ovid concerns the poems themselves as "ethical" works, useful in the moral education of the Christian reader.[33] The *accessus ad auctores*, in addition to providing the *vitae*, offer a systematic guide to the ethical interpretation of the texts they introduce. After the name of the author and of the work, they uniformly provide an explanation of (1) the work's subject (*materia*)—for instance, the "boys and girls" addressed by the *Ars Amatoria;* (2) the occasion—in the case of the *Tristia,* for example, to "appease Caesar"; (3) the work's utility (*utilitas*); and (4) its classification in philosophy—ethics. The *accessus* see the *Tristia* as a story of woe and misery, the *utilitas* of which is to teach the reader to avoid the "same mistake" that Ovid made. Ovid's intention, they say, was to dissuade poets from writing "anything shameful" [*aliquid indignum*] through which "they would suffer the same punishment."[34] We can understand Chaucer's interest in Ovid's biography because of its dramatic and narrative appeal, but the interpretive apparatus of the *accessus* seems too rigid to have been of any use to a poet of uncertainty and flux. The fall of a love poet who wallowed in weakness and lust, the stormy journey into exile, the elegiac laments of the man separated from his faithful wife—we can imagine that Chaucer was enraptured by this. But how can the ethical grid, the workmanlike, moral classifications of Ovid's words and deeds, play a role in Chaucer's poetry? The *accessus* may indeed be rigid and predictable: the clerical commentators tried to show that Ovid was an "ethical" poet and should be kept in the curriculum. But they are also at times provocative, even strangely playful, and can indeed aid us as we contextualize Chaucer's work. The moral evaluations offered by the *accessus* form part of the entanglement of scholastic, theological, and poetical reactions to the *Ars Amatoria* that shape Chaucer's "medieval Ovid."

Let us consider the *accessus* to the *Ars Amatoria*. The common *accessus* tell us that the *Ars* teaches ethics and gives "a complete guide for loving." It is a work, as Ghisalberti summarizes, "concerning love, toward the composition of an art, designed to establish the foundation of a full and perfect art of love."[35] One commentator, aware that the art of love caused Ovid's downfall, tells us that the *Ars Amatoria* was misread. It seems, he says, to teach adultery (the emperor's claim), but in actuality "it scorns lust and love and describes how we may love honestly" (Ghisalberti, "Medieval Biographies of Ovid," 57). If the *Ars Amatoria* was so healthful and fine a work, we may wonder why Ovid wrote the *Remedia Amoris*. To resolve this contradiction, commentators revise their reading of the *Ars Amatoria*, claiming now that it fired a destructive passion that led Roman youths to despair and suicide. In the *Remedia*, Ovid becomes a divine agent of grace, because "the ruler of all things did nothing that did not have a remedy" (ibid., 45).[36]

The schoolmasters, in their "hasty baptism" of pagan authors, knew how to play with rhetoric and reality, making Ovid serve, in Douglas Bush's phrase, as "all things to all men."[37] Ovid could be a corruptive, lascivious love poet or an agent of spiritual health. In this fluid interpretive context, vernacular poets had to evaluate the love poems themselves—in their own poetry. They had to do more than simply follow the interpretive rules established by their culture and by the shifting classifications of Ovid's work. Chaucer read Ovid's poems, the commentaries written between the lines and up and down the page, and Boccaccio's, Petrarch's, and Jean's Ovid. Then he turned to confront the poet, to address Ovidian love in his own *artes amatoriae.* Chaucer neither swallowed whole, nor could he ignore, ethical commentary.

But how specific a part did these ethical rules and categories of the *accessus* system play in Chaucer's confrontation with Ovid's poems? When we consider the *Troilus,* for example, we will want to know what it means that Chaucer's characters adopt Ovidian doctrines and read life with an "Ovidian" perspective. Can Ovid's poems actually function as ethics? Can they teach the young women and men in Chaucer's poetry anything about love, as the commentaries say they can? If the *Remedia Amoris* was inspired by God, can it also help the lovesick, pagan Troilus?

Furthermore, since Chaucer knew Ovid's poems as "ethics," we have to ask what it meant for Chaucer himself to be a love poet, a "new Ovid." Did Chaucer see himself as a moral philosopher? If so, was he a successful one in his own judgment? Did he (and should we) read his own poems as "ethics," in the way the schoolmasters read Ovid's? Although the *accessus* offer no answers to these questions, they do show us that as we study Chaucer's Ovid and read his medieval Ovidian poetry, we must at least ask them.

Antiovidiana

This overview of the medieval scholastic reception of Ovid allows us to understand some of the basic concerns that Chaucer would have had as he read and rewrote his favorite poet. We see that Ovid's whole life, the utility of his works, and their role in his political fortunes would all have been part of Chaucer's experience of the medieval Ovid. I want to turn to some specific points raised by the commentaries and by related texts.

One aspect of the medieval Ovid involves what we might generally call antiovidiana—those texts that teach us that not everyone loved or even tolerated Ovid in the Middle Ages. Two of Chaucer's contemporaries occasionally offer such anti-Ovidian comments. Petrarch complains that Ovid acted "womanly" before and after exile and that herein lies the chief defect of his poems: "That man seems to me to be a great genius, but he was beset by a prurient and lubricious nature and, ultimately, a female weakness of spirit."[38] As Boccaccio does in his commentary on Dante, Petrarch detects

Ovid's "female weakness" in the love poems, but Petrarch also criticizes Ovid for not bearing his misfortunes and exile more bravely. As Hexter puts it, Petrarch sees Ovid's laments as "one final example of his unmanliness" (*Ovid and Medieval Schooling*, 97).

At times, medieval authors could attack Ovid by associating him with their own youthful frivolities and their attraction to both art and love—crimes that Ovid linked to each other and to himself for all time. The twelfth-century abbot, Guibert de Nogent, discusses his misguided adoration of Ovidian rhetoric, which he links to the wicked stirrings of his own fleshly desires:

> After steeping my mind unduly in the study of
> versemaking, with the result that I put aside for
> such ridiculous vanities the matters of universal
> importance in the divine pages, I was so far guided
> by my folly as to give first place to Ovid and the
> pastoral poets and to aim at a lover's urbanity in
> distributions of types and in a series of letters.
> Forgetting proper severity and abandoning the
> modesty of a monk's calling, my mind was led
> away by the enticements of a poisonous license.
> . . . By love of it I was doubly taken captive, being
> snared by both the wantonness of the sweet words
> I took from the poets and by those which I poured
> forth myself, and I was caught by the unrestrained
> stirring of my flesh through thinking on these
> things and the like.[39]

For Guibert, Ovidian art inspires pride and vile self-indulgence, distracting the monk from the healing gravity of Scripture. In this paradigm, Ovid is a dangerous influence whose sweet words lure the holy man from sacred duty.

More severe than Guibert's monastic critique is the attack on Ovid provided in the anonymous fourteenth-century poem, the *Antiovidianus*—a text never before brought to bear upon Chaucer. After dedicating the work to his master, and before addressing Ovid's corpus, the poet places Ovid's poetry in the context of Christian history, linking Ovid's "pleasing verses" to the false words of the Devil, who tempted man to fall. The poet particularly attacks Ovid for using the beauty of his art to hide his foul and dangerous matter—for "gilding dung." "My muse strikes Ovid," he writes, "because taking up dung, with his shining muse he made it gold, and in his pleasing verses made gall into honey, night into light, death into life, and labor into rest." Because of this vile duplicity, "[Ovid] wrote nothing that was not false," and his works "separate the pious from piety."[40]

This critique of Ovid is an extreme one. An *accessus*, by contrast, would never hope that Ovid be "nurtured with the odor of putrid dung" and "refreshed by the air that crackles out of his behind" (Kienast, ed., *Antiovidianus*, ll. 85–86).[41] But when we put this critique next to the *accessus*, we see a vivid doubleness of attitude toward the Ovidian love poem. On the one hand, we have its acceptance into the curriculum, and, on the other, its condemnation by Christian writers. This tension is reflected in Chaucer's own acceptance of Ovid in his "curriculum" and his final rejection of Ovidian art at the end of the *Troilus*. In chapter 4 I will bring this anti-Ovidian attack to bear on Chaucer's Ovidian Wife of Bath, who takes her own place in the history of love language and artful rhetoric.

The *Antiovidianus* also offers a fascinating reading of the poems of exile: "Nam fles exilium, fles excidium, gemis vrbe / Te pulsum. Non fles, te quod Avernus habet" [You lament your exile, you lament your downfall; you groan that you have been driven out of the city. {But} you do not lament yourself, whom Hell has] (ll. 121–22). According to the poet, Ovid was not aware of his spiritual state, and so, misguided and ignorant, he can only moan. The poet elaborates this point in his evaluation of the *Ex Ponto:*

> Vt tua perlegeres memorando crimina, penam
> Hanc dederat iustus tis [*sic*] miserando deus.
> Sed male morbosus, moriturus morte perhenni,
> In medium surgis obprobriando deum.
>
> (ll. 131–34)

> [A just god had given you this punishment so that
> you would be exiled remembering your crimes.
> But, sick in spirit and about to die an eternal
> death, you rise complaining against a healing god.]

The poet does not associate Augustus with the Christian God, but is sensitive to the way Ovid views the emperor, for Ovid himself regularly refers to Augustus as his "god" while appealing to him for mercy in the *Tristia*. Not all commentaries on the *Tristia* emphasize this point; some merely report that Ovid sought a pardon he never received. Indeed, reverence for Augustus is not uniform; some commentaries theorize that Ovid's "error" was seeing

Augustus with a young boy—thus violating "godes privitee," as it were.[42]

In juxtaposition to scholastic glosses, then, the *Antiovidianus* illustrates the range of interpretation that could be applied to Ovid's exile. We must wonder if the poet's observation that Ovid's spirit was sick and that the exile writings offended a "just," "healing god" can help us understand Ovid's function in Chaucer's career. Hexter, acknowledging that the evidence is slight and late, cites these lines from the *Antiovidianus* as part of an association of the *Tristia* with *tristitia*, the "spiritual sadness that wears men down and is in direct opposition to the Christian virtue hope."[43] To what extent does Troilus, who wanders in the false "worldes brothelesse," or the Pardoner, the social, spiritual outcast, suffer from this same sickness of spirit? Could Chaucer have seen in Ovid's exile an image of despair, a despair that comes from love-longing or from a love of fallen language?

Since Chaucer's rhetoricians, and Chaucer himself, ultimately consider the relation between their words and "God," medieval moral condemnations of Ovidian rhetoric must have been part of Chaucer's concern as he presented characters who spout Ovidian doctrines. Whatever his personal understanding of Ovid and Augustus, whatever stories he believed, Chaucer could not have helped seeing that Ovid faced a divine audience and felt the wrath of divine power. The legends of Ovid's conversion to Christianity also indicate, from a different perspective, that readers were compelled to address, in their imaginations, Ovid's connection to the divine.

We witness here a certain confluence of Chaucer's poetry and a Latin poetic condemnation of Ovid. The *Antiovidianus* is a uniquely thrilling text, and I think it repays study. However, in scholastic commentaries we most often find not confluence but tension between moral philosophy and vernacular poetry. Some commentaries, in an effort to sanitize or rationalize Ovid, and thus to adopt him gently into a Christian curriculum, often "falsify the poetry," as Ghisalberti starkly puts it.[44] Faced with the need to classify Ovid's love poems as "ethics," one commentary, for example, sees *Ars Amatoria* III as a guide for women to "learn how to be retained" by men.[45] The statement is based on Ovid's own description of the work as a guide for women to learn "to love well so as to avoid being dumped" (my paraphrase, see *Ars* III, esp. 41ff.). But the commentary, in its need to classify, misses the wit, irony, and power of Ovid's art of "arming the Amazons." Ideologically, the commentary fears the strategy that empowers women and thus makes the poem seem like a simple cosmetic guide. One would hardly know from reading this gloss that Ovid's poem, among other things, accuses men of being treacherous and teaches women how to deceive lovers and guardians with notes, tears, and blandishments. The commentary restricts meaning and suppresses Ovid's poetry.

By contrast, Jean de Meun's La Vieille and after her Chaucer's Wife of Bath, as they revise and refocus *Ars Amatoria* III, take on the power relations implicit in both Ovid's text and in the commentary and create a new feminine "ethics" beyond the scope of either Ovid or the *accessus*. For each of these mistresses of love, *Ars Amatoria* III becomes much more than a book about how women can be retained. When we juxtapose scholastic and narrative treatments of Ovidian art in this way, we see that "Chaucer's Ovid" does not directly correspond to academic commentaries but, rather, grows out of the tensions implicit in his culture's inconsistent approaches to the poet it alternately adored, studied, and scorned.[46]

We can see from this brief overview that scholastic commentary can serve as a useful tool for understanding Chaucer's Ovid. It does not, however, definitively represent his Ovid, for Ovidian sexual and poetic issues were fully treated in vernacular poems we know Chaucer studied deeply— the *Filostrato* and the *Roman de la Rose*. Drawing heavily from Ovid, these poems provide dramatic depictions of love doctrine and of gender and marriage relations that often shadow Chaucer's treatment of Ovid. Our understanding of Chaucer's use of Ovid as a source and as an influence must include his reading of these discourses on, from, and about Ovid in the books closest to his mind and heart. Both Ovid and Jean de Meun, and Ovid *in* Jean de Meun, were indispensable to Chaucer as he created characters with artistic, social, and sexual ambitions. But Chaucer is writing his own art of love as he weaves images, ideas, mythic stories, and the names of actual texts of Ovid in a new poetic universe. Often he develops Boccaccio's or Jean de Meun's use of Ovid by going back to the original text to create some tension or irony and to exploit the potentials of the passage, sometimes playing off both immediate and ultimate sources.

My interest in textual interplay is based on my reading of Ovid's love poems and the particular inheritance they provided these medieval writers. John Fyler's *Chaucer and Ovid* views Ovid's works synchronically, as if they were more or less interchangeable, all pointing to the failure of systems. Fyler's theme is that both poets offer "skeptical explorations of the sources of human knowledge."[47] One of the strengths of his theory is his provocative pairing of Ovid and Chaucer against Virgil and Dante, who *do* see themselves as capable of providing answers about the nature of knowledge and human experience. Chaucer read and understood Ovid and was skeptical in ways that Virgil and Dante were not.

However, in the Wife's *Prologue* or in the *Troilus*, where rhetoric and sexual/textual power erupt from and around Ovidian texts, we have to look for more than just epistemological worry. In an effort to come to terms with the shifting material in these, perhaps Chaucer's greatest works, I offer a reading of Ovidian art, beginning with the playful, magical world of the *Ars Amatoria*.[48]

Chaucer saw the *Ars* as a poem not, *pace* Fyler, about failure but about infinite *success* through protean, rhetorical artistry and craft. The scholastic commentaries state that the *Ars* offers a "complete art of love." The commentaries do not, however, tell us that this success comes from lying and from Ovid's infinite control of reality through his control of language. In almost every piece of advice Ovid offers, we see how craft can overcome any deficiency or difficulty a young lover may encounter.[49] While discussing seduction strategy, for example, Ovid recommends taking one's lover to the races and brushing the dust from her dress just to get a chance to touch her thigh. And if there is no dust, he says, brush it off anyway [tamen excute nullum] (*Ars* I, 151). Another plan is to take her to a military procession and impress her by naming all the heroes. And yet the names need not be the real ones, so long as they have, in one translator's words, "the ring of truth":[50] "[Say that] this one or that one is a leader, and they will be whatever names you say; if you can, be truthful; if not, nevertheless say something convincing."[51] These words define Ovidian rhetoric well—things are what you name them; the act of naming (dicere nomina) controls reality; no external "truth" need interfere in or prevent this process.[52]

Along the same lines, Ovid advises men to entreat their women with promises, because "what harm will there be to promise? Anyone can be rich with promises" [quid enim promittere laedit? / pollicitis diues quilibet esse potest] (*Ars* I, 443–44). As Ovid says elsewhere, always be prepared to give a gift of words, using the Latin idiom for lying (*dare verba*). Talk is cheap, and that is its great benefit, because it can bring success. We see the same play with "names" in Ovid's advice to tell the woman that "you only want to be friends" and then maneuver from there: "Let your secret love sneak in under the name of 'friendship.' I have seen words deceive severe women in this way. He who was once a friend became a lover."[53] "Dare verba" is Ovid's creed, for words are one's best weapons against the limits of knowledge and the stubborn elusiveness of the objects of desire.

Words can get one into and also out of love, as Ovid shows in two opposing passages from the *Ars* and the *Remedia* that sharply display the fluidity of his grand system of illusion and deceit. If your lover is less than ideal, Ovid says, use names to make her seem attractive, for "faults may be softened with names" [nominibus mollire licet mala] (*Ars* II, 657). If she is too dark, call her "nicely tanned"; if fat, call her "full-figured," and thus "let a vice be hidden in its proximity to good" (1. 661). Ovid reverses the process in the *Remedia*. If one wants to fall *out* of love, he must let beautiful features be called vices:

> profuit adsidue uitiis insistere amicae,
>   idque mihi factum saepe salubre fuit.
> "quam mala" dicebam "nostrae sunt crura puellae"
>   (nec tamen, ut uere confiteamur, erant).
>
> (*Remedia*, ll. 315–18ff)

> [It is useful to dwell continually on the faults of
> your girl. This often worked for me. "How ugly," I
> would say, "are her legs," even though, to tell the
> truth, they were not.]

The physician was sick, but he healed himself with words, turning his girlfriend's beauty into ugliness.[54] Truth is what one says is true, and reality must answer to the names one gives it. As the master of this system, Ovid never admits failure, never shows where the game stops. He is forever a teacher, a doctor, an artist. Problems of love may be endless but so are his methods.[55] In this passage he even uses his own past lovesickness and sorrow not as signs of weakness or limitation but as selling points for the remedies he is marketing. Ovid is not only the *magister amoris*, he is also a client.

Everything is a system; some sort of art comes to the rescue every time. Although Ovid admits that passion can sometimes force one into submission to Cupid, he nonetheless creates a remedy for love, a bizarre means of liberation through excess:

> Mollior es neque abire potes uinctusque teneris
>   et tua saeuus Amor sub pede colla premit:
> desine luctari; referant tua carbasa uenti,
>   quaque uocant fluctus, hac tibi remus eat.
>
> (*Remedia*, ll. 529–32)

> [You are weak and unable to leave; you are held
> captive, and cruel Love presses your neck under
> his foot. Stop fighting it; give your sails to the
> wind. Let your boat go to wherever the waves call
> you.]

Ovid tells his pupil to give up control of his vessel, to make love until he is beyond need or desire; excessive indulgence eradicates passion:

> Explenda est sitis ista tibi, qua perditus ardes:
> cedimus; e medio iam licet amne bibas.
> sed bibe plus etiam quam quod praecordia poscunt;
> gutture fac pleno sumpta redundet aqua.
> i, fruere usque tua nullo prohibente puella;
> illa tibi noctes auferat, illa dies.
> taedia quaere mali: faciunt et taedia finem;
> iam quoque, cum credes posse carere, mane,
> dum bene te cumules et copia tollat amorem
> et fastidita non iuuet esse domo.
>
> (*Remedia*, ll. 533–42)

> [Your thirst, which has made you burn miserably,
> must be satisfied. I submit; it's fine to drink from
> the middle of the stream. But drink more than
> your stomach demands; let the water overflow
> from your full throat. Go, enjoy your girl with no
> prohibitions; let her steal your days and your
> nights. Seek tedium for your woes; even tedium
> makes an end. Furthermore, when you think you
> are ready to be without her, stay anyway, and while
> you fill yourself well, let excess destroy love, and
> then her house will seem revolting to you.]

Here Ovid ventures into complex psychological waters, trying to root out sexual *jouissance,* to convert it into disgust.[56] Sexual revulsion does play a big part in Ovid's remedies, and medieval medical texts will use disgust as a cure for lovesickness.[57]

The efficacy of medieval medicine aside, in Ovid's world of love the imaginary pupil cannot get hurt because all Ovid's Roman roads lead to remedy. Even surrender, he contends, ultimately brings victory over passion. Ovid's boat may go out of control, but as Robert Durling states, "the effect of such pretenses of doubt and lack of control is obviously a function of the general pose of absolute control."[58] "Since spirits vary," says Ovid, "we vary our arts, a thousand types of ills, a thousand cures" [Nam quoniam variant animi, variabimus artes; / mille mali species, mille salutis erunt] (*Remedia*, ll. 525–26). In the *Ars Amatoria* and in the *Remedia*, Ovid has offered a closed, safe world of words in which, as Peter Allen says, "it is possible to play."[59]

Ovid's bravado reaches back into mythic history; he would have saved Phyllis, Dido, and Medea, and would have stopped the Trojan War itself:

> uixisset Phyllis, si me foret usa magistro,
>   et per quod nouies, saepius isset iter.
> nec moriens Dido summa uidisset ab arce
>   Dardanias uento uela dedisse rates,
> nec dolor armasset contra sua uiscera matrem,
>   quae socii damno sanguinis ultra uirum est . . .
> redde Parin nobis, Helenen Menelaus habebit
>   nec manibus Danais Pergama uicta cadent.
> (Remedia, ll. 55–60, 65–66)

> [Phyllis would have lived, if she had had me as a
> teacher, and would have traveled more often the
> road she took nine times. And Dido, dying, would
> not have had to see, from the high castle, the
> Trojan ships, giving their sails to the wind. Nor
> would sorrow have armed the mother against her
> children when she sought revenge on her husband
> by spilling her own blood. Give me Paris:
> Menelaus will have Helen and Troy will not fall to
> Danaan hands.]

Of course Ovid knows this is all a game. He tips his hand by telling us that he could have stopped the Trojan War; he need not admit, in a moment of sobriety or rhetorical failure, that this is not so.

Ovid discusses the comic essence of the love poems in the *Tristia*, when he looks back over his career at the poem that brought him to ruin and exile. He addresses a "trusted friend":

> Utque tibi prosunt artes, facunde, severae,
>   dissimiles illis sic nocuere mihi.
> vita tamen tibi nota mea est. Scis artibus illis
>   auctoris mores abstinuisse sui:
> Scis vetus hoc iuveni lusum mihi carmen, et istos,
>   ut non laudandos, sic tamen esse iocos.
> (Tristia I, ix, 57–62)

[As your serious art, eloquent friend, is profitable
to you, just so has a different art harmed me.
Nevertheless, you know my life; you know that
the habits of the author remain separate from
these arts. You know that this old song of mine is a
game from my youth. These verses ought not to
be praised, but should, rather, be seen as jests.]

The great drama of Ovid's poetry unfolds, both for Ovid himself and for his medieval disciple Chaucer, when these "jests" can no longer be isolated in an amoral world of illusion and artifice.

As we study various characters—Ovid's exiled persona, Pandarus, Criseyde, Troilus, and the Wife of Bath—we see that dramatic conflict arises when someone misreads the barriers between art and reality or what we can call history. When one reads these barriers correctly and can "play the middle" expertly, as the Wife can, he or she wields great power. The Wife knows that Ovid's arts are a game, and she becomes expert at the game of "giving words" in her "real-life" battles with her husbands and with a very real tradition of antifeminist texts by men. For Troilus, however, tragedy comes when he takes art too seriously, putting all his hope in a proto-Ovidian buddy. Conflict in the poem also arises when Troilus eventually refuses to adjust to change, instead maintaining some sort of "stedfastnesse" and "trouthe." In Ovid's and in Chaucer's poetry, Ovidian "art" fails when the rules of the universe seem to change before a character's eyes and verbal craft simply does not do what it should. Characters who think they live in the world of the *Ars Amatoria* find that they live in the *Metamorphoses*.

Ovid himself creates just such a new, uncaring universe both in his "book of bodies changed" and in his exile poetry. The *Metamorphoses* is in many ways about failed artists—Daedalus, Arachne, Orpheus—and in the *Tristia* and the *Ex Ponto*, no words can halt the poet's tragic sorrows. As Chaucer shapes his own poetic universe he accordingly draws from the *Metamorphoses*, and, to a lesser degree, from the exile corpus, by reference, parallel, and allusion. In this way Chaucer balances the infinite verbal pretensions of his characters and reflects in his own works the movement from game to earnest, from *iocus* to *severus*, that he saw in Ovid's poems and knew clearly from the Ovidian vitae. As a medieval Christian reader of Ovid, Chaucer was compelled to address this dramatic conflict and to confront human rhetoricity and desire in a world of revealed truth. But since he was a vernacular poet, a "new Ovid," and a self-appointed clerk of Venus, to do so must also have been his passion and his joy.

2
Love, Change, and Ovidian "Game" in the *Troilus*
Books I and II

He that me broghte first unto that game,
Er that he dye, sorwe have he and shame!
For it is ernest to me, by my feith.
   Canon's Yeoman's Prologue, VIII, ll. 708–10

What Else Chaucer Did

T THE OPENING of the *Troilus*, the narrator, appealing to the fury Tisiphone for inspiration, calls himself the "sorwful instrument, / that helpeth loveres . . . to pleyne." He continues:

For I, that God of Loves servantz serve,
Ne dar to Love, for myn unliklynesse,
Preyen for speed, al sholde I therfore sterve,
So fer am I from his help in derknesse.
But natheles, if this may don gladnesse
To any lovere, and his cause availle,
Have he my thonk, and myn be this travaille!
                    (Book I, ll. 15–21)

Here, at the outset, Chaucer draws attention to himself as a servant of the servants of the pagan God of Love. He depicts his work as a source of comfort that may help those who have suffered for love and "availle" their "cause." It is not clear how exactly the poem will help lovers to "pleyne" or do them any "gladnesse," but certainly the stanza promises some sort of succor for lovers—the chosen audience of a poet who has cast himself as their servant.

Ovid opens the *Ars Amatoria* and the *Remedia Amoris* with similar claims to provide succor for lovers. "If anyone in town does not know the art of love, let him read this and, guided by my song, let him love" (*Ars*, ll. 1–2).[1] The *Remedia* says: "Come to me for precepts, deceived youths, all you whom love has betrayed" (*Remedia*, ll. 41–42).[2] In the lines preceding this offer, Ovid displays his commitment to be a servant of the servants of love when he negotiates, successfully, with this very God of Love simply for permission to compose this book of cures for those in pain.

Planning "art" and "remedy," Ovid offers "precepts"; Chaucer, comfort and advocacy. These self-appointed servants perceive that lovers need help, and they set out to provide it. Each promises to improve the lover's lot, to bring ease where there is pain. As we consider Chaucer's Ovidianism in the *Troilus*, we must wonder if Chaucer's aid will take the form of Ovidian "art" or "remedy." Will this new Ovidian servant of lovers teach strategy or cure? Will he use Ovid's own texts? How will we measure his success in antique romance against Ovid's in amatory elegy? Has Ovid offered, in Chaucer's view, universal ethical precepts, as the commentaries claim?

To get at these questions, we must first examine the *Troilus* and its immediate and primary source, Boccaccio's *Filostrato*. Chaucer's adaptation of the Italian poem reveals how he read and absorbed Ovid's instructional works and brought them to bear on the ancient story. By studying Chaucer's "translation" of the *Filostrato*, we will see how the actual texts and the various medieval manifestations of Ovid serve Chaucer as he fashions his story of the many "arts of love" practiced by Pandarus, Criseyde, and Troilus. Putting Ovid, Boccaccio, and Chaucer side by side throws "Chaucer's Ovid" into relief and shows us Ovid's role in Chaucer's medieval Christian vision.

Studying Chaucer's sources, critics have worked hard to determine "what Chaucer really did" to the *Filostrato*. The general thrust of this scholarship has been to assess how Chaucer intensified Boccaccio's poem, making it more serious, vehement, and philosophically profound. Generally, critics argue that there is much more at stake in Chaucer's poem, that we are on a deeper level of discourse.[3] But what does Ovid, particularly the frivolous poet of the *artes* of love, have to do with this Chaucerian intensification?

One of the most prominent recent students of the two poems, Barry Windeatt, explores what he calls the "paynted proces" by which Chaucer translates Boccaccio.[4] Windeatt explains that though dramatically the *Filostrato* is close to the surface of Chaucer's *Troilus*, the character and the implications of the poem have been thoroughly reshaped by Chaucer's art of translation and interpolation. Chaucer consistently intensifies the

Filostrato by adding references to death and sorrow and by emphasizing the "contrast between the lovers' assumptions and the nature of reality" ("Italian to English," 100). Windeatt tells us that there is more weeping in Chaucer's text, more "intensified contrasts and antitheses," a greater interest in nature and in the "process" of the characters' inward feelings (ibid., 79, 90–91, 85). Windeatt notices too that Chaucer has added an "Ovidian sense of a universe implicit with a historic texture of personal unhappiness" (ibid., 99), finding a natural, historical literary framework for the emotional process his characters—as opposed to Boccaccio's more static versions—must undergo.

Windeatt is right to describe part of what is going on as Ovidian, for in the process of "medievalizing" the Italian story and making it more grave and vehement, Chaucer also, to coin an ugly word, "Ovidianizes" it, by alluding to and echoing passages from Ovid. Chaucer's characters seem to turn to Ovidian rhetoric to attempt to calm flux and harness love—as Shakespeare's Cleopatra so perfectly puts it, to "shackle accidents and bolt up change." Armed with Ovidian handbooks, they combat an unpredictable Ovidian universe.[5] Boccaccio certainly brought Ovid into the story of Troilus, but Chaucer, as we will see, develops and expands Boccaccio's use of Ovid. Through such additions, Chaucer brings to the fore a conflict that in Boccaccio's poem is only embryonic and not specifically Ovidian: the struggle between protean rhetorical strategy and the grievous world of flux and mutability, in Chaucer's terms, between "game" and "ernest."

As we study how Chaucer brought Ovid into the *Troilus*, we must also notice the special significance of Chaucer's allusions to the *Metamorphoses*, for the *Filostrato* includes virtually no references to the sufferers in Ovid's epic.[6] By tracing the evolving role of Ovid's poems in the *Troilus*, we see how Chaucer presents two separate attitudes toward love and art, attitudes exemplified by two Ovids: the young, brash, urbane poet of the *Ars Amatoria* and the older victim of impending, or imposed, exile in the *Metamorphoses* and the *Tristia*. By using cruel fortune to temper the playful rhetorical world, Chaucer asks if Ovid's love manuals will be of any value in the world of the "metamorphoses." The poem shows that though the characters constantly employ rhetoric to counter flux, rhetoric, due to its limitations, becomes part of the problem and fails to deliver more than mere temporary success and safety.[7]

The focus of this conflict is really Troilus. In his lovesickness, he turns to the Ovidian Pandarus for help, but Troilus does not want to live and love by quick fixes and clever scams, does not want to see everything as "game." We have to wonder, finally, if his fidelity to "trouthe" is wisdom or foolishness. Is there something wrong with Troilus or, rather, with everyone else in his universe? All the characters in this poem struggle and suffer, burdened by fear, war, and impending doom. Yet Pandarus and Criseyde seem to know so much more about living in this world than Troilus does. Even if we do not speak of his death, Troilus suffers more than anyone else in the poem. What is it that prevents him from attaining happiness and success?

Perhaps life would be easier for Troilus if he could believe that the only problem in the world was "finding a girl" and that the solution to losing a girl was simply to "find another." To Pandarus, these *are* the only problems, the only possible ones he can recognize. Because of his Ovidian literary genealogy, Pandarus is not designed to address human desire on any other level. For thousands of lines, however, Troilus has no way of knowing this. He does not know what Pandarus—or, for that matter, Criseyde— really is. Chaucer's entire poem, his art of love, is in many ways the story of Troilus's education, and the lessons it teaches go far beyond what we hear in the snappy epigrams of Ovid's original *artes amatoriae*. The rest of this chapter examines Ovidian game as both Pandarus and Criseyde employ it in the first two books of the poem. Rhetorical play and protean strategy distinctively mark Chaucer's rendering of Boccaccio's story. But Chaucer also works here to prepare us for the onset of earnest that will overwhelm the hopes of the lovers and finally dispel Troilus's illusions.

Learned and "Lewed"

With one notable exception, the main characters in the *Troilus* are examples of *homo rhetoricus* or *femina rhetorica*, relying on craft and confident that their art will create or amend reality as needed. Discussing the *Ars Amatoria* in *The Motives of Eloquence*, Richard Lanham describes this art and its boasts: "The ability to construct reality . . . is finally a skill, a talent, a principle of dynamic balance against change" (51). Lanham's words apply equally well to the *Troilus*, where a character's ability to manipulate events is based on his or her rhetorical skills. In the *Troilus* this ability most often depends, seemingly, on how much Ovid the character has read and can employ.

Chaucer showcases various characters' Ovidian power throughout the work, but one thing remains constant: Troilus's inability to employ language as effectively as the others do, forcing him to rely on and be controlled by their games and rhetorical power. John Speirs has called Troilus the "least Chaucerian of the trio," and to this we must add that he is the least Ovidian, too. Troilus suffers in this poem, ultimately, because he pledges and maintains "trouthe" (see III, 1296ff.). However we may see that insistence *sub specie aeternitatis,* belief in "trouthe" has no place in an Ovidian universe. This issue of "trouthe" brings up a question we will have to confront: In what kind of poetic world has Chaucer set his Trojan "art of love"? Is it a world of fiction and Ovidian play, like the *Ars Amatoria,* or a world in which history and "reality" confound play and verbal fantasy, as they do in Ovid's later poetry? Perhaps that depends on a given character's perspective, and on that character's apparent Ovidian learning.

As he shapes the world of the poem, Chaucer takes pains to show that Troilus, for one, has not read much Ovid. The first explicit indication of his ignorance comes as Pandarus, explaining his own unhappy love life, asks Troilus if he has read Oenone's letter to Paris, the one that tells how Apollo's medicinal powers fail to heal the god's own love wounds. "Nay nevere yet, ywys" (I, 657), Troilus replies, because unlike learned Pandarus he has not read Ovid's *Heroides,* from which Oenone's letter comes (*Heroides* V). The scene does not occur in Boccaccio's poem. A few stanzas later, using a reference that also has no parallel in the *Filostrato,* Pandarus tells the young lover that it is fruitless to weep over his sorrows "as Nyobe the queene, / Whos teres yet in marble been yseene" (I, 699–70). When Troilus finally responds, he expresses his distaste for Pandarus's proverbs and learned allusions: "What knowe I of the queene Nyobe?/ Lat be thyne olde ensaumples" (ll. 759–60). Already we see a clear pattern. Pandarus, in his use of mythic exempla and in his self-characterization as the "sick physician" of love, adopts the voice of the Ovidian love counselor. Troilus, on the other hand, is the young student, uneasy, but in dire need of instruction in the basics.

Later, in an amateurish attempt at constructing a fanciful alibi for his whereabouts, Troilus incorrectly refers to Apollo speaking from the laurel (in Ovid's story it is Daphne who is so transformed). Winthrop Wetherbee considers the "elaborate" nature of the alibi, its awkward details, and its passionate closing couplet as evidence of "spontaneity," "urgency," and the "spiritual tendency of Troilus's feelings," providing "vivid insight into the instinctively religious element" of Troilus' character. Windeatt claims that the error is Chaucer's and indicates that the poet "is less interested in the details of what happened in the classical story than in evoking the kind of personified natural world where trees are alive with gods."[8] But given Troilus's statements about Niobe and Oenone's letter, I think we are to see his alibi as further evidence of his amateur rank as a verbal artist. Pandarus knows his Ovid well, as does Criseyde, who later quotes from the very letter that Pandarus has asked Troilus about (IV, 1548ff.). Since none of these references, to Oenone, Niobe, or Apollo and Daphne, is in the *Filostrato,* we see that Chaucer is adding to Boccaccio's poem an Ovidian vocabulary that develops an important contrast between Pandarus's knowledge and Troilus's ignorance.

In accord with Chaucer's distribution of Ovidian learning, Troilus has not read the *Ars Amatoria* either. Even though Ovid advises young men to seek women in temples, Troilus goes there to scorn the lovers and only accidentally catches sight of the enchanting Criseyde. Chaucer makes Troilus a prime subject for an Ovidian counselor by denying him the romantic experience that Troilo has in Boccaccio's poem and denying him Troilo's Boethian awareness of mutability.[9] Contemplating the initiation of this new affair, Boccaccio's hero wonders:

> Che è a porre in donna alcuno amore?
> Che come al vento si volge la foglia,
> Cosi in un di ben mille volte il core
> Di lor si volge . . .
> O felice colui che del piacere
> Lor non è preso, e sassene astenere!
>
> (*Filostrato* I, 22)

> [Why give love to any woman? For even as the leaf
> flutters in the wind, so in one day, fully a thousand
> times, do their hearts change. . . . Oh, happy is he
> who is not caught by their delights and can hold
> himself aloof.][10]

Troilus has no such insight but says only that he *has heard* of the woes of getting, maintaining, and, ultimately, losing a woman:

> I have herd told, pardieux, of youre lyvynge,
> Ye loveres, and youre lewed observaunces,
> And which a labour folk han in wynnynge
> Of love, and in the kepyng which doutaunces;
> And whan youre prey is lost, woo and penaunces.
> O veray fooles, nyce and blynde be ye!
> Ther nys nat oon kan war by other be.
>
> (I, 197–203)

The game of love is going to be new to Troilus, whose swaggering scorn is no substitute for experience. And in his testimony here he unconsciously refers to the Ovidian program that Pandarus will put him through, for his three-part statement reflects the function of *Ars* I, *Ars* II, and the *Remedia*, respectively. Somewhere he has heard of the woes of winning, keeping, and losing love, but he has no idea of what is in store for him, no idea that Pandarus will become those texts to try to help him adjust to every fluctuation in the game of love. It seems that Chaucer wants to prepare us for Troilus's detailed lessons and eventual suffering because of these specific texts designed to aid a lover at each stage.

In line with these changes to Boccaccio's poem, Chaucer transforms a passage in which Boccaccio describes Troilo's engagement and even delight at the prospect of his love. After Troilo is smitten, Boccaccio tells us: "He was anxious only to cure his amorous wounds, and to the task he now devoted his every thought and in it he found his delight" [Sol di curar l'amorose ferute / Sellecito era, e quivi ogni intelletto / Avea posto, all' affanno ed il diletto] (I, 44). Chaucer's Troilus, however, only desires that "she of him wolde han compassioun, / And he to ben hire man while he may dure. / Lo, here his lif, and from the deth his cure" (I, 467–69). The English eliminates Troilo's sense of action, intellection, and delight, all of which indicate control and confidence independent of his reliance on Pandaro. Chaucer eliminates this *jouissance*, expressing instead Troilus's fear and anxiety. Chaucer wanted not a veteran to play his Troilus, but a novice, a *iuvenis*, like those whom Ovid teaches. Throughout the poem Chaucer continually distinguishes Troilus by his unfamiliarity with Ovid, keeping him out of step with other characters, making him the poorest strategist in the poem, and, most important, making him the object of the learning and rhetoric used by others. As the "game" of love unfolds in these first two books, we see that Troilus is at best a poor player.

Uncle Amoris

Just as Chaucer emphasizes Troilus's ignorance of Ovid, he correspondingly reveals Pandarus's vast Ovidian wisdom, as we have already seen in Pandarus's use of the *Heroides* and his reference to Niobe. And like the Ovid of the love poems, Pandarus is experienced and expert, though not always himself successful.[11] His familiarity with Ovid makes him, in the early books of the poem, an *Ars Amatoria* incarnate that provides the necessary advice and stratagems for the young lover to win the woman. He is the author of "game," and the drama of the poem hinges on his imagined vision of love and truth.

Pledging his loyalty and his aid, Pandarus tells Troilus: "Wherfore I am, and wol ben, ay redy / To peyne me to do yow this servyse" (I, 989–90).

The offer originates in the *Filostrato*, where Pandaro, also admitting he is unlucky in love, makes a similar promise (I, 28). But Pandarus's next advice comes not from Boccaccio but from Ovid, and from an unexpected Ovidian source at that. Pandarus tells the young, sorrowing lover that though Criseyde is now his woe, she may soon be the cause of his joy:

> For thilke grownd that bereth the wedes wikke
> Bereth ek thise holsom herbes, as ful ofte
> Next the foule netle, rough and thikke,
> The rose waxeth swoote and smothe and softe.
>
> (I, 946–49)

The image comes from the *Remedia*, where Ovid tells his pupils that the same poet who taught love can now teach the cures for the wounds they may have suffered. The students should not be concerned about this seeming paradox because "the earth nourishes herbs both healthful and harmful, and the nettle is often next to the rose" [terra salutares herbas eademque nocentes / nutrit, et urticae proxima saepe rosa est] (*Remedia*, 45–46).

Ovid here addresses, as we saw earlier, "deceived youths . . . whom love has betrayed" and who need healing. In Chaucer's passage Pandarus, like Ovid, pretends to be the master of paradox, deftly dancing on the border between rose and nettle. But this early in the poem the voice of "remedy," particularly a remedy for those betrayed by their love, strikes an ominous note. Pandarus unconsciously points us toward Troilus's betrayal and the need for a "remedy" before the lovers have even met. We begin to wonder all too early just whether Pandarus can keep the rose and the nettles separate and keep Troilus safe, both now and also when the need for remedy really arises. We also begin to wonder what kind of art of love this poem will be and how it will "availle" the cause of lovers, as Chaucer has promised. Is Pandarus the vehicle of comfort and aid?

If he is, then this comfort, for Troilus and for eager listening lovers, comes in the form of game. As part of his complex Ovidian identity, Pandarus, unlike his Italian counterpart Pandaro, flaunts a specific interest in "game." When Troilus blushes before finally revealing the name of his beloved, Pandarus cries out, "Here bygynneth game" (I, 868), a line that has no counterpart in Boccaccio. In the *Filostrato*, Pandaro is a good companion and a useful go-between, helping his friend and peer. He and Troilo are two Trojan youths, eager for war and love. But Pandaro is no Ovidian artist, and, accordingly, he will employ none of Pandarus's mechanisms, the rumors about Criseyde or the meeting at Deiphebus's house. Pandarus's words and actions display the important gap between Troilus's hope for truth and Pandarus's own addiction to play. He later uses "game" twice, as Chaucer transforms Pandaro's friendly pledge of support into an ambivalent scheme. Discussing his role in the lives of the lovers, Pandarus says he has "bigonne a gamen pleye" (III, 250) and has acted "Bitwixen game and ernest" (III, 254).[12] Unlike his counterpart, the worried Pandaro, he makes no indignant mention of the disgrace of having thrown his honor to the ground; he is not concerned with honor, with losing or gaining it.

Troilus's anxious worry and Pandarus's love of play develop a tension between the two men that will become most powerful as they each react to Criseyde's departure later in the poem. Chaucer heralds this conflict early on, by giving Pandarus his stark and ominous declaration, "Here bygynneth game." The poem progresses to the point at which Troilus sees the folly of this Ovidian-Pandarian game. Like the hapless Yeoman quoted in the epigraph to this chapter, he will sadly lament, "It was no game to *me*."

To develop this dramatic tension elsewhere in Book I, Chaucer employs images and ideas from Ovid's love manuals and at the same time challenges their ability to combat the God of Love and the heavy change he brings. In the "Bayard the horse" passage, for example, completely Chaucer's addition to Boccaccio's story, the narrator compares Troilus's inevitable submission to Love to the horse's submission to the law of the whip:

> As proude Bayard gynneth for to skippe
> Out of the weye, so pryketh hym his corn,
> Til he a lasshe have of the longe whippe—
> Than thynketh he, "Though I praunce al byforn
> First in the trays, ful fat and newe shorn,
> Yet am I but an hors, and horses lawe
> I moot endure, and with me feres drawe"—
>
> (I, 218–24)

Troilus, who never imagined that any force could control him "ayeyns his wille," must suddenly fall "subgit unto love" (I, 225ff.). The scene recalls Ovid's own many battles with the God of Love. Early in the first book of the *Amores*, Ovid concedes that he must surrender to Cupid, just as oxen and horses must surrender to yoke and bit (*Amores* I, ii, 13–16). At this point in the *Amores*, brash Cupid had just routed Ovid's plans to write epic by "lopping off a foot" from his hexameter, reducing Ovid's second verse to pentameter and turning his epic into elegy. Similarly, Ovid also counters Cupid at the outset of the *Remedia*, where the god grudgingly allows Ovid to save poor stricken lovers as long as he promises not to defame love itself.

Despite all these defeats, in the *Ars Amatoria* itself Ovid is the one who makes the rules, equating humble ox and horse not with submissive lovers but with Love himself:

> Sed, tamen et tauri ceruix oneratur aratro,
> frenaque magnanimi dente teruntur equi:
> et mihi cedet Amor.
>
> *(Ars* I, 19–21)

> [But nevertheless, even the ox's neck must feel
> the weight of the plows, and the bit is chafed by
> the teeth of the proud horse. And thus even Love
> must submit to me.]

In light of Ovid's battles with Cupid, how can we read Troilus's encounter? Chaucer's image gives Love, not craft, the upper hand, indicating that the *Troilus* is not set in a rhetorical, Ovidian world where art harnesses Love. In the *Filostrato* at this same juncture Boccaccio only warns his readers that "worldly minds are blind" and "often do things fall out not at all as we planned" (I, 25; see *Troilus* I, 211ff.). As Troilus falls in love, Chaucer expresses the events in particularly Ovidian terms, amplifying Boccaccio's concern for failure and hinting that the "art of love" we are going to witness, unlike Ovid's, may not work.[13]

Throughout Ovid's love poems, Cupid polices the world of lovers and shows Ovid, as he shows Troilus, that his bow is not broken (*Troilus* I, 208). Accordingly, Ovid pays his respects to him from time to time. But it is all play. Ovid offers contradictory accounts of his love battles in the *Ars* and the *Amores* because his is the realm of infinite verbal possibility, a world of poetic "pro wrestling," just for show with a new winner every week. At one moment Love has mastered Ovid, and at the next he has torn off his yoke and proudly slapped it on the neck of his would-be conqueror. Anything goes. Ovid's poetry teaches the art of love not only to men but also to the women whom he has just taught the men how to deceive. He offers a guide to finding love, and also a remedy if one has found love too distressing. He covers every angle and fearlessly embraces contradiction. Chaucer loves game too, but in the *Troilus* he wants to know the limits of rhetorical arts, and he seeks to define the boundaries of game. Trouble begins, then, when Troilus believes that Ovidian strategy can really bring him truth in love, when he tries to makes *severas* out of *iocos* and earnest out of game, an error that lies at the heart of his experience in the poem.[14]

Seize the Day

In Book II as Pandarus continues to "play," Chaucer prepares us for Fortune's turn and the imminent sorrowful "changes" of the later books. To convince Criseyde to welcome Troilus's love, Pandarus uses Ovid's argument about the frailty of beauty:

> Thenk ek how elde wasteth every houre
> In ech of yow a partie of beautee;
> And therfore, er that age the devoure,
> Go love; for old, ther wol no wight of the.
>
> (II, 393–96)

Pandarus knows Ovid's warning that "beauty is a fragile good" that "declines with time and is consumed by its own duration" (*Ars* II, 113–14).[15] His following warning that "crow's feet" (*Troilus* II, 403) will appear under Criseyde's eyes is modeled on Ovid's image of "wrinkles that furrow your flesh" [rugae, quae tibi corpus arent] (*Ars* II, 118) as the hair turns gray and the body gives way to age.[16] These warnings have their parallel in the *Filostrato*, but Boccaccio makes no mention of crow's feet. Chaucer recognized Boccaccio's use of Ovid and then went back to Ovid's text to explore possibilities that Boccaccio was not interested in developing. His addition of an Ovidian detail here illustrates the overall process we have been tracing and indicates that Chaucer was working not only from Boccaccio's text but from Ovid's too.

We also learn something about the origins of rhetoric. At this point in the *Ars Amatoria*, Ovid tells young men that they need more than fleeting beauty to win a lover. A man should thus cultivate himself, learn "two languages" [duas linguas] or be "articulate" [facundus] like Ulysses, who, though not handsome, captivated Calypso with his tales of Troy (*Ars* II, 121ff.). Ovidian eloquence arises from this need to compensate for the transience of physical beauty. Would-be lovers need something more flexible and reliable. Pandarus, *facundus* as any man, turns to rhetoric to counter whatever instability befalls him and the lovers he serves. Both he and his master Ovid believe that words can overcome experience.

The context and implications of Pandarus's "carpe diem" message, however, differ from Ovid's. Ovid fashions the capable young lover and in the process mentions the limits of beauty as a tool in the game. Protean flexibility will amend this easily enough; Odysseus did it and so can anyone. Age, misery, even the Trojan War itself are no match for Ovid's art. Chaucer, however, insists that they are. Pandarus speaks more urgently than the Ovidian master does, depicting a race against time and age, particularly in the imperative "Go love" and in the active verbs "wasteth" and "devoure."

Most significant, in the *Filostrato*, Pandaro's version of this Ovidian argument actually works. Criseida agrees with Pandaro and immediately asks for further report of Troilo:

> "Alas," said Criseida, "thou sayest truly. Thus do
> the years carry us away little by little; and most do
> die ere they tread the path of love to the end. But
> now leave thinking of this and tell me if I can yet
> have the solace and sport of love, and in what
> manner thou didst first take note of Troilus."
> (Gordon, "The Story of Troilus," 46)

Criseyde's reaction to Pandarus's version of the same warning offers not agreement but sorrow and anxiety:

> With this he stynte, and caste adown the heed,
> And she began to breste a-wepe anoon,
> And seyde, "Allas, for wo! Why nere I deed?"
> (II, 407–9)

Chaucer creates this contrast by doing some smart cutting and pasting with the *Filostrato*. He has shifted and intensified Criseida's tearful concern for her honor from *Filostrato* II, 47, to make it directly follow Pandarus's discussion of beauty's transience. Boccaccio uses Ovidian doctrine as a successful incitement for Criseida to give in; to Pandaro, to her, and to the narrator, it simply makes sense. By contrast, Chaucer's "edition" of the episode investigates how the characters respond to change and examines the emotional cost of their responses.[17]

Pandarus's letter-writing instructions to Troilus work similarly, for here also Chaucer plays with the Ovidian context of Pandarus's counsel in order to convey a heightened sense of urgency. In the *Filostrato*, even though Pandaro advises Troilo to write to Criseida, he offers no stylistic guidelines. Pandarus's advice that Troilus keep his letters free of condescension and learned pretension, however, is sound craft from the *Ars Amatoria* (I, 459 ff.) with an added detail borrowed from the *Heroides* (III, 3):

> Towchyng thi lettre, thou art wys ynough.
> I woot thow nylt it dygneliche endite,
> As make it with thise argumentes tough;
> Ne scryvenyssh or craftily thow it write;
> Biblotte it with thi teres ek a lite;
> And if thow write a goodly word al softe,
> Though it be good, reherce it nought to ofte.
>
> (II, 1023–29)

His warning that Troilus not write "dygneliche," "scryvenyssh or craftily" translates Ovid's advice not to use legalistic "labored words" [molesta verba] and not to be "too eloquently highbrow" [in fronte disertus][18] for fear of seeming pompous. Pandarus knows Ovid well, but further comparison to the original Ovidian text adds an interesting twist to this sequence in Chaucer's art of love. Ovid's advice ends as he encourages his pupil to remain confident even if the woman either "will not accept your letter or sends it back unread" [si non accipiet scriptum inlectumque remittet] (*Ars* I, 469). Troilus too fears the "return to sender" stamp on his letter, for he asks Pandarus what to do if Criseyde "nolde it for despit receyve" (*Troilus* II, 1049). Ovid and Pandarus, the officiating doctors of love in these respective texts, respond to this problem differently, and their responses illustrate the new context that Chaucer has given Ovid.

Ovid tells his student that if the woman refuses the letter, he should keep trying because all things change in time. Be patient, he says, because "though you see it took a long time for Troy to fall, nevertheless it did fall" [capta vides sero Pergama, capta tamen] (*Ars* I, 478). Ovid advises his students to look forward to victory, but since Troilus is a Trojan, Chaucer cannot use this historical example of the rewards of patience.[19] By having Pandarus adopt Ovid's letter-writing advice but not this image of conquest, or from a Trojan perspective defeat, Chaucer again juxtaposes Ovidian art and cold, uncaring history. What sounds so hopeful in Ovid's poem becomes ironic and ominous in Chaucer's. This shift from victory to defeat is emblematic of Chaucer's use of Ovid's love poetry throughout the *Troilus*. The fall of Troy, stripped of epic solemnity and gravity by Ovid's playful optimism, becomes powerful and pathetic once again in the *Troilus*.

When the letter is written, Pandarus promises to hand deliver it and ensure a response: "For by that Lord that formede est and west, / I hope of it to bryng answere anon / Right of hire hond" (II, 1053–55). Just as when he drags Troilus into bed with Criseyde, Pandarus takes an active, almost desperate approach to love, displaying once again an urgency that we do not sense in Ovid's poem. Pandarus tries to leave no room for error; he walks through every step with his pupil, almost obsessed with guaranteeing each detail of the pursuit. Pandarus is an "ars," but he is not exactly Ovid's *Ars* because Chaucer toys with Pandarus's Ovidian roots to create a less assured *doctor amoris*, working in a less secure world, and teaching a more passionate and ultimately less malleable young man.

Helenic Art

Book II sees the rise of another Ovidian whose rhetorical skills continue to develop the tension between Ovidian art and Chaucerian drama. Throughout the book, Criseyde's words echo those of Ovid's Helen in her letter to Paris (*Heroides* XVII); here she vacillates between indignation and passionate submission as she debates accepting the Trojan Paris's love. The complex resonances of this Helenic language allow Chaucer to bring into the poem a greater sense of history and also to develop Criseyde as a skillful Ovidian. Helen's epistle is at once part of the history of Troy, part of Ovid's poetic project of telling a new history of women, and, for medieval scholastic commentators, part of Ovid's ethical project of stigmatizing base desire.[20] The Helen of the *Heroides* would have been many things to Chaucer: a sign of doom; a source of verbal power and art; and also an example, according to the *accessus*, of "corrupt desire" [*amor incestus*].[21]

Chaucer folds these conflicting identities into his inherited material as he simultaneously empowers Criseyde and undermines her power by locating it in history—in the tragic history of Troy. This "power" arises because the *Heroides*, not formally part of the *Ars Amatoria*, share many features with it and in many ways create the same sealed world of free play. The *Heroides* take part in Ovid's plan to "arm the Amazons" (*Ars* III) and must be seen in the context of his comprehensive study of men and women negotiating desire through language.

Chaucer subtly, but unmistakably, associates Criseyde and Helen. These parallels insist that it is dangerous to consider either woman "fidelem," because they both respond to change with change, adjusting to new situations expediently.[22] Criseyde's concern for keeping her "honour sauf" (see *Troilus* II, 479 ff.; III, 159), fear of fickle, deceitful men (II, 786–87), and her dubious claim that she is new at love-letter writing (II, 1212ff.), all appear in Helen's text.[23] The first two have analogues in Boccaccio,[24] but her claim about letter writing is Chaucer's own addition from Ovid's poem:

> "Depardieux," quod she, "God leve al be wel!
> God help me so, this is the firste lettre
> That evere I wroot, ye, al or any del."
>
> (*Troilus* II, 1212–14)

Examining these parallels, one critic argues that Criseyde learns from Helen how to act without acting and how to decide without deciding.[25] Such a view is by no means anachronistic, for as Hexter has shown, at least one medieval commentary on the *Heroides* displays an appreciation for Helen's rhetorical art. The commentary states: "[Helen] speaks as a lover because now she wants to and now she doesn't."[26] This insightful and sensitive comment allows us to broaden our view of the commentary tradition on Ovid's poem, seeing that medieval teachers were not restricted to a dry moral interpretation of the letters as promotions of chaste love or criticisms of impure [incestus] love. It is useful and important for our analysis of Criseyde to note that Helen commonly exemplifies the latter.[27] However, the clever commentator could go deeper, discovering the verbal arts and strategies that make a character an accomplished lover and a skilled rhetorician.[28]

Ovid's Helen and Chaucer's Criseyde are both. Although taken aback by their respective suitor's advances, neither is unaware of her own beauty. Criseyde says she is "oon the faireste, out of drede" (II, 746), recalling Helen's claims that though she may doubt Paris, it is "not because I lack confidence or because I am unaware of my appearance" [non quod fiducia desit, / aut mea sit facies non bene nota mihi] (XVII, 37–38). Accordingly both Ovid and Chaucer give their heroines an appreciation and appetite for men, expanding their historical, literary identities and giving them independent will and "taste." Criseyde does not fail to notice Troilus's "shap," as her spontaneous intoxication upon seeing him makes clear, and Helen recognizes the mutual attraction that captivates her and Paris: "My husband is away, and you too sleep alone, and we are seized in turn by each other's beauty" [Et vir abest nobis, et tu sine coniuge dormis, / inque vicem tua me, te mea forma capit] (XVII, 179–80). This extraordinary verse wraps the lovers together between their possessive pronouns.

Helen adds that Paris's beauty just might lead her to forget her modesty and surrender, since, though he pretends he is a warrior, he is really made for love: "Perhaps, forgetting shame, I might become wise and, finally conquered, give my hesitating hands" [Aut ego deposito sapiam fortasse pudore / Et dabo cunctatas tempore victa manus] (XVII, 259–60). Helen is quite capable of "getting down to business," and so is Criseyde, who interrupts one of Troilus's labored pledges to "trouthe" to take him finally as her lover:

> But lat us fall awey fro this matere,
> For it suffiseth, this that seyd is heere,
> And at o word, withouten repentaunce,
> Welcome, my knyght, my pees, my suffisaunce!
>
> (III, 1306–9)

Helen, for her part, acts out an Ovidian paradigm, for her last statement about surrender echoes Ovid's letter-writing advice that women will submit to craft and "give their hands to eloquent men" [tam dabit eloquio victa puella manus] (*Ars* I, 462). We are not surprised, then, that Helen's description of Paris's flirtatious behavior at the banquet—tracing love letters in wine and drinking from the place her lips touched the goblet—comes right out of the *Amores*, where the master himself is flirting with his mistress under her husband's nose.[29]

In the Paris-Helen sequence, then, we witness a successful, textbook, Ovidian seduction. But Helen is no abstract object of pursuit, not the nameless victim of *Ars Amatoria* strategy; she is, rather, a qualified Ovidian herself. In this exchange of letters, Paris and Helen clash without either of the Ovidians losing self-respect or verbal control. Their mutual goal is mutual enjoyment. In other letters in the *Heroides*, we hear formerly suppressed emotional histories. In this pair, Ovid imagines the artistry and the wit of a woman not lamenting her naïveté and scorning her betrayer, but thinking, desiring, negotiating, well armed with Ovid's gift of words.

Criseyde's echoes of Helen thus portray her too as crafty and able to adjust to circumstances without ever losing verbal control or dropping her rhetorical guard. Criseyde, like Helen, is a player in the game of love and change, a competent Ovidian, a true niece of Pandarus, and rhetorically far beyond Troilus, who, unlike his distant brother, the Paris of the *Heroides*, can only mangle logic about free will and sigh Petrarchan sonnets. In fact, later in the poem Troilus himself becomes a composite of the scorned women in the *Heroides*, waiting endlessly for the return of his lover, recalling past promises, writing letters, and wishing for death.

A feature of Paris's own letter in this sequence has added significance for the *Troilus*, bringing into the story a hint of the large historical movement that will ultimately confound all hopes. Paris ends by ominously assuring Helen that no one will try to rescue her and if anyone does, his men will easily repel them (see XVI, 341ff.)—famous last words indeed. Chaucer's implied association of Criseyde with Helen, then, again brings into his poem the overarching theme of Troy's fall. Helen's affair leads to the fall of Troy and Criseyde's to the fall of Troilus. Criseyde's musings, like Helen's, thus conceal a cataclysmic situation, for behind each of their rhetorical displays is the reality of war, failure, betrayal, and death.

But here we must maintain one important distinction between the *Heroides* and the *Troilus*. The *Heroides*, despite the epic magnitude of the names "Helen" and "Paris" and the verbal irony in the discussion of war, are still, like the *Ars Amatoria*, set in a world of play. Ovid's celebration of language and the characters' emphasis on their personal, emotional lives neutralize the gravity of epic situations. By re-creating Helen's artful monologues and romantic spirit in Criseyde, a character in a tragic story that extends beyond the boundaries of the closed Ovidian love-world, Chaucer puts gravity back into the Troy story by putting love-language back into the world of change. And by throwing Helen's voice into Criseyde, Chaucer continues the dramatic question he began to explore in Book I with Pandarus: Can a character lift Ovidian craft outside the shielded fantasy world of "art"? As the poem progresses we will be anxious to see if Criseyde's verbal power can help her when she and Troilus have to part. Will her Ovidian training come into play when she meets the crafty, Ovidian lover, Diomede? The next chapter will try to answer this.

Stepping back from the first two books of the *Troilus*, we see how Chaucer throws Ovidian voices into his characters almost as if they were unconsciously turning to Ovidian texts for guidance and identity. Yet in this game of love we see constant signs of sorrow and doom—in this last example, the inevitable fall of Troy and Trojan—as Chaucer darkens the world of play with the threat of failure and tragedy. Verbal games are powerful, and those who master them can control any set of circumstances, changing as the external world does. But because rhetoric sustains happiness and control only until new circumstances demand a new plan, it wins many battles, but can never win the war, never subdue what Ovid in the *Metamorphoses* calls the "tanta . . . rerum inconstantia" [the great inconstancy] that twists men, or what Chaucer or Boethius would call mutability or Fortuna.

Mutability should logically pose no problem for an Ovidian, who would simply fight change with change, reshaping himself or herself in amoral, protean fashion. However, great folly comes when one uses Ovidian rhetoric but takes it for truth, forgetting that all things change and that a successful Ovidian lover has to change too. And at a certain point even the best Ovidian shape-shifting and the sweetest of lies fail to stop Fortune's wheel. The world of art and fantasy has to give way to history and tragedy. As the rest of the poem unfolds, Chaucer will continue ever more powerfully to make earnest out of game and expose the frailty of the love-world Pandarus has built on Ovidian doctrine. Chaucer does this in part by turning again to Ovid, not in his incarnation as the playful doctor of love, but as the author of metamorphosis and as the man of many sorrows, buffeted himself by change and exile.

3
Change and Remedy
Books III, IV, and V of the Troilus

 HE CHARACTERS frantically search for "remedy" in the final books of the Troilus, as Ovidian game encounters Ovidian mutability. Before we trace this confrontation, however, we must acknowledge that Pandarus's arts do indeed bring the lovers together. An elaborate, pretentious dinner party, the invention of Troilus's imaginary rival "Horaste," a "secre trap dore" and a little leading "by the lappe" finally unite the lovers. Ovid would have been proud of such devices, for to win a love, he says, one must adopt "a thousand devices" [mille modis]. "Whoever is wise," he continues, "will be infinitely versatile" (*Ars* I, 756ff.).[1] Pandarus is busy being a good Ovidian. Yet in the course of Book III, Chaucer undermines Pandarus' scheming and the union his devices have created. In this book and continuing toward the poem's tragic climax, Ovidian art becomes more and more dubious and less and less capable of keeping Troilus and Criseyde together. As the rest of the poem unfolds, the characters seem to grow farther apart. Of course, Criseyde's leaving Troy contributes to this separation, but the divisions between her and Troilus and between Troilus and Pandarus reveal themselves as essential divisions of belief. Simply put, Chaucer will separate Troilus from his friend and from his lover, both of whom remain disciples of Ovid.

Success and Myrrha

Let us first look at the lovers' union to see how even in success Ovidian art appears out of harmony with human love. Pandarus's fabrication of a rival of Troilus, for example, is an excessive tactic in this case and almost backfires. Pandarus tells Criseyde that Troilus fears a competitor, Horaste, and needs a sign of security. Making one's lover fear a rival is a solid Ovidian device, and Pandarus must assume that the general air of jealousy will bring the lovers closer. He is right, but it does not happen so easily. In the *Amores,* Ovid's opponent, the old woman Dipsas, tells her female pupils: "Do not let [your suitor] love free from anxiety, fearing no lover; / love will not endure well if you eliminate conflict" (*Amores* I, viii, 95–96).[2]

Pandarus, as a third party, adopts this love-enhancing device, but it does not suit the needs or wishes of either of the lovers. Criseyde, the object of Pandarus's trickery here, explodes with dismay and grief; she knows no Horaste and has no desire to make Troilus jealous. Later, necessity will compel Criseyde herself to employ Ovidian survival strategy, but at this point, unlike Pandarus, she is no cynical plotter. She denies that "jealousy is love," and she cries to think that some fool has told Troilus this nonsense and that he has believed it (see III, 806ff., 988ff). Troilus, whom Pandarus intends to benefit by the story of the false rival, instead suffers because of the ploy. The tears Criseyde sheds over this accusation make Troilus feel the "crampe of deth" upon his heart, and he begins to regret Pandarus's plot:

> And in his mynde he gan the tyme acorse
> That he com there, and that, that he was born;
> For now is wikke torned into worse,
> And al that labour he hath don byforn,
> He wende it lost; he thoughte he nas but lorn.
> "O Pandarus," thoughte he, "allas, thi wile
> Serveth of nought, so weylaway the while!"
> . . . .
> Than seyde he thus, "God woot that of this game,
> Whan al is wist, than am I nought to blame."
>
> (III, 1072–78, 1084–85)

Troilus thinks the Ovidian "games" worthless, but he cannot yet fully articulate his feeling, even though his sorrow shows that the poem is building toward this realization. Despite the tears shed, Pandarus's little device does work; it so upsets the lovers that they fall into mutual consolation that culminates in the heavenly bliss of sexual consummation. Even so, the plan would have failed if Pandarus had not thrown Troilus into bed with Criseyde. By having Pandarus employ the Horaste strategy, Chaucer exploits the tension between the pretense of rhetorical strategy and the pathos of human pain. Every Ovidian game demands an emotional price in the *Troilus*, but Pandarus does not understand this. Incapable of what are now called value judgments, he operates from radical contingency. If a strategy is "useful" he uses it, with no regard for anything but victory.

In essence I am arguing for "Chaucerian gravity" in these later books of the poem, and to understand the specifically Ovidian terms with which Chaucer expresses this gravity, we have to consider the role of Ovid's poem about "bodies changed." To discuss the *Metamorphoses*, we should first define what "change" means in Chaucer's text. As Wetherbee points out in his discussion of Ovid and the *Troilus*, it does not mean mere physical change: "There is change in Chaucer's Ovidian world, but no true metamorphosis." Wetherbee rightly makes this distinction between the two poets, for though Chaucer alludes directly to many stories of metamorphosis, such as Niobe and Daphne, change in the *Troilus* is not physical or mythic. Chaucer's characters never escape their plights by turning into something else.[3]

Equally important, however, is the poets' *shared* vision of change, for often in the *Metamorphoses* itself, there is "no true metamorphosis," no mythic escape or liberation. Instead, Ovid focuses on the same type of instability and flux that fills the *Troilus*, the movement from woe to weal to woe. Who, for example, recalls the "metamorphosis" in the story of Orpheus? The episode ends with his female murderers turned to trees by Bacchus, but the point of the story is the fragility of happiness and the ever-present threat of loss, culminating in Eurydice's disappearance: "Loving, he turned his eyes to see her and she suddenly vanished" [Flexit amans oculos: et protinus illa relapsa est] (*Metamorphoses* X, 57).[4] Similarly, we all, like Pandarus, know that Niobe was turned to stone, but the true "change" in her story is from the presumptuous pride of abundant motherhood to the misery and sorrow of childlessness (see VI, 146ff.).

The daughters of old Anius in Book XIII are turned to doves by Bacchus so they may escape captivity, but the most important transformation in the story is that of Anius himself, from a father of five to a man "nearly bereft." When Anchises wonders if he errs in thinking Anius a father of several children, the old man replies:

Non falleris, heros
maxime; vidisti natorum quinque parentem,
quem nunc—tanta homines rerum inconstantia versat—
paene vides orbum.

(XIII, 644–47)

[No, you do not err, O greatest hero. You once saw
the father of five children, whom now—so does
the great inconstancy of things twist men—you see
nearly bereft.]

The great inconstancy of things that twist men—this mutability constitutes metamorphosis for both Ovid and Chaucer. Ovid testifies to this conception of "change" not only throughout the *Metamorphoses* but also in the *Tristia*. From exile Ovid writes that his own life story is fit to be in his book of "bodies changed," since his freedom and renown have been transformed into exile and despair. He too is a victim of the *rerum inconstantia;* he too has fallen "out of joie," as he tells his poem before sending it to Rome:

Sunt quoque mutatae, ter quinque volumina, formae,
nuper ab exequiis carmina rapta meis.
his mando dicas, inter mutata referri
fortunae vultum corpora posse meae.
namque ea dissimilis subito est effecta priori,
flendaque nunc, aliquo tempore laeta fuit.

(*Tristia* I, i, 117–22)

[And there are, in fifteen volumes, the changed
forms, songs lately snatched from my funeral rites.
Tell them the face of my fortune can be consid-
ered among the bodies changed, for things are not
now what they were before. Now there is cause for
woe, where there once was joy.]

Though Chaucer's Ovidian allusions in themselves are relevant, his complex crafting of stories in which joy turns to woe requires attention.

But I do not want to reduce either Ovidian or Chaucerian metamorphosis to simple "mutability." Metamorphosis can indicate a great many types of change, social, sexual and emotional, as Leonard Barkan demonstrates so thoroughly in his study of Ovid's poem.[5] To understand better

Chaucer's use of Ovid and the function of Chaucerian metamorphosis, let us examine one scene in some depth, looking at a story about mutability and about mythic and human change, a story about sexual experience that is one of the most unsettling in Ovid's poem. In Book IV, Chaucer compares the sorrows of the lovers to those of Myrrha, whose story comes from the *Metamorphoses:*

> The woful teeris that they leten falle
> As bittre weren, out of teris kynde,
> For peyne, as is ligne aloes or galle—
> So bittre teeris weep nought, as I fynde,
> The woful Mirra thorugh the bark and rynde—
> That in this world ther nys so hard an herte
> That nolde han rewed on hire peynes smerte.

(IV, 1135–41)

Chaucer's allusion, which has no counterpart in the *Filostrato*, is particularly striking because the tale of Myrrha strangely parallels the story of the lovers in Book III of the *Troilus*. Chaucer uses an elaborate series of images that force us to fear for the lovers' fate. The important "change" in Ovid's story is not Myrrha's transformation into a tree, though this is how Chaucer *explicitly* recalls her. The focus is, rather, the movement from youthful desire to incest and exile, a tale of unrestrained and unquenchable passion in which a young lover, led by an older, wiser counselor, is finally united with her love object.[6] Examining the specific imagery in Ovid's and Chaucer's episodes shows us just how Chaucer has employed this tale of change.

Having spent his first night with Criseyde, Troilus awakes and curses "nyght," whose departure signifies the end of the lovers' pleasure:

> O blake nyght, as folk in bokes rede,
> That shapen art by God this world to hide
> At certeyn tymes wyth thi derke wede,
> That under that men myghte in reste abide,
>
> . . . .
>
> Thow doost, allas, to shortly thyn office,
> Thow rakle nyght! Ther God, maker of kynde,
> The, for thyn haste and thyn unkynde vice,
> So faste ay to oure hemysperie bynde
> That nevere more under the ground thow wynde!

For now, for thow so hiest out of Troie,
Have I forgon thus hastili my joie!

(III, 1429–32, 1436–42)

As Robinson long ago pointed out, Chaucer models much of Troilus's speech (not found in the *Filostrato*) on *Amores* I, xiii, which also mentions the night-time affair of Jove and Alcmena (ll. 45–46). However, Ovid's poem exclusively invokes accursed Dawn, who comes too soon because she will not lounge with her old husband, Tithonus, but Troilus addresses night only, emphasizing its blackness and its ability to hide the world. Troilus laments not that dawn has come but that the protective covering of night is gone. Similarly, in the *Metamorphoses*, Myrrha, as she joins with her father, is protected from recognition by darkness: the incest occurs when "the golden moon had fled the sky, dark concealing clouds covered the stars, and night was lightless" (*Metamorphoses* X, 448–50).[7]

The father's curiosity leads him to bring in a torch and with "light brought in" [inlato lumine] (l. 473) he discovers the crime [scelus]. The "change" occurs as the father pulls his sword and chases the daughter away into exile and she begs the gods to transform her, to take her beyond her plight. They turn her into a tree—the image that Chaucer uses to recall the primary themes of the story: the advent of young, forbidden desire, the power of an uncontrollable human will, and the fragility of the secret affair wrought by deceit in darkness. When Chaucer compares the lovers' sorrows to those of Myrrha, then, he does not offer a sympathetic or romantic reflection of their "exploitation" by Pandarus. Rather, he provides a darker, more severe coloring to their affair, deflating their lofty language and hopes, particularly Troilus's, during their night of indescribable bliss. The direct reference to Myrrha summons a world of change that breaks the illusions of love poetry and love strategy. The story of Myrrha serves particularly well here because in the context of Ovid's corpus it functions as Ovid's own deflated version of the "art of love," the earnest version of the game and play we find in the *Ars Amatoria*.

How does Myrrha appear in Ovid's love poetry? In her two appearances there, she serves as nothing more than an amorous exemplar, first of lust, then of bad timing. In the *Ars Amatoria*, she exemplifies female aggression, proving "that all women can be caught" [prima tuae menti ueniat fiducia, cunctas / posse capi] (*Ars* I, 269–70). "If we males did not ask the woman first, the woman, already won, would play the aggressor" [Conueniat maribus, ne quam nos ante rogemus, / femina iam partes uicta rogantis aget] (277–78). In the *Remedia*, Myrrha appears as proof of Ovid's argument not to delay starting one's therapy. Do not keep saying, "I'll start tomorrow," says Ovid, because delay is dangerous: "If you had sensed early, Myrrha, how great a crime you were preparing, you would not be hiding your face in bark" [Si cito sensisses quantum peccare parares, / non tegeres uultus cortice, Myrrha, tuos] (*Remedia*, ll. 99–100). As usual, Ovid's bravado purges the myth of gravity and turns tragedy into bold hope.

But in the *Metamorphoses*, as in the *Troilus*, characters *are* left to their fates.[8] The game of love stops and experience overcomes art. Chaucer saw this movement in the poems of Ovid and casts it in his own poem by comparing his lovers to Myrrha. The one-line allusion alone does not do all the work. But by allowing his own story, in its imagery and detail, to recall Ovid's story of darkness, pandering, and incest, Chaucer invokes the world of metamorphosis that lies behind the simple comparison at IV, 1139. He shows that the lovers are doomed and that Pandarus's plans, like those of Myrrha's nurse, but unlike those of the *magister* in the *Ars Amatoria*, will ultimately fail.

In darkening the expectations of game by conjuring Ovid's *Metamorphoses* in Book III, Chaucer neither judges the lovers directly, nor makes it easy for us to do so. He invites us to rethink the Ovidian rhetoric that has brought them together.[9] Chaucer, having the advantage that the texts of Ovid's career are simultaneously before him, mingles the playful world of the *artes amatoriae* and the world of grievous change in ways that Ovid in his early poetry could not.

But Chaucer's complex allusion to Myrrha and metamorphosis neither negates nor ironizes the "hevene blisse" of the lovers, celebrated in one of the greatest Middle English praises of human sexuality:

> Of hire delit or joies oon the leeste
> Were impossible to my wit to seye;
> But juggeth ye that han ben at the feste
> Of swich gladnesse, if that hem liste pleye!
> I kan namore, but thus thise ilke tweye
> That nyght, bitwixen drede and sikernesse,
> Felten in love the grete worthynesse.
>
> (III, 1310–16)[10]

Rather, Chaucer exploits the tension between the bliss and the power of change. Ovid himself, in a unique passage in the *Ars Amatoria*, also celebrates mutual sexual joy. After endless catalogs of strategy, Ovid offers a moment of quiet repose: "Behold how the bed consciously accepts the two lovers. Stay outside the closed doors, Muse. Without you and following their own desires, they will speak those oft repeated words. Nor will hands lie idle in the bed, but fingers will find what they might do in those places where Love moistens his secret dart" (*Ars* II, 703–8). This is the time for neither game nor sadness, but for a seemingly perfect moment. So too in the night of bliss shared by Troilus and Criseyde we find no game and no woe. Here we have a free, still, sexual paradise, beyond the poet's scope, beyond language. Ovid's love scene is "extra-musical," for the lovers themselves need no inspiration, no craft to prompt them to do and say the right things. Words, craft, and wit create these strangely parallel passages in Ovid's and Chaucer's respective arts of love. The bliss of Ovid's lovers is timeless and perfect; that of Chaucer's lovers is qualified and soon to be bound up in woe.

Chaucer's addition to the *Filostrato* of other, explicit references to the *Metamorphoses* contributes to the sense of impending doom in Book III. In Book II, the "swalowe Proigne" wakes Pandarus with the story of the disaster that befalls her and her sister (II, 63ff.), preparing us for Criseyde's ominous comparison to the "newe abaysed nyghtyngale" (III, 1233).[11] Troilus, praying for strength and success in love, calls Venus and Apollo to help him for the sake of "Adoun" and "Dane" (Daphne). Although Troilus here seems to finally display some knowledge of Ovid, his innocent references to disastrous, even fatal love ironically point to the mutability and the calamity that will befall him.[12]

Chaucer employs Ovid's stories of change as an inventive philosophical "remedy." Ovid balanced his own works: he led his pupils to love, then gave the wounded ones healing remedies. Chaucer provides a comparable balance, but on a graver level. In the later books he invokes the powers of change in specifically Ovidian terms to counter the power of the love strategy that he had also portrayed in specifically Ovidian terms. Chaucer seems to be following the view of one medieval commentator who reports that Ovid wrote the *Remedia Amoris* to offset the *Ars Amatoria* because "the highest creator of all things did nothing without providing a remedy."[13]

Chaucer knew well from Boethius and from Jean de Meun that bad fortune provides the soul a better remedy than good fortune does, because it alone gives true wisdom, revealing the mutability and frailty of the world.[14] Chaucer's references to the *Metamorphoses*, in that they reflect the many changes that Troilus suffers in his double loss of Criseyde, have the potential to become this corrective, showing the reader that Ovidian change is overcoming Ovidian art. The reader can see this, but Fortune's many changes serve to frighten the lovers without necessarily enlightening them. At the very end of the poem, Chaucer expresses the Boethian remedy to the problem of change in explicitly Christian terms. But before he does, he depicts how the three central characters variously respond to change as they test out several types of Ovidian remedy.

Change, Pandaro, and Pandarus

In Book IV, which opens with Fortune at her wheel, change becomes formidable and rapid. Previously, in the first change of the poem, the cynical Troilus became a stricken would-be lover; sudden shock made the scoffer at love into a disciple. But Troilus is never comfortable with change. Steadfast and true, even as an opponent of love, how did he cope with his new status? Pandarus, as master of the *Ars Amatoria* and therefore a master of flexibility, helped Troilus deal with change and fulfill his desire. As master equally of the *Remedia Amoris*, Pandarus will attempt again to succor his friend when the next change occurs, when Criseyde must leave Troy. But any hope for his success fails as the imagery of mutability begins to dominate the poem and to devastate the lovers. Ovidians can only do so much when the rules of the universe change, when the "playing" field evolves into a battlefield of history. Pandarus cannot help Troilus, and Criseyde, realizing that the world is changing quickly, can only hope to save herself.

At the Trojan council's discussion about exchanging Criseyde for Antenor, Troilus hears the fateful proposal: "For which ful soone chaungen gan his face, / As he that with tho wordes wel neigh deyde. / But natheles he no word to it seyde" (IV, 150–52). In the *Filostrato*, Boccaccio tells us that Troilo is "pierced to the heart" by the news and thinks he will die, but Boccaccio does not offer the vocabulary of "change" or focus on Troilus's visage as Chaucer does.[15] Boccaccio dramatizes mutability in his poem, especially in Troilo's complaint, "La mia letizia s'é voltata in pena" [My joy has turned to woe] (IV, 45). But Chaucer intensifies the theme and portrays it in explicitly Ovidian terms whenever he can, in these lines and throughout the final two books.

Therefore, a few lines later in Chaucer's poem, in a passage that has no parallel in the *Filostrato*, Troilus becomes a tree "Ibounden in the blake bark of care, . . . So sore hym sat the chaungynge of Criseyde" (IV, 229, 231). He is thus Myrrha again, as he was in Book III, or Daphne, driven to this new form by disastrous love. At this point we do not have to pin down the association because we see clearly what is happening: Chaucer is saturating Boccaccio's story with an Ovidian vocabulary that overwhelms the language of the poem as the characters fall into a maelstrom of change.

Of course, the changing referred to in this passage is the *e*xchange of Criseyde for Antenor, but it foreshadows the next change—Criseyde's betrayal of Troilus in Book V. These changes together bring on Troilus's own neo-Ovidian transformation, for in the *Troilus*, as in the *Metamorphoses*, "the inconstancy of things" transforms life, replacing joy with sorrow. And despite the fantastic nature of Ovidian change, the subject's consciousness does not stop; the transformed one always knows what has happened. As Ovid says of the unlucky hunter Actaeon when Diana turns him into a stag, all was changed but "his mind alone remained the same" [mens tantum pristina mansit] (III, 203). Troilus feels but still does not understand the power of change that betrays him but does not obliterate his consciousness.

And yet, he hopes for escape, telling Pandarus that to relieve him of his sorrows, Pandarus must first "transmewen" him "in a ston" (IV, 467). In Book I, Troilus impatiently asks Pandarus, "What knowe I of the queene Nyobe?" and now he seeks to be turned into stone, as she was, to escape his sorrow. Buffeted by change and swirling in allusion, Troilus is finding that he lives in an Ovidian universe from which Pandarus can offer him no escape. The vocabulary of transformation dominates Criseyde too. Through her distress over the exchange, Criseyde's face "was al ychaunged in another kynde" (IV, 865). Chiding Pandarus for first bringing her into love's service, she calls herself "Criseyde, / That now transmewed ben in cruel wo" (IV, 829–30). Criseyde cannot escape the sorrow of separation, but, as we will soon see, she can and will, as Pandarus advises, "take care of herself" by embracing change in ways that Troilus simply cannot.

Although everything looks bleak for Troilus, his friend Pandarus becomes for him the *Remedia Amoris*, a handbook designed to aid suffering lovers. Pandarus's transformation from the *Ars Amatoria* into the *Remedia* directly reflects the medieval academic understanding of the relationship between these two texts. According to commentary on the *Remedia*, Ovid wrote the work to relieve the misery and to stop the suicides of his pupils who had fallen into "error" and despair because of the doctrines of the *Ars Amatoria*.[16] Similarly, William of St. Thierry's twelfth-century theological treatise *De natura et dignitate amoris* contends that Ovid was compelled to write the *Remedia* by his suffering disciples.[17] Troilus certainly qualifies as a pupil whom an "art of love" has led into error and distress; thus, like Ovid's students, he needs the "remedies." As Ovid begins the *Remedia*, he tells his worried pupils not to fear and not to be surprised that the same man who taught love now proposes its cures. Pandarus displays this same fluidity, the ease and delight of a rhetorician changing styles to accommodate a new set of circumstances.

Pandarus first encourages the Trojan youth to "fight change with change," telling Troilus to find someone else:

> And ek, as writ Zanzis, that was ful wys,
> "The newe love out chaceth ofte the olde";
> And upon newe cas lith newe avys.
> Thenk ek, thi lif to saven artow holde.
> Swich fir, by proces, shal of kynde colde;
> For syn it is but casuel plesaunce,
> Som cas shal putte it out of remembraunce.
>
> (IV, 414–20)

The doctrine originates in the *Remedia* (ll. 441ff.) in a passage that culminates in advice to follow the example of a certain protean lover who lost one woman but immediately found another. After the lover's speech defending his actions, Ovid tells us:

> dixit et hanc habuit solacia magna prioris,
> et posita est cura cura repulsa noua.
> ergo adsume nouas auctore Agamemnone flammas,
> ut tuus in biuio distineatur amor.
>
> *(Remedia,* ll. 483–86)

> [He spoke and had her as a great solace for his
> former loss, and so a rejected love was replaced by
> a new interest. Therefore, follow new flames
> according to the example of Agamemnon, so as to
> divide your love into two.]

The context of this passage in the *Remedia* makes it particularly appealing to see Ovid as Chaucer's source here. For Ovid's model protean lover, wise enough to find another woman, is Agamemnon. When Chryseis's priestly father demands that she be returned to him, her lord Agamemnon capitulates and casually appropriates Achilles' lover, the captive Briseis, in her stead. We cannot determine if Chaucer knew the complex history of Criseyde's name, but it is hard to ignore the fact that Pandarus's advice echoes an Ovidian passage about how to get over Criseyde's literary great-grandmother. Finding a new woman should be no problem, both Pandarus and Ovid agree, for the "town is ful of ladys al aboute" (IV, 401), and "as many are the stars in the heavens, so are the women in your Rome" [quot caelum stellas, tot habet tua Roma puellas] (*Ars* I, 59). Furthermore, as Ovid tells his readers at the end of this section on the judgment of Agamemnon, if you read Ovid's books, "your boat will be full of girls" [plena puellarum iam tibi nauis erit] (*Remedia*, l. 488).

In Chaucer's development and deflation of Ovidian strategy, we see the deep rift between the fantasy of the "arts of love" and the gravity of the *Troilus*. "Getting over" a lost love is no problem in the *Remedia*. The epic situation is characteristically diffuse, Ovid speaking of his exemplar Agamemnon as if his "new care" [cura nova] were without consequences. Ovid forgets, or rejects as unimportant, the rest of the story—the wrath of Achilles and the disaster it brings down upon the Greek troops. But such details, an incursion of "history," would only distract us from Agamemnon's stroke of amorous wisdom. All we know and all we need know are the quick fixes that calm the stricken lover. Agamemnon's political identity, later life, and ultimate fate, like those of Achilles, Odysseus, Romulus, and all the other hero-lovers in the poem, do not concern us.

Much of Pandarus's advice on this subject comes directly from Boccaccio, for Pandaro tells his friend much the same things, particularly that "the new love chases out the old" [il nuovo amor sempre caccia l'antico] (IV, 49), and "the town is full of women" [questa città si vede / piena di belle donne e graziose] (IV, 48). However, his additions to Boccaccio's Ovidian scene invite our comparison of Chaucer's text with Ovid's original verses, for they make Pandarus more of an Ovidian than his Italian counterpart. To support his "new love" argument, Pandarus tells Troilus something about the other fish in the sea:

> What! God forbede alwey that ech plesaunce
> In o thing were and in non other wight!
> If oon kan synge, an other kan wel daunce;
> If this be goodly, she is glad and light;
> And this is fair, and that kan good aright.
> Ech for his vertu holden is for deere,
> Both heroner and faucoun for ryvere.
>
> (IV, 407–13)

This elaboration grows naturally out of Boccaccio's Ovidian verses because it too is Ovidian, modeled after one of the *Amores:*

> haec quia dulce canit flectitque facillima uocem,
> oscula cantanti rapta dedisse uelim;
> haec querulas habili percurrit pollice chordas:

tam doctas quis non possit amare manus?
illa placet gestu numerosaque bracchia ducit
et tenerum molli torquet ab arte latus.

(*Amores* II, iv, 25–30)

[One, most skilled, sings sweetly and modulates
her voice. I would like to have given snatched
kisses to that singing mouth during its song.
Another runs over the complaining strings with
graceful fingers; who can fail to love those clever
hands? That one pleases with gestures and
rhythmic movements of her arms, and with her
soft art sways her delicate sides.]

In this particular lyric, Ovid suffers from what we might call *amor synech-dochus*—he loves each woman according to some partial attribute, and cannot or will not allow any woman a complete identity.

Pandarus, perceiving that Troilus has fetishized Criseyde as the "only woman" for him, tries to show him the appeal of shifting, "casual" Ovidian love. "Artow for hire and for noon other born?" Pandarus asks him (IV, 1095), incredulous that Troilus would believe in romantic destiny. Indeed, Ovid's problem in this love lyric is not that he is smitten but that his desire floats freely, incapable of fulfillment—"so many women, so little time." In this context "getting over" a lost love could not possibly pose a problem, but sticking to one would.

Romantic relief does not come so easily in the *Troilus*. Pandarus tells Troilus, as Troilus distills it into a epigram, "Thenk not on smart, and thou shalt fele noon" (IV, 465). Pandarus argues, in Ovidian fashion, that the willful embrace of illusion is just as powerful as any reality that Troilus experiences. But Troilus is no Ovidian; he cannot see the world as fiction and play and maintains that his love is real and true:

She that I serve, iwis, what so thow seye,
To whom myn herte enhabit is by right,
Shal han me holly hires til that I deye.
For Pandarus, syn I have trouthe hire hight,
I wol nat ben untrewe for no wight,
But as hire man I wol ay lyve and sterve,
And nevere other creature serve.

(IV, 442–48)

Sorrow does not simply go away, and Troilus cannot, in his own metaphor, play "raket," switching lovers "to and fro" in a careless game of romantic tennis (see ll. 456ff.). Troilus even hopes to carry on his lament after he dies, pledging to "eternaly compleyne" after he is "down with Proserpyne" (470ff.). Pandarus does not want him to cry for even another minute, since the world abounds with potentially new lovers. The narrator himself interjects this point as he begins to perceive how the gap between Ovidian teacher and "trouthe"-loving pupil widens. Commenting on Pandarus' advice about replacement lovers, he tells us:

> Thise wordes seyde he for the nones alle,
> To help his frend, lest he for sorwe deyde;
> For douteles, to don his wo to falle,
> He roughte nought what unthrift that he seyde.
>
> (IV, 428–31)

More strongly here than at any time before, a voice in the poem explicitly confronts Pandarus, whose strategy now unravels.[18] By comparison, Boccaccio shows no interest in criticizing his Pandaro, who has functioned as an intermediary but not as a strategist, as a friend but not as a merchant of *unthrift* advice.

This distinction between the panderers is worth developing. As we saw, Pandaro advises Troilo to write letters but sets up no guidelines in matters of style. He arranges meetings for the lovers but does not contrive an elaborate plan and a false story about Criseyde's plight. He horastes no Horastes, borrows no Ovidian verses about roses, nettles, and the trials of love. Because he is less of an artist, he is less responsible for uniting the lovers. Pandaro never physically drags the lovers together or shoves a hesitant Troilus into bed. He does not represent an "ars amatoria" as Pandarus does. Boccaccio's narrator has no reason to turn against Pandaro or challenge his advice, particularly in light of Pandaro's anti-suicide speech—his valiant call-to-arms that wakes Troilo from his self-indulgent torpor.

Chaucer's complete omission of this martial exhortation displays his major reworking of the character of Pandaro. Pandaro tells the sorrowing Troilo not to betray himself to death but to talk of fighting and, if he must die, to die in war. Let us go to the battlefield, he says:

> quivi, sì come giovani pregiati,
> combatterem con loro, e virilmente
> loro uccidendo, morrem vendicati . . .
>
> (*Filostrato* VII, 45)

[There shall we, like well famed youths, fight
against them, and slaying them we shall manfully
die, not unavenged]
(Gordon, *The Story of Troilus*, 112)

Pandaro's tone is rational, strident, dutiful. He exhorts Troilo as one noble
Trojan youth to another, not as an Ovidian love counselor to his pupil. This
speech would have added an epic gravity to Pandarus that would have
clashed with his identity as Ovidian *magister amoris*.

Pandaro's words bring into the *Filostrato* the larger issue of the Trojan
War, not as an ironic reflection of Troilo's ultimate doom, his link to the
falling city, but rather as a hearty slap in his morbid, lovesick face. Such a
"remedy" did not fit into Chaucer's Ovidian world. The *Filostrato* does not
seek to trace the limitations of Pandaro's art or of his rhetorical perspective
on reality. Pandaro never plays a game for his own benefit, does not pry
under the sheets after the lovers' night together, and has no obsession with
game. Since Boccaccio does not develop Pandaro as *homo rhetoricus*, he does
not offer us a divine perspective on rhetoric, as Chaucer does in Troilus's
apotheosis to the eighth sphere. Chaucer, rather than Boccaccio, forges this
opposition between worldly words and transcendent wisdom.[19]

At this point in Chaucer's poem, Troilus, like the narrator, begins to
take the offensive and challenge his friend and counselor: "Whi hastow nat
don bisily thi myght / To chaungen hire that doth the al thi wo?" (IV, 486–
87). Troilus's disgust culminates with "Nay, God wot, nought worth is al thi
red" (IV, 498), finally articulating a sentiment that in Book III he could only
contemplate. We do not find this last phrase, this bold attack, in Boccaccio's
version of the encounter. In the *Filostrato*, Pandaro continues to try to provide comfort for Troilo; he cries with him, "and he often offered comfort as
lovingly as he could" [e nondimen sovente il confortava / quando poteva il
piùpietosamente] (IV, 63). Chaucer's Pandarus, however, has no reply to
Troilus's accusations and can only "holde his tunge stille" (IV, 521). Faced
with Pandarus's silence, and beset by his own disillusionment and anger,
Troilus becomes even more desperate in his search for a "remedie" for his
suffering.

"No Remedie"

As the poem progresses, however, it becomes clear to everyone that there
will be "no remedie" for Troilus. For now that the lovers separate, Troilus's
search for comfort abounds with ironic references and parallels to the *Remedia
Amoris*. Ovid's poem offers remedies that apply to all sorts of love-related

sorrows: separation, betrayal, anxiety, excessive desire. Ovid can heal whatever wound Love has made, calming the troubled heart and preventing suicide. He teaches the lover, essentially, to change with circumstances, to leave the past behind, and to look with hope to the future. This plan works well in witty epigrams but not in Chaucer's poem. Chaucer thus must build a definition of "remedy" that transcends Ovidian illusion and game.

But resolution comes slowly, as Chaucer meticulously explores the characters' various responses to change. All three protagonists must decide how best to combat mutability, but Troilus has the worst time of it. What keeps him specifically in pain, through both separation and betrayal, is his hope— he refuses to believe that Criseyde does not love him. Thus Troilus falls into a classic Ovidian error: "We keep delaying" our liberation, Ovid says, "because we hope that we are still loved; as long as we are pleased with ourselves, we are a gullible bunch" (*Remedia Amoris*, ll. 685–86). "Do not believe women's words, for what could be more deceptive?" And do not believe, he warns finally, "the authority [of their oaths] to the eternal gods" (ll. 687–88).

Troilus, however, does just this; he believes he is still loved because he believes in Criseyde's words and in her oaths. Criseyde certainly believes in him and loves him. But as we have seen in her Helenic rhetoric, Criseyde can play the game of love and can play it in specifically Ovidian terms. In a world of change and without many options available to a woman in her position, Criseyde has to save herself, even if it means betraying Troilus. She speaks in an Ovidian voice as she explains to Troilus her need to depart. After pledging fidelity by swearing "on every god celestial . . . On satiry and fawny more and lesse" (IV, 1541, 1544), she then tells the river Simois to "retourne bakward" to its source on "thilke day that [she] untrewe be / To Troilus" (IV, 1548ff.).[20]

In Ovid's *Heroides*, Oenone, in a letter discussed earlier, quotes Paris's oath to her. Paris's pledge differs from Criseyde's only in the river he invokes: "When Paris abandons Oenone and still breathes, let the waters of Xanthus return to their source" [Cum Paris Oenone poterit spirare relicta / Ad fontem Xanthi versa recurret aqua] (*Heroides* V, 29–30). Paris's faithlessness naturally leaves Oenone anxious to see this phenomenon—"Hurry back, Xanthus, return to your source" [Xanthe, retro propera, versaque recurrite lymphae] (V, 31). In Book I, Troilus admits to Pandarus that he has not read Oenone's letter; if he had, he would have realized its dubious nature. As usual, Troilus's unlearnedness makes him prey to the verbal arts of Ovidian rhetoricians. He is simply not "textual" enough to identify Criseyde's allusions and see their implications for his future.

Criseyde's use of this letter displays that she, however, is indeed textual enough to respond well to change. In the stanzas leading up to her oath to Troilus, she offers him a series of pledges and promises, her "gift of words." Criseyde must know, as Ovid says, that "anyone can be rich with promises." Among the encouraging words comes the hope that her exchange will perhaps bring peace to the Greeks and Trojans. We remember Ovid's boast that he could have stopped the war by curing Paris of his desire. Criseyde enters here into a world of Ovidian illusion; her words alone create hope, and her imagination invents reality.

In Book V, Criseyde will adopt the final Ovidian remedy—welcoming a new lover. But even in Book IV we are prepared for her actions and learn of her skill. Discussing the problem of separation with Troilus, she claims that she has "art ynough" to "slen this hevynesse" (IV, 1266–67). Here she is talking about the lovers' mutual concern and of her plan to trick her father, but her confidence in her art shows that she intends to survive any way she can.

Pandarus senses this, encouraging her with a reminder that "Women ben wise in short avysement" and standing anxious to see "how [her] wit shal now availle" (IV, 936ff.). Again, Pandarus refers to the problem of separation, but his emphasis on wit looks forward to Criseyde's self-preserving "changes," her expedient, protean decision to find another lover. She believes—as Pandarus and Ovid do, but as Troilus does not—that lovers can be exchanged. Drawing unfortunate attention to the issue of Criseyde's sincerity, the narrator tells us that all she said was spoken in "good entente" and that "hire herte trewe was and kynde" (see IV, 1415ff.). Troilus, to his credit, is skeptical of her forecast and still fears that she will meet some "lusty knyght" among the Greeks (see IV, 1485ff.). But he soon puts his doubts aside and keeps his faith in her words and oaths.

In accord with this delusion, and in contrast to the "remedies" Criseyde is preparing, Troilus systematically violates Ovidian dicta on how to survive a lost love. In all these instances, just as in his blind faith in Criseyde's oaths, Troilus seems foolish, incompetent, and hopelessly incapable of employing the healthful Ovidian cures that should be able to save him. However, as the rift between Troilus and Pandarus grows, and the difference between the lovers' responses to change sharpens, these seeming failures allow Chaucer to depict most starkly the confrontation between game and earnest, between illusion and reality, and between Ovidian flexibility and human "trouthe."[21]

First, Troilus rereads Criseyde's old letters (V, 470ff.). Ovid explicitly condemns this act: "Beware the stored-up letters from your sweet lover;

old letters can affect even the strong willed" [Scripta caue relegas blandae
seruata puellae: / constantis animos scripta relecta mouent] (*Remedia*, ll.
717–18). Troilus then surveys Criseyde's house and various places of sentimental importance for the lovers:

> Lo, yonder saugh ich last my lady daunce;
> And in that temple, with her eyen cleere,
> Me kaughte first my righte lady dere. . . .
> And yonder ones to me gan she seye,
> "Now goode swete, love me wel, I preye."
>
> (V, 565–67, 571–72)

Again, Ovid is very clear on what to do in this situation:

> et loca saepe nocent; fugito loca conscia uestri
> concubitus; causas illa doloris habent.
> "hic fuit, hic cubuit, thalamo dormiuimus illo;
> hic mihi lasciua gaudia nocte dedit."
> admonitu refricatur amor uulnusque nouatum
> scinditur: infirmis culpa pusilla nocet.
>
> (*Remedia*, ll. 725–30)

> [And often places can be harmful; flee sites that
> knew your lovemaking; they are causes of woe.
> "Here she was, here she lay, in this room we slept
> together; here in the playful night she gave me
> her joys." Suggestion can make love burn again,
> and a wound, newly healed, can be reopened. A
> small thing can be harmful to the infirm.]

Troilus applies no clever remedies. Instead, he deliberately and actively
seeks to keep the flame alive, in ways that Ovid depicts as very dangerous.

Boccaccio first lifted this material from Ovid (see *Filostrato* V, 54ff.),
but Chaucer's addition to the scene reveals his art of adaptation. In the
"Canticus Troili," Troilus calls Criseyde his "sterre" whose "bemes bright"
can guide him away from Charybdis (V, 638–44). Chaucer here makes further use of the passage in the *Remedia* that discusses avoiding the sites of
love, immediately after which, Ovid warns of the dangers of reminiscing:

> tu loca, quae nimium grata fuere, caue.
> haec tibi sint Syrtes, haec Acroceraunia uita;

hic uomit epotas dira Charybdis aquas.

(*Remedia*, ll. 738–40)

[Beware the places that once brought you great joy.
These may be your Syrtian quicksand; avoid this
Acroceraunian peak; here ferocious Charybdis
vomits up her waters.]

Ironically, then, Troilus heads for the very disaster he hopes to avoid, un-aware, as usual, of the Ovidian context of his words and actions. In Boccaccio, Troilo's actions may be sad, but they are not ironic. Chaucer not only makes them ironic, but by fleshing out the Ovidian context in ways that Boccaccio did not, he depicts Troilus's actions as explicit violations of the *Remedia*. Boccaccio gives Troilo no such song; he exposes no such ignorance because he is not interested in developing Troilo's unlearnedness or his victimiza-tion by Ovidians. He borrows from Ovid a scene of particular pathos, but he does not reveal any games.

All this verbal irony seems to indicate that Troilus would be better equipped to survive his loss if he had read more Ovid. He would know the ominous context of his actions and wisely stay away from dangerous memo-ries. Since Pandarus has led Troilus according to Ovid's *Ars Amatoria*, the *Remedia* now appears his only hope. However, at this point, we wonder if reading Ovid would actually help him. We begin to see now that no de-fense could ever prevent him from remembering the sights and sounds of his lost love. Ovid's words seem a desperate shout from far away, strident yet hopeless. Troilus's actions do, however, remind us that there is an "Ovidian" way of responding to change, a code or plan or perspective that either fails or is impossible to reconcile with "trouthe." Thus we would be fooled, as Troilus is throughout most of the poem, if we think that reading the *Remedia* would help him at all. By this point, the limits of Ovidian art for Troilus are clear. Change overcomes game, confounding the system that all along has only countered flux with imperfect and transient solutions.

As Book V unfolds, it obliterates any remaining notions we may have that the *Remedia* will work or that any remedy exists for Troilus, as the al-most choral repetition of the phrase "no remedie" hauntingly shows.[22] Ap-propriately it is Diomede who tells Criseyde, "Lat Troie and Troian fro youre herte pace! . . . For Troie is brought in swich a jupartie, / That it to save is now no remedie" (V, 912, 916–17), making explicit the connection between man and city that has been implicit all along. Here Chaucer's trans-lation adds the concept of "remedy," for Boccaccio's character says to Criseida only that "Troy has now come to such a pass that all hopes that men have there are lost" (VI, 20) [Ch'a tal partito omai Troia é venuta, / ch'ogni speranza ch'uom v'ha é perduta] (Gordon, The *Story of Troilus*, 104). Chaucer translates the *Filostrato* so as to develop the involvement of Ovid's *Remedia* in ways that Boccaccio did not pursue.

Later, the narrator, speaking of Troilus after his long, futile wait for Criseyde's return, says, "He kan now sen non other remedie / But for to shape hym soone for to dye" (*Troilus* V, 1210–11). Here Chaucer again intensifies the *Filostrato,* for Troilo only "wastes away" [Troilo se ne consumava] (VII, 16), and Troilus prepares himself for death. But equally important is the addition of the ominous phrase "no remedy." Troilus then tells Pandarus that he now seeks only his own death, "Syn that ther is no remedye in this cas" (V, 1270). In this context, Pandarus's final words in the poem reveal the same sentiment. Although he echoes Pandaro, Pandarus speaks also as the incarnated voice of the *Remedia Amoris*. However, we would never find his words in Ovid's poem:

> If I dide aught that myghte liken the,
> It is me lief; and of this tresoun now,
> Got woot that it a sorwe is unto me!
> And dredeles, for hertes ese of yow,
> Right fayn I wolde amende it, wiste I how.
> And fro this world, almyghty God I preye
> Delivere hire soon! I kan namore seye.
>
> (V, 1737–43)

Here the *Remedia Amoris* confesses that he is out of his depth; game has become earnest, and he can do no more for Troilus. Pandarus must do what Ovid would not—give up the battle and fall into vengeful verbal attacks on the woman.[23]

Yet the failure of the *Remedia* for Troilus does not chase Ovid from the poem, for Ovidian rhetoric reappears in the language of Criseyde's new suitor.[24] We have heard Diomede say that there is no "remedie," but obviously he knows that there *is* an "ars." The narrator describes him as a fisherman who "leyde out hook and lyne" (V, 777), recalling Ovid's image of the smart lover as a crafty fisherman (*Ars* I, 47–48).[25] He is of "tonge large," and he muses that in the wooing of Criseyde, all he has to lose is his "speche" (V, 798), echoing Ovid's notion that the only gift a poet can offer a woman is "words" (dare verba, "to deceive") and proving himself a suitable vehicle for all Ovid's strategies. Diomede drinks wine with the woeful Criseyde, for like Ovid he knows that "wine prepares the spirit and incites the fire of love; good strong wine chases cares away" [uina parant animos faciuntque caloribus aptos; / cura fugit multo diluiturque mero] (*Ars* I, 237–38). Diomede is not above deceit: he "feyned hym with Calkas han to doone" and speaks to Criseyde "with double wordes slye" (846, 898). Boccaccio's Diomede has, in contrast, an "honorable purpose" [cagione onesta] (VI, 9) in talking to Calkas. Indeed, none of Chaucer's "Ovidiana" comes from the *Filostrato*, where Boccaccio says Diomede is "fluent of speech" (VI, 23). Chaucer has added these details to portray Diomede as a textbook Ovidian lover. The line between rhetoric and falsehood is a thin one, as Chaucer's poem shows again and again. Diomede already knows and can do everything that Pandarus has to teach and do for Troilus. As a rather comic coincidence, Ovid at the opening of the *Remedia* says, in humble supplication, "Non ego Tydides" [I am not Diomedes], attempting to appease Cupid, whose mother Diomedes wounded in the Trojan War. In Chaucer's poem, to his great misfortune, Troilus is no Diomedes either.

In Diomede's speech, we see that Chaucer undermines and exposes Ovidian rhetoric, but his characters summon it anew, in his depicting men and women as ceaselessly rhetorical. Ovidian rhetoric perpetuates itself throughout the poem because in a limited sense it works; it brings Troilus and Criseyde together, and it certainly works for Diomede. Likewise, Criseyde shows herself a fine student of Ovid when she enacts the Ovidian axiom, "The new love chases out the old." The love of Diomede and Criseyde has no "celestial" pretensions, and both characters know it. Rather, this love is born from a shift in circumstance; it is a lean-to, slapped together with good Greek wine and a "tonge large." We witness here the genesis of stock Ovidian love, and we suspect that the dreadful, endless cycle of woe and weal is starting up again, as it will later in Robert Henryson's continuation of the story. Chaucer takes us beyond Ovid's amorous games by asking us to think about this prisonlike cycle and to doubt the merits of the rhetorical system that invigorates it. The neo-Ovidian couple in which Criseyde has taken refuge, however, lacks pathos, innocence, and hope— features that give Troilus and Criseyde's love humanity and, unfortunately, open it to all sorts of doom-filled Ovidian ironies.

"Worldes Brotelnesse"

Troilus's apotheosis to the "eighthe spere," from which he can look down upon "this wrecched world" and curse "al oure werk that foloweth so / The blynde lust, the which that may nat laste" (V, 1823–24), celebrates his escape from language and desire. Throughout the poem he has been manipulated by other characters who are skilled in Ovidian craft. But what in the mundane sphere amounts to bumbling unlearnedness becomes innocence and genuineness when cast in celestial light. Chaucer does not argue that salvation or wisdom comes from ignorance of Ovid, but he does put rhetoric and fiction in Christian perspective, as he will do again at the end of the *Canterbury Tales*, exposing them as tools of worldly "vanite" or, at the very least, the lot of *homo rhetoricus*.

Believing all along in the truth of love, Troilus now sees the foolishness of Ovidian game. The survivors, Pandarus, Criseyde, and Diomede, will go on creating reality for themselves with words. They adjust and readjust in protean fashion to circumstances, never hoping for or even perceiving something higher, truer, and eternal. Chaucer's appeal to the Trinity "eterne on lyve" is thus more than a simple contrast between worldly and divine joy; it is the poet's appeal to something above the chaotic world of words. In making this appeal, the narrator must reject Ovid and all that Ovidianism implies about flux, desire, and human experience. Criseyde herself, as a surviving Ovidian woman, must bear much of this condemnation, both in Pandarus's forced words of comfort to Troilus and in subsequent literary history.[26]

Troilus's final vision implies a certain reading of Ovid, one based upon Chaucer's medieval Christian apprehension of Ovid's life and art and of the relationship between earthly love and exile. Part of Chaucer's reading is based upon the way Ovid read himself, for Ovid in his *Tristia* discusses both his love poems and his *Metamorphoses*.[27] We are fortunate to have such self-reflexive commentaries, something that Chaucer, who enjoyed court favor and was certainly no exile, never had to write. To comprehend Chaucer's use of Ovid and his sensitivity to the ethical concerns that arise in Ovid's texts, we can make an extended parallel between Ovid's political fortunes and Troilus's romantic life. Chaucer's Book V, like Ovid's *Tristia*, confronts the *Ars Amatoria* and tries to make sense of its fictive language of desire.

To understand this comprehensive analogy between the classical and medieval reflections on the arts of love, we have to recall something about Chaucer's reception of Ovid through medieval *accessus* and through the comprehensive *vitae* that introduced Ovid's poems.[28] As we have seen, the medieval *accessus* link all Ovid's works as part of one logically developed history. Accordingly, the ethical implications of the young Ovid's play, the *Ars Amatoria*, reveal themselves in the old man's lament, the *Tristia*. Chaucer knew what happened to Ovid because of the *Ars Amatoria*, and here at the end of the *Troilus* we see the sorrow, the *tristitia*, of a young lover who has, despite his own innocence and steadfastness, been guided by an Ovidian "text" incarnate. In Ovid's "story," the author of the art of love suffers and is punished; in Chaucer's poem, the naive pupil absorbs the disaster. Troilus did not write a playful yet misunderstood poem about love; he led a life of misunderstanding allegiance to both Ovidian love and to "trouthe." This indecorous mix mires him in sorrow and propels him into exile.

Chaucer's awareness of the overall shape of Ovid's poetic career allows us to see how Book V of the *Troilus* may parallel the *Tristia*. Although the *Tristia* is an autobiographical elegy and the *Troilus* a long narrative poem, both works study how fortune can change powerfully and tragically when one takes game for earnest. Ovid repeats over and over that his love poetry was not at all "real," just a joke and a trifle.[29] The *Ars Amatoria* had no effect on reality, he says, despite what people might fear:

> sed neque me nuptae didicerunt furta magistro,
> quodque parum novit, nemo docere potest.
> sic ergo delicias et mollia carmina feci,
> strinxerit ut nomen fabula nulla meum.
> nec quisquam est adeo media de plebe maritus,
> ut dubius vitio sit pater ille meo.
> crede mihi, distant mores a carmine nostro—
> (vita verecunda est, Musa iocosa mea)
> magnaque pars mendax operum est et ficta meorum:
> plus sibi permisit compositore suo.
>
> (*Tristia* II, 347–56)

> [No wives perpetuate any deceit because of my
> teaching. No one who knows so little could
> possibly teach such arts. And so I wrote delightful
> things and light songs in such a way that no
> scandal has ever been attached to my name. Nor
> are there any married men, even among the plebs,
> who doubt their fatherhood because of any crime
> of mine. Believe me: my life is not like my song.
> It's modest, but my muse is playful. A great part of
> my work is lies and fiction, and it has given itself
> more freedom than its author ever had.]

Ovid argues that the strategies and conceits of the love poems are not, finally, true doctrine or a design for living.

Chaucer, like Ovid, knows the dangers of the art of love and the dangers that arise if one takes play for high seriousness. Prince Troilus, by putting faith in Pandarus's doctrines and by stubbornly insisting on his faith in Criseyde, makes just this error. The exile he suffers is spiritual, as he wanders in the "false worldes brotelnesse" (V, 1832), far from the true home of God's love. Both Troilus and Ovid undergo the pain of separation; Troilus from his only love, and Ovid from the sweet joys of his beloved Rome.[30] Troilus's exile on account of the *Ars Amatoria* can thus be regarded, at least in part, as a "medieval" or "Chaucerian" version of Ovid's. Chaucer makes the connection powerfully stark by giving Troilus a lament that recalls Ovid's proposed epitaph from *Tristia* III:

> O ye loveris, that heigh upon the whiel
> Ben set of Fortune, in good aventure,
> God leve that ye fynde ay love of stiel,
> And longe mote youre lif in joie endure!
> But whan ye comen by my sepulture,
> Remembreth that youre felawe resteth there;
> For I loved ek, though ich unworthi were.
>
> (IV, 323–29)

> HIC • EGO • QVI • IACEO • TENERORVM • LVSOR • AMORVM
> INGENIO • PERII • NASO • POETA • MEO
> AT • TIBI • QVI • TRANSIS • NE • SIT • GRAVE • QVISQVIS •
>   AMASTI
> DICERE • NASONIS • MOLLITER • OSSA • CVBENT[31]
>
> (*Tristia* III, iii, 73–76)

> [I, who lie here, once played with tender loves.
> Naso, the poet, I was destroyed by my own wit.
> And to you who pass let it not be any burden,
> lover, to say "may the bones of Naso rest softly."]

Ovid is not only a lover but the too playful poet of love, destroyed by his own wit, and he addresses lovers who would pity his plight. Troilus, as a lover, addresses lovers; he, too, hopes for pity.

In this lament, Chaucer has given Troilus the "sickness of spirit" that the fourteenth-century *Antiovidianus* perceives and chastises in Ovid. As we saw earlier, the anonymous poet tells us that Ovid was sent into exile to think about his crimes, but he responded foolishly: "*sick in spirit* and about to die an eternal death, you rise complaining against a healing god" (Kienast, ed., ll. 133–34; my emphasis).[32] The poet goes on to contrast Ovid to Boethius, an exile who overcame complaint and distinguished himself. Both Ovid and Troilus suffer from what medieval moral philosophers called *tristitia;* in Hexter's words, that is "the spiritual sadness that wears men down and is in direct opposition to the Christian virtue hope" (*Ovid and Medieval Schooling,* 98). And both, now at the bottom of Fortune's wheel, think on their graves.

To express the change from weal to woe that has led to tragic loss in their respective works, Ovid and Chaucer each allude to episodes from the *Metamorphoses.* Discussing the mysterious "error" that helped lead to his banishment, Ovid asks:

> cur aliquid vidi? cur noxia lumina feci?
> cur imprudenti cognita culpa mihi?
> inscius Actaeon vidit sine veste Dianam:
> praeda fuit canibus non minus ille suis.
>
> (*Tristia* II, 103–6)

> [Why did I see anything? Why did I make my eyes
> guilty? Why to my unsuspecting self was the fault
> made known? Actaeon was unaware when he saw
> Diana naked: nevertheless he was prey to his own
> dogs.]

Earlier on, Ovid gives himself the lament that the mute and metamorphosed Actaeon is denied: "Me Miserum" (see *Tristia* I, ii, 19ff.). Explicitly and implicitly Ovid lives out the changes in fortune suffered by his mythic characters. Like Chaucer, Ovid looks for a vocabulary to express the sorrow of unforeseen change and finds it in the *Metamorphoses.*

In the *Tristia,* Ovid has taken us far from the world of the love poems, as we can see when he compares himself to Ulysses (I, v, 57ff.). He tells his readers: "Write, learned poets, about my sorrows instead of Ulysses's: I have suffered more evils than he has" [Pro duce Neritio docti mala nostra poetae / scribite: Neritio nam mala plura tuli]. Ulysses, like Troy and all its sect, was only an amorous exemplar in the *Ars Amatoria:* Ulysses was not handsome, so he used words to seduce women. Now, in Ovid's new world of sorrow, Ulysses gets his identity back as an exile, a man of many sorrows. The deep difference underlying the two, Ovid hastens to add, is that Ulysses' suffering was false, a fiction, and Ovid's own is all too real: "Remember that the greatest part of that man's labors are fiction; there is no fable in my sufferings" [adde, quod illius pars maxima ficta laborum, / ponitur in nostris fabula nulla malis] (*Tristia* I, 79–80). Ovid concludes that in any case Ulysses did get home, something he can at this point only remotely hope for. Ovid uses Ulysses here to balance the great wanderer's playful appearance in the *Ars* and to indicate Ovid's own "change" from one poem to the other. Once the powerful and popular poet of the *Ars Amatoria*, Ovid is now in exile.[33] So too is Troilus; once catapulted into bliss by his own personal "ars amatoria," he has now been metamorphosed into a sorrowing wanderer.

Ovid's use of the *Metamorphoses* continues in the short but stunning fourth poem of *Tristia* I, where Ovid recounts his trials aboard ship on his way to Tomis. During a storm, the ship goes out of control, and the frightened sailor must submit to the sea:

> navita confessus gelidum pallore timorem,
> iam sequitur victus, non regit arte ratem.
> utque parum validus non proficientia rector
> cervicis rigidae frena remittit equo,
> sic non quo voluit, sed quo rapit impetus undae,
> aurigam video vela dedisse rati.
>
> (Tristia I, iv, 11–16)

> [The sailor's pale face confessed a frosty fear:
> conquered, he follows, unable to rule the boat with
> his art, as a rider, less than powerful, slackens the
> useless reins on the rigid neck of the horse. Thus,
> I see that not where he wishes, but where the
> force of the waves takes him, the helmsman gives
> the boat the sail.]

Ovid expresses lack of control in the metaphor of the charioteer giving up the reins, as if the literal image of the foundering ship were not concrete enough to convey the sense of futility and disorder. Ovid is not simply logging in his experience; he is finding imagery to express his change in fortune, the shifting circumstances that have sent his life tragically out of control. He is writing an "art of exile."

Ovid uses a similar image in the *Metamorphoses* in the story of Phaeton. As he depicts Apollo's son, he reverses the comparison offered in the *Tristia:*

palluit et subito genua intremuere timore . . .
iam Meropis dici cupiens ita fertur, ut acta
praecipiti pinus borea, cui victa remisit
frena suus rector, quam dis votisque reliquit.

(Metamorphoses II, 180, 184–86)

[He grew pale and suddenly his knees began to
tremble with fear. . . . Desiring to be called
Apollo's son, he is thus borne along like a boat by
the north wind whose helmsman lets the conquered steering fall, as he relinquishes the vessel
to the gods and prayers.]

A few lines later, Phaeton himself, like the fearful pilot in the *Tristia*, gives over: "Mentis inops gelida formidine lora remisit" [Mad with icy terror, he lets the reins fall] (l. 200). This passage and *Tristia* I, iv, share strikingly similar imagery: *pallere, remittere, frenum, gelidus, vincere.* The *Metamorphoses* provides for Ovid a vocabulary that closely describes his own "real-life" battles with the "the inconstancy of things" [rerum inconstantia] that has routed his hopes and ambitions.[34] Ovid means what he says when he claims that in exile he now is fit to take a place in his own poem, for he tells his story of exile as a story of metamorphosis.

His play with nautical images becomes significant to our understanding of the unity of imagery across Ovid's works when we look at the opening words of the *Ars Amatoria:* "By art, sail, and oar, swift craft are driven—light chariots too—and thus Love ought to be guided by art" [Arte citae ueloque rates remoque mouentur, / arte leves currus: arte regendus Amor] (ll. 3–4). In the *Remedia,* too, it is smooth sailing with Ovid at the helm: "With me as the leader, men, put off your harmful cares; with me leading, it's steady as she goes for ship and crew" [Me duce damnosas, homines, conpescite curas, / rectaque cum sociis me duce nauis eat] (ll. 69–70). As Ovid spins his love doctrines, he sails carelessly through calm seas. But in the *Tristia*, art is at a loss, and he himself becomes a victim of metamorphosis and nautical disaster. As art and power submit to fortune and chaos, Ovid is lost at sea.

So too is Troilus, already described as "steerless" without his beloved lodestar Criseyde. Troilus fears further that should Criseyde leave, he would not know where fortune would take him: "If that Criseyde allone were me laft, / Nought roughte I whider thow woldest me steere" (IV, 281–82).[35] These images of fragile, fearful voyaging in which only hope guides him show that Troilus is bound for disaster. The Ovidian Pandarus promised the control and artistic power of the *Ars* and later the *Remedia,* but Troilus must face the *Metamorphoses* and *Tristia* instead. In both the *Tristia* and the fifth book of the *Troilus,* then, loss and separation obliterate art and leave their respective protagonists "steerless" and fearful.

The parallels continue. Ovid's most elaborate analogy for his night of banishment is the fall of Troy: "If it is possible to compare great things with small, it was like Troy, when it was being taken" [Si licet exemplis in parvis grandibus uti, haec facies Troiae, cum caperetur, erat] (see *Tristia* I, iii, 21–26). In the playful context of the *Remedia,* Ovid tells us he could have *saved* Troy if he had been called in to clear up the vicious triangle: "Give me Paris: Menelaus will have Helen, and Troy won't fall to Danaan hands" [Redde Parin nobis, Helenen Menelaus habebit / nec manibus Danais Pergama uicta cadent]. But no art can save Ovid from suffering his own fall. Ovid's Trojan War analogy marks a serious reversal in the tone and nature of the reference in his poetry. Now that his own fortunes have turned, Ovid gives the fall of Troy back its power and pathos. Just so, late in the *Troilus,* the reality of the Trojan War asserts itself powerfully as Chaucer's references to it multiply and intensify.[36] Warlike Achilles, not a broken heart, kills Troilus.[37] Men have died, from time to time. . .

These parallels and shared themes, particularly in the context of Chaucer's awareness of Ovid's tragic career, suggest that Chaucer may have had the *Tristia* in mind while composing Book V. But Chaucer, finally, does something that Ovid does not and indeed cannot do. Through Pandarus, Troilus has taken the *Ars Amatoria* seriously, and it leads him to a love that brings sorrow and death. And the narrator rejects this "feyned" Ovidian love in favor of the Trinity. Follow God, he tells us, and since "he nyl falsen no wight. . . . What nedeth feynede loves for to seke?" (V, 1845, 1848).

In the *Tristia* we learn that the *Ars,* a game, was taken seriously by its readers, or at least by the humorless emperor who sent Ovid into exile. Responding to the charge, Ovid repudiates his love poetry: "{Having failed at epic} I returned to a light task and stirred my breast with fictional love" [Ad leve rursus opus, iuvenalia carmina, veni, / et falso movi pectus amore meum] (*Tristia* II, 339–40).[38] The crux of the matter lies in these two words, Ovid's "falsus" and Chaucer's "feynede." In the *Troilus,* feyned means "simulated, counterfeit, spurious, false, not real."[39] Chaucer uses the word morally, contrasting the human and the divine. Ovid's *falsus,* however, means "fictive," "non-mimetic," and thus implies no moral universe. Far from rejecting the *Ars Amatoria,* Ovid uses its falseness as his defense: If read with an "upright mind," his poem is harmless.[40] As Ovid tells the emperor:

"{If you had read my poem} you would have found no crime in my Art" [nullum legisses crimen in Arte mea] (*Tristia* II, 240).[41]

For Ovid, poetry brings personal dangers; for Chaucer, moral ones. Chaucer believes that falsus ("fictional") does not excuse poetry because it cannot be separated from the other sense of the word, what Chaucer means by feyned—"unreal," "ingenuine," "deceitful." Ovid, anxious to return to Rome, regrets his love poems for what they did to him. Chaucer rejects these same Ovidian poems for the false understanding they bring to his hopeful lovers. The medieval *accessus* classify the *Ars Amatoria* as a "complete guide for loving," but Chaucer exposes it as a false and dangerous game. His address to "yonge, fresshe folkes" at the end of the *Troilus* becomes a new version of Ovid's paternal address to the youth of Rome (*iuvenes*) in the *Ars* and the *Remedia*.[42] At the end of his work, Chaucer turns to his young audience, teaching them about a love beyond Ovidian art, one that will never "falsen" them.

Chaucer's reevaluation of Ovid thus finally provides the real "remedia amoris." Instead of looking for a temporary, fragile cure for an entangling passion, Chaucer repudiates carnal love. Ovid tells his pupils that to remedy love, one must pretend his lover is fat even though she is not, or that he must go to her house unexpectedly and see how unattractive she is without makeup. Further, he advises that when one is already exhausted and disgusted by sexual frenzy, he should contemplate the blemishes and flaws of his lover's body.[43] Chaucer sees no remedy here, or in any of the Ovidian techniques suggested by Pandarus or trampled by Troilus. And so, at the end of the *Troilus*, he redefines love and points his readers away from the protean, rhetorical world to the Trinity, unchanging and eternal, asking them to learn what Troilus only glimpses after death and what Ovid, an exile and a pagan, could never learn.

We have seen how Chaucer's revision of the *Filostrato* creates a dramatic conflict between Ovidian game and different types of truth—the truth of human emotion, the truth of history, and the truth of the divine Word. The world of the *Troilus* evolves from the *Ars Amatoria* and the *Remedia Amoris* into the *Metamorphoses* and the *Tristia*. As the universe of the poem becomes more and more dire, what do the Ovidian disciples do? Pandarus disappears, since he is not designed to negotiate real emotion, and Troilus's inability to change with circumstances dooms their teacher-student relationship. Criseyde, for her part, survives through Ovidian strategy: She makes false promises, swears false oaths, "travels," accepts a new love, and leaves the past behind. But the un-Ovidian, unprotean Troilus pays an emotional price, suffers, and finally dies. All told, what has language done for lovers in the *Troilus?* Seemingly everything and nothing, depending on the beliefs and the perspective of the given lover.

In the following chapter, we turn to a new question, one that Chaucer asks later in his Ovidian career. What would happen if Ovidian art could be mastered by someone who is willing to change, has no nostalgic allegiance to "trouthe," and makes the rules of the universe herself, immune from the reality of history and war that burdens the cast of the *Troilus?* What if one uses Ovidian art not just to get, keep, and "get over" a lover but to wage a battle for romantic and marital justice? In the *Canterbury Tales,* Chaucer attempts to answer these questions by creating the Wife of Bath, his greatest Ovidian scholar and disciple. She tells all about her verbal craft and her consummately successful arts of love in one of medieval literature's greatest battles of books and authorities. But what role exactly does this gritty, contemporary, bourgeoise play in this battle, and what might "success" actually mean?

4
New Armor for the Amazons
The Wife of Bath and a Genealogy of Ovidianism

Chaucer and His Ovid

 N HIS IMAGINARY letter of consolation to the exiled Ovid, the bishop-poet Baudry offers this lament: "What we are is crime, if it is a crime to love, / For the God who made me, also made me love."[1] "Allas," says the Wife of Bath some 250 years later, "that evere love was synne," expressing a sentiment inherent to medieval lovers, who are subject to judgment just as Ovid, the servant of the servants of love, was subject to exile and ban. Those in a Christian universe, like the twelfth-century bishop and the fourteenth-century fictional weaver, find themselves confronting forces of authority that are in conflict with their art and their experience.

As a prominent document in the history of this struggle between love and authority, and specifically in the literary history of Ovidian love, the *Wife of Bath's Prologue and Tale* examines the ambitions of a uniquely constructed master of Ovidian art. The Wife is the most deeply embroiled of all Chaucer's characters not only in Ovid's texts themselves but in their medieval manifestations and implications.[2] She is, like Ovid, the master of "experience" (usus).[3] She applies an explicitly Ovidian strategy from both the *Ars Amatoria* III and from Ovid's Old Woman of the *Amores,* and she tells a story from the *Metamorphoses.* In addition, her husband owns a copy of the *Ars Amatoria* in his book of wicked wives. The interplay between these many "Ovids" constitutes one of Chaucer's most profound dramatizations of sexual and marital power and authority. More than any other poet in Chaucer's library, Ovid was concerned with the power of men and women in the games of love. And so to understand fully the literary historical significance of the Wife and to perceive the full extent of Chaucer's interest in the gendering of authority, we must understand the Wife's Ovid, the Venerean's use of "Venus's clerk."[4]

The Wife's "Ovid," furthermore, is in many respects Jean de Meun's, for the "art of love" that sprawls across thousands of lines of allegory in the *Roman de la Rose* lies behind much of Alison's own art and struggle. This clash of not so ignorant armies helps Chaucer shape the Wife, her many husbands, Jankyn's book, and the battles that ensue. As many scholars have seen, the Wife draws from the advice to lovers offered by her literary "mother," La Vieille. Equally important to our study of the Wife's marital battles is the discourse of Ami, the Ovidian "friend" of Amant whose Jealous Husband's speech is a close analogue and indeed a source for the antifeminist material in the Wife's *Prologue.*[5]

In the entire discourse of Ami we find a "genealogy of Ovidianism" that shows how female greed and male domination caused the end of the Golden Age by creating the need for trickery and fraud—that is, for Ovidian art.[6] This genealogy is explicitly based on Ovid's story of the decline of the Golden Age and the origins of his own love doctrines as described in the *Ars Amatoria* and the *Amores.* As the Wife takes on the antifeminist tradition, she attempts, ultimately, to depict a model for returning to that "golden age" by getting beyond treachery and the claims to authority and power that prevent love. Chaucer's use of Jean's poem not only allows us to comprehend "Chaucer's Ovid" but also illustrates how Chaucer transforms parts of Jean's diffuse allegory into a compressed narrative monologue.[7] As Chaucer reimagines the work of his literary fathers, Ovid and Jean de Meun, he allows the Wife to reimagine the words of her own literary ancestors and to become, finally, his most powerful Ovidian artist.

An artist and a protean rhetorician, the Wife invents reality as both Ovid and her most immediate precursor, Pandarus, do. She enacts various stratagems of Ovidian deceit and basically "holds her husbands on hand" in any way necessary. She "twists" them and extracts, as both Dipsas and La Vieille advise, money and gifts. In return, she offers her husbands what Ovid would call a gift of words, openly lying (ll. 226 ff.) and at times feigning appetite (l. 417). She twice tells the pilgrims that all she says to her husbands "was fals" (ll. 382, 582), and she sums up her art thus: "Atte ende I hadde the bettre in ech degree, / By sleighte, or force, or by som maner thyng" (ll. 404–5), for God gave women the arts of "Deceite, wepyng, [and] spynnyng" (l. 401).[8]

The vital dynamic of the Wife's *Prologue* comes in part because Ovid's love poems are the source, not only of the Wife's craft, but also of much of the conventional antifeminism she embodies. As we will see, her drinking, sexual appetite, trickery, and callousness in looking for a new husband at the last one's funeral are all common antifeminist complaints rooted in Ovid's poems. For the Wife, as for any medieval reader, Ovid was both an ancient *auctor* who knew the wiles of women and also a crafty counselor who knew the "art of love." Ovid is, then, at once her adversary and her benefactor, the founder of the tradition that opposes her and also, ultimately, her own creator.[9] The origins of this duplicity lie in Ovid's own double agency, for in the *Ars Amatoria* he arms both "Greeks" and "Amazons." In the *Troilus* we saw how Chaucer exploits the tension between two Ovidian "moments"— the youthful love poetry and the poetry of change and exile. In the Wife's *Prologue*, Chaucer orchestrates a battle between two opposing Ovidian incarnations—the antifeminist founder and the savior of disempowered women.

In the thick of the battle is Jankyn's book of "wykked wives"—that bound version of the Jealous Husband's speech in the *Roman de la Rose*. The false authority it assumes demands that it be surrendered and burned, despite Jankyn's anxieties over losing his source of male power. Throughout her *Prologue and Tale*, the Wife combats the subjection that arises from the definitions of sexual difference generated by antifeminist texts. As she strips Jankyn of the book, she strips him of what he thought was his warrant of wisdom and superiority. As the Wife becomes a new Ovid and composes a new art of love, we can tell that Chaucer's concerns with authority, experience, and textual power create a drama that we did not see in Troy. But we must wonder if "trouthe," which both doomed and ennobled Troilus, will play a part here too.

Ovid and Marriage: *"Then Let the Bride Read Nothing"*

To understand better Ovid's diverse role in the Wife's battles, we should examine Ovid's own views on marriage relations—views that contributed to his scandalous reputation and eventually to his exile and ban.[10] He was charged with teaching men to corrupt married women through seduction, and with teaching women to deceive their husbands and commit adultery. The corruption of married women, the *matronae*, is at the heart of each accusation, but the crimes refer to Books I and II of the *Ars* (which arm the

Greeks) and to Book III (which arms the Amazons). These teachings were unpopular with Caesar Augustus. Medieval schoolmasters commonly observed that Ovid was exiled in part because "Roman matrons were corrupted" [corruptae fuerant romanae matronae] by his *Ars Amatoria*.[11]

Ovid had tried to preempt controversy by specifying his audience for the *Ars*—high-class courtesans only, the *hetaerae*, and *not* the *matronae*.[12] A letter to Maximus (*Ex Ponto* III, iii) addresses the accusation that men—armed with the *Ars Amatoria*—were nonetheless seducing the higher class of women. Ovid contends that he has "not disturbed lawful wedlock," and he asks the God of Love: "Have you at any time, by following my law, learned to deceive brides and to make descent uncertain?" (III, iii, 53–54). Nevertheless, to Rome his games were serious matters, shifting marital power relations and endangering the future of the patriarchal social order.

Ovid was aware that some might think his guidance in *Ars Amatoria* III would dangerously empower the *matronae* to seek secret love for themselves. He tried again to specify his audience while teaching the newly freed slaves to deceive their men and guardians. So that no one will think he intends these arts for the *matronae*, he pointedly announces a politically correct Roman marital doctrine: "Let the bride fear the husband" [nupta uirum timeat], "for this is what law, right, and modesty command" (III, 613–14). As Wilkinson observes, "Ovid is at pains to emphasize that his poem has nothing to do with married or "respectable' women."[13] Augustus felt, however, that "respectable" women were learning from Ovid how to deceive their husbands anyway. The emperor did not believe Ovid's claim that Roman fathers "need not fear the legitimacy of their children," and he may even have felt that Ovid's games led his own granddaughter Julia into disgraceful adultery.[14]

In the *Tristia*, Ovid addresses these charges by distinguishing his poetry from the popular mime plays that "show" women how to deceive men (*Tristia* II, 497ff.). He repeats his claim to an unmarried audience (II, 253ff.), and states explicitly that "no brides learned deception" from him as teacher (II, 347). In response to Augustus's statement that matronae might learn adultery despite Ovid's innocent intentions (II, 253), Ovid issues the bold, even Miltonic challenge, "Then let the bride read nothing" [Nil igitur matrona legat] (II, 255). If poetry translates immediately into behavior, then almost any poem ever written could prove dangerous. The only way to protect the public, if individuals cannot choose for themselves, is to ban all poetry. As Ovid says elsewhere, "Any text can corrupt" (see *Tristia* II, 255–56, 264).

In this entire controversy, we learn something about Ovid's teachings that will prepare us to consider the literary historical context of the Wife's encounter with authority. In banishing Ovid, Augustus was trying to protect Roman law and mores; the issue of antifeminism does not arise. Despite his place in medieval antifeminist texts, Ovid never wrote explicitly about the evils of women, not even in the *Remedia Amoris*, where Amor, not femina, provides the opposition. If a pupil gets too deeply embroiled in love and flirts with suicide, then Ovid can liberate him from this self-destructive passion.[15] Indeed, part of the *Remedia*'s advice is to find another woman, and Ovid explicitly states that though he addresses the *Remedia* to men, his words will help women as well.[16] Ovid has no committed agenda or antifeminist burden. Unlike church fathers and medieval clerks, he does not argue an ecclesiastical position exhorting celibacy. Rather, he plays— and plays so as to *join* lovers, not keep them apart. It is the manner of "joining" that brought on Roman wrath.

Even though Ovid is not essentially an antifeminist author,[17] medieval intellectual and literary history saw the *Ars* and the *Remedia* as antifeminist texts. Christine de Pizan makes this clear in her treatment of Ovid in the *Book of the City of Ladies*, which she wrote specifically to counter the excesses of antifeminism. Christine asks the character Reason why Ovid (a renowned poet, though inferior to Virgil) would write such foul things about women in these two poems.[18] Later, Rectitude responds to a similar question, saying that since Ovid and other antifeminist writers armed men against deceitful women, these writers ought to have done the same for women— arming them against the wiles of deceitful men (II, 54, 1).[19] These passages tell us that the love poems, though not initially designed, of course, as misogynist or misogamist texts, were appropriated as such by the medieval authorities whom Christine battles. Accordingly we find Ovid's works included in antifeminist anthologies, as Chaucer's index to Jankyn's book of wicked wives indicates. The Wife's and Christine's specific references to Ovid's status provide our best evidence that Ovid, despite his intentions and despite the rhetorical complexities of his gendered voices, was a founding father of the medieval antifeminist tradition.

A survey of the works in Jankyn's book further indicates Ovid's role in the antifeminist tradition and shows precisely what the Wife of Bath must confront.[20] The book contains, among many others, "Valerie," "Theofraste," and "Seint Jerome." Valerius, the fictional name of Walter Map, refers to his *Discourse to Ruffinus the Philosopher Lest He Take a Wife*. Theophrastus wrote a tract against marriage, known only because it is preserved by Saint Jerome, whose *Epistola Adversus Jovinianum* is one of the founding texts of medieval antimarital literature. And, of course, the anthology includes "Ovides Art" (Wife's *Prologue*, l. 680). Ovid appears here (and is the focus of Christine's attack) because the antifeminist texts draw from Ovid's love poems and make them, like the *Metamorphoses,* sources for sordid details about mythic women such as the incestuous Myrrha and Pasiphaë, the bride of a bull. Ovid's poems, furthermore, sometimes describe woman as greedy, vain, and given to "that fierce female lust" [ista feminea libidine] (*Ars* I, 341). Despite Ovid's supposed fairness in arming both Greek and Amazon, many of his comments on sex, however playful, rhetorical, and, indeed, contradictory, lend themselves easily to antifeminist use.[21]

Jankyn's book offers us a definitive example: the wife lists for us the characters her husband has studied, including Pasiphaë, who is grouped with Eve, Delilah, and Clytemnestra—women who brought their men to disaster. Jankyn reads to the Wife:

> Of Phasipha, that was the queene of Crete,
> For shrewednesse, hym thoughte the tale swete;
> Fy! Spek namoore—it is a grisly thyng—
> Of hire horrible lust and hir likyng.
>
> (ll. 733–36)

In the margins of a *Canterbury Tales* manuscript, we find a gloss on this passage from one of the actual texts in Jankyn's book—Jerome's own catalog of wicked wives:

> Why should I refer to Pasiphae, Clytemnestra, and
> Eriphyle, the first of whom, the wife of a king and
> swimming in pleasure, is said to have lusted for a
> bull, the second to have killed her husband for the
> sake of an adulterer, the third to have preferred a
> gold necklace to the welfare of her husband, etc.,
> thus Metellius Marrio according to Valerius.[22]

In its manifestations as Jankyn's reading and as an actual gloss to a fifteenth-century manuscript of Chaucer, Jerome's short catalog indicates that women's lusts bring their husbands to disaster.

Ovid alludes to the story in the *Metamorphoses* but tells it in full in *Ars* I, among a series of catastrophes brought on by "female lust." Ovid offers here not a vote for celibacy but proof that women can be had: "Come, then," he encourages his students, "do not doubt that all women can be won" [Ergo age, ne dubita cunctas sperare puellas] (*Ars* I, 343). Ovid is playing—*sperare* may also mean "to fear"—but the context is winning women, not rejecting them, as an antifeminist text would. Ovid says that women are lustful and therefore all the more *available* to the eager seeker. Jerome converts Ovid's advice into a misogamist argument: Women are lustful and therefore *dangerous*, so stay away. Jankyn has not only the original story of Pasiphaë in his copy of the *Ars Amatoria* but also Jerome's comments, giving him both text and gloss and allowing him access to the details that Jerome omits.

The Wife's refusal to tell the "tale" in any detail—a tale Jankyn thinks "swete"—hints that she knows the full, "grisly" version of the story found in the *Ars Amatoria*. Furthermore, her phrase "horrible lust" may be an echo of Ovid's "ista feminea libidine," for it accurately translates the scornful Latin intensifier "ista." In this episode, then, Ovid's hopeful, albeit rather bestial, assertion of a man's chances of sexual conquest becomes a frightening argument against marriage and a fitting inclusion in Jankyn's antifeminist book. We see here why the Wife has to do battle with glossators and clerks in this complex combat of words and authorities, a medieval battle of the books that seriously studies gender and power.[23] We also see here the power inherent in collections like Jankyn's that include both primary Ovidian material and patristic glosses; the book's diversity and cross-referencing make it a dynamic, elastic force.

As we move through the *Prologue* and look at the Wife's defenses against this book, we have to try to determine which antifeminist texts lie behind her words. Displaying rhetorical genius and sound scholarship, the Wife uses Ovid against the antifeminist texts that themselves, as in the case of Pasiphaë, form another part of the medieval Ovidian tradition. Ovid provides power to whomever can use him well, and as the Wife herself says, the first one at the mill is the first to grind the wheat (l. 389).

Ars and the Woman

To begin to understand the intertextual complexity of these Ovidian battles, we must examine in detail the Wife's use of Ovid to see just how comprehensively Chaucer has shaped the *Prologue* into a neo-Ovidian art of love. By embodying details from the antifeminist tradition and incarnating the sterile bits of academic detail from Jankyn's book, the Wife becomes what men fear most, the fully armed, nimble Amazon, wise through experience yet still skilled at the "olde daunce." She reclaims parts of Ovid's *Ars Amatoria* III and employs its stratagems against men. However, when Ovid's arts are insufficient or counterproductive, the Wife bends them to suit her own needs. Her protean flexibility in this regard does not surprise us, for it is itself an Ovidian hallmark.

I would like to look at five primary instances of the Wife's use of Ovid in her *Prologue*. In the first, she renders some Ovidian verses on the function of the woman's body in sexual economics. In the next four, I will first, if possible, consider the Wife's words in the context of antifeminist ideology, and then examine the original Ovidian verses behind what she says. Tracking down both text and gloss reveals the ideological assumptions and conventional imperatives of the Wife's play and illustrates that she knows how to set Ovid and the antifeminist conventions against each other. Prominent in some of these instances is the Wife's use of the body: Although she is a "text," she is also a "body," powerfully asserting her physicality in sexual politics. As Hélène Cixous says of women writers, "A woman without a body . . . can't possibly be a good fighter."[24]

1. After her long disquisition on Scripture and virginity and after the interruption of the Pardoner, the Wife offers the pilgrims a sample discourse on how to control a husband, in the course of which she takes on and refutes a long series of antifeminist accusations. One issue is woman's freedom—as the Wife attacks her theoretical husband for wanting to "Be maister of my body and of my good" (ll. 308ff.). "We love no man," says the Wife, "that taketh kep or charge / Wher that we goon; we wol ben at oure large" (ll. 321–22). He cannot control both her body and her goods; if he locks up her goods, he must be ready to say, "Wyf, go wher thee liste; / Taak youre disport, I wol nat leve no talys" (ll. 318–19). At the end of this assertion of independence, the Wife tells her husband that as long as she continues to please him, he should not worry about what she does with her body on her own time: "Have thou ynogh, what thar thee recche or care / How myrily that othere folkes fare?" (ll. 329–30). She continues:

> For, certeyn, olde dotard, by youre leve,
> Ye shul have queynte right ynogh at eve.
> He is to greet a nygard that wolde werne
> A man to lighte a candle at his lanterne;
> He shal have never the lasse light, pardee.
> Have thou ynogh, thee thar nat pleyne thee.
>
> (ll. 331–36)

Editors are fond of citing Cicero's *De Officiis* and the *Roman de la Rose* for this passage.[25] The version in the *Roman* is a difficult one in which Ami criticizes Jealousy and says that she is so greedy that if she had to share anything, she would still want to retain the whole of her initial portion, the way a lantern retains its entire flame. There is no concrete sexual application here, and the Wife's use of the passage must be based on Ovid, who like the Wife discusses sexual relations.

Ovid's words come in the context of advice to women in *Ars Amatoria* III: "Do not refrain from giving your "joys of Venus' to men," Ovid says, "and if they deceive you, what did you lose? It's all still there" [Gaudia nec cupidis uestra negate uiris. / ut iam decipiant, quid perditis? omnia constant] (III, 88–89). And then he offers the image "quis uetet adposito lumen de lumine sumi" (III, 93), further encouraging his pupils not to be shy or "dangerous" but to seek pleasure and forget about the instability of men. "I am not prostituting you," says Ovid tellingly, "just stopping you from fearing false loss" (III, 97–98).

Ovid's masculine persona here seems to "care" but speaks an oppressive sexuality. However, Ovid's verses also imply that women are compelled to use their bodies as sexual tender. This "false loss," the generous rendering of the *gaudia*, allows men to fulfill their desires without feeling they are taking anything from the woman. Ovid assures women that they will continue to be taken, that they will not lose their ability to please. Men never tarry, of course, but women will always have the means to draw men to them. Behind this "comfort" we must see woman's fear of rejection and isolation, for if the vagina were actually to be depleted, what would a woman do next? The *gaudia veneris* indicates female dependence on male desire; it has no value until man begins to partake of it. In Ovid's verses, we see that "what women want most" is of no value or interest; all they are allowed to be are bodies that serve male pleasure.

The Wife's use of the image reveals that she will be no victim of male deceit but will do the deceiving herself. She uses her "instrument" as part of her plan for control over her husbands—part of her argument that they should *leave her alone*, let her do what she wants, stop being so suspicious: "Have thou ynogh, thee thar nat pleyne thee." She does not care if men never tarry, because she will not tarry either. Not waiting to be "taken" by men, she reclaims the body as her own, not as the tender that cedes the precious *gaudia*—the only coinage left to a woman deceived—but as her own source of freedom. The Wife effectively silences men by giving them what they want most, because it is this silencing, this abdication of male power, that gives the Wife what *she* wants most—to control her own body and use it as she wishes. She needs no assurances, fears no loss, and turns her *gaudia veneris* into her own gain.

2. Farther on in her sample discourse, the Wife explains another technique by which she keeps her husbands under control. She accuses them of flirting with other women ("Of wenches wolde I beren hem on honde")

and tells them that her own nighttime wanderings are "for t'espye wenches that [they] dighte" (ll. 393, 398). The Wife admits that these techniques are a bit harsh, acknowledging the "peyne" and the "wo / Ful giltelees" that she put the men through. However, she contends ultimately that "Whoso that first to mille comth, first grynt" (l. 389)—it is best to be in control by striking first.

Looking at the ideological context here, we see that Chaucer's immediate source is Deschamps's *Miroir de Mariage,* and Deschamps's source is, in turn, Theophrastus, included, not surprisingly, in Jankyn's (as yet unintroduced) book. In the *Miroir,* which seeks to dissuade its readers from marriage, women's whining accusations prove that they cause too much trouble to be of any positive value. They complain all night about where the man has been, his being late, and his flirting with the maid:

> Vous regardez, quant elle vient,
> No voisine, bien m'en perçoy,
> Car vous n'avez cure de moy;
> Vous jouez a no chamberiere:
> Quant de marchié venis arriere,
> L'autre jour, que li apportas?
> Las! de dure heure m'espousas!
> Je n'ay mari ne compaignon.
> Certes se vous me fuissiez bon,
> Et vous n'amissiez autre part,
> Vous ne venissiez pas si tart
> Comme vous faictes a l'ostel.
>
> (*Miroir,* ll. 1600–11)

> [You look at our neighbor when she comes—I can
> see this easily—since you have no concern for me.
> You toy with our maid. When you returned from
> the market the other day, what did you bring her?
> Alas, the sad hour that we wed; I have neither a
> husband nor a companion. Certainly if you were
> good to me and if you didn't love others, you
> wouldn't come home so late, as you do.][26]

But if we look to Ovid, and to the *Roman de la Rose,* we see the Wife's strategy *as* strategy, not as antifeminist warnings. Ovid says that a sure way to control a man is to make him feel loved:

efficite (et facile est) ut nos credamus amari:
prona uenit cupidis in sua uota fides.
spectet amabilius iuuenem et suspiret ab imo
femina, tam sero cur ueniatque roget;
accedant lacrimae, dolor et de paelice fictus,
et laniet digitis illius ora suis.

(Ars III, 673–78)

[Make it, and this is easy, so that we think ourselves loved. Desire makes a man gullible. Let the
woman look at him kindly and sigh deeply. Then
let her ask why he comes late; let her shed tears as
well, feign sorrow over a rival, and scratch his
cheeks with her nails.]

La Vieille adds vehemence to the advice and says that the woman should feign anger (*semblant aïrer*), run at the man and say she knows that he is not late without a reason (*Roman*, ll. 13823 ff.). In both passages these actions are ruses, ways of "getting to the mill first," as the Wife would say.

The relations between the several texts are immediately apparent. Neither of the canonical antifeminist sources—Theophrastus or Deschamps—reports that women do such complaining as strategy; it is, rather, "nagging." As Theophrastus says, they go on "all night long with babbling complaints" [deinde per noctes totas garrulae conquestiones].[27] Thus, by harassing her husbands, the Wife does not simply fulfill a female stereotype but employs an Ovidian *strategy*, filtered through La Vieille's added violence. She tells the pilgrims she *pretends* to nag, that she knows "al was fals." Chaucer certainly knew and used the *Miroir de Mariage* here, but the specific power and function of the Wife's actions come through Ovid and Jean de Meun. She knows that the male claims against women are constructs, as her scornful "thou saist" indicates. She knows there is no "real" authority here, but rather a fabricated force, and so she plays a game herself—summoning her own authorities, Ovid and La Vieille, who empower women. We begin to see, really, that the *Prologue* recounts a medieval battle of the books, with the Wife marshaling texts designed for women (of course still written by men) against the texts in the antifeminist arsenal.

3. After her long discourse, the Wife turns specifically to her fourth husband, who was a "revelour." This leads her to reminisce a bit about her salad days when she was "yong and ful of ragerye" (see ll. 453ff.). Here, in

words rooted in Ovid's *Ars Amatoria* III, the Wife freely admits that she likes to drink and that when she drinks, she must think on love:

> And after wyn on Venus moste I thynke,
> For al so siker as cold engendreth hayl,
> A likerous mouth moste han a likerous tayl.
> In wommen vinolent is no defence—
> This knowen lecchours by experience.

(ll. 464–68)

Again, let us consider the ideological and textual contexts of the Wife's allusions.

MS Egerton 2864, Add. 5140, contains a gloss on the passage: "A drunken woman is filled with great anger and pride, and has no defense against sin."[28] The gloss moralizes the Wife's drinking and, indeed, like the gloss from Jerome, can probably be found in Jankyn's book, since it is derived from Ecclesiasticus, the following chapter of which Jankyn himself quotes. The text is biblical, but its application here constitutes a medieval gloss in itself that betrays the same attitude toward women as the book of wicked wives does. The Wife is right when she says that men gloss "up and doun," but little did she know that her own text would be glossed—behind her back as it were.

Turning once again to Ovid, we see that (as in the case of the advice to feign distress at a rival) Ovid directs his words *to* women, as part of a passage on self-presentation, with a caution that excessive drink is unbecoming and, like sleep, makes a woman vulnerable to all sorts of unexpected sexual encounters (*Ars* III, 761ff.). The advice parallels Ovid's telling men to go to banquets where they "might find something more than wine" [est aliquid praeter uina, quod inde petas] (*Ars* I, 230). Ovid here praises wine as a giver of strength and relaxation, but warns that drunken men cannot judge beauty and are vulnerable to wanton women who can at this time "snatch their spirits" (I, 243).

Both men and women who drink are vulnerable, and so the warnings seem parallel—except that Ovid says women *deserve* whatever happens to them while drunk, but says no such thing about men: "Digna est concubitus quoslibet illa pati" (*Ars* III, 766). The object in each case is optimum union of the sexes, not celibacy and rejection. But it is the optimum for the man only. Taken together, the two passages say that men do not want either ugly or drunk women, and so neither sex should drink. As often happens, when we look closely at Ovid's "fair" distribution of power, it disappears. But the notions of pride, anger, and sin—the focus of the gloss—are absent from Ovid's and indeed from La Vieille's advice (see *Roman*, ll. 13452ff.), which warns against excessive drink but makes no Bacchus-Venus connection. In that the Wife, like Ovid, refers specifically to Venus, her passage shows a direct link to the *Ars*. Chaucer read the *Roman*, must have liked its use of Ovid, as he liked Boccaccio's in the *Filostrato*, and went back to Ovid to exploit fully the implications of the passage in light of the Wife's struggle with authority.

She drinks, despite her husband's restrictions, and she turns to love—one of her weapons of control against men. In that she refuses to be disciplined by her husband, she converts Ovid's decorous warning into a source of power and freedom, overcoming not only her husband's control but also the gloss's accusations of "sin." The gloss has turned "love" into "sin," simply substituting one word for the other. But they are not the same. Who knows this better than the Wife, whose famous lament, "Allas that evere love was synne," exposes the false conclusions of the gloss.

One medieval commentary on the *Ars*—exhibiting the scholastic tendency to disarm the work by classifying it as ethics—says that the purpose of Ovid's discussion of feminine *mores* is that women can learn "how to be retained" [quibus modus retineri valeant], reflecting Ovid's own comment that he is going to teach women how to love so that men will not leave them.[29] The Wife does not worry about how to be "retained"; she has her own agenda and her own desire to "win." Thus, when she asserts her knowledge of both Bacchus and Venus, she converts what to Ovid is an embarrassing faux pas, what to the antifeminist mind is "sin," and what to a school commentator are "mores," into an expression of freedom and an assertion of the body, which is, for her, not simply something a woman grooms to please men.

4. The Wife's next discussion, which extends to the end of the *Prologue*, concerns Jankyn the clerk, husband number five. One of her early meetings with him occurs during Lent, when her husband "was at Londoun," and in the course of discussing her freedom that spring, the Wife tells us that she "hadde the bettre leyser for to pleye, / And for to se, and eek for to be seye" (ll. 551–52). The detail has its immediate source in the Jealous Husband's speech and also appears in Deschamps's *Miroir de Mariage*. In the *Roman*, the Jaloux complains that women, "vont traçant par mi les rues / Pour voeir, pour estre veües" (ll. 9029ff.), and Deschamps entitles a chapter "Comment femmes procurent aler aux pardons, non pas pour devocion qu'elles aient, mais pour veoir et estre veues" [how women seek pardons {at church}, not because of their devotion, but in order to see

and to be seen].[30] Both of these antifeminist diatribes use this detail as evidence of female pride.

But the ultimate source for these writers (Deschamps refers to Ovid by name) and for Chaucer is *Ars* I, 99, where Ovid tells men to go to public shows because women go there "to see and to be seen" [spectatum ueniunt, ueniunt spectentur ut ipsae]. Ovid, far from warning men of female vanity and inciting them to celibacy, is trying to tell them where to find lovers. Female vanity reliably starts the whole hunting process. If Ovid were reading Chaucer, he would want to argue that Criseyde went to that temple that day for the same reason.

Ovid does not condemn women, but we can see how easily his "essentialist" generalization could become an antifeminist comment, and so it seems the Wife is just playing her part as the vain female of the antifeminist texts. But she makes Ovid's advice to men part of her own art of love, freely venturing out while her husband is away. Although she is not, as she speaks to the pilgrims, married, her presence on the Canterbury pilgrimage also displays her freedom, for she tells them that her trips include "these pilgrimages."[31] The Wife has taken a shred of attack and stereotype from the male tradition and converted it from "they do" to "I do," affirming craft and will. In relation to Ovid's text, she becomes much more than merely a reliable prey that makes itself present so that male hunting season can begin. She does the hunting herself, clearly emphasizing the "seeing" over the being seen.

5. After describing this secret meeting with Jankyn, the Wife then explains how at her husband's funeral her eye was again on Jankyn, whom we know she later marries:

> To chirche was myn housbonde born a-morwe
> With neighebores, that for hym maden sorwe;
> And Jankyn, oure clerk, was oon of tho.
> As help me God, whan that I saugh hym go
> After the beere, me thoughte he hadde a paire
> Of legges and of feet so clene and faire
> That al myn herte I yaf unto his hoold.
>
> (ll. 593–99)

Deschamps's *Miroir* seems to be the direct source for these lines. It explains that women will take a dead husband's possessions, offer only a short service [*courte messe*], and look for another husband among the crowd of mourners: "Et regardera en le presse / A parter le deffenct en terre, / Quel mari elle pourra querre / Et avoir après ceste cy" (ll. 1974–77).[32] Frightened antifeminists, like the persona of this text, see these actions as evidence of woman's insensitivity and evil.

But when we turn to Ovid's handbook, we find a quite different context. In *Ars* III, he explains to his widow-pupils that "Often a man is found at a man's funeral; it is best to go in tears, with your hair tousled" [Funere, saepe uiri uir quaeritur; ire solutis / crinibus et fletus non tenuisse decet] (ll. 431–32). The Wife takes this tip and eyes Jankyn at her fourth husband's funeral, *restoring* its Ovidian function and status as advice to women. One of the great ironies of the whole situation is that the husband she finds at the funeral is the clerk who has all this material in his book and, perhaps, has already read about the Wife's strategy in his version of the *Ars Amatoria*. On one level, he and the Wife are both victims and products of inherited texts, scripts in which each must play a role. The drama comes in the Wife's simultaneous fulfillment of and restlessness with that role.

In the various dramatic instances I have analyzed, the Wife creates herself out of antifeminist fragments of fear and ignorance, those things that men say women are made up of—lechery, trickery, garrulousness, and pride. When she displays these "wicked" features, she illustrates that she herself is a product of a male literary tradition. But by manipulating the texts in this tradition and by "spoiling" Ovid's armaments, she empowers herself to shape her own art of love in the tradition of *Ars Amatoria* III and La Vieille. In this way she takes control of both man and text, or, rather, of man *through* her control of texts and of her own body. Most important, perhaps, her arts reveal that Chaucer is aware of at least two Ovids, one a founder of antifeminism, the other a father of an opposing tradition that is born within the *Ars Amatoria* and advanced by La Vieille. It is not altogether clear that we should call this tradition "feminist," which in this case would be a hopelessly anachronistic term. But Chaucer has intricately reimagined his *auctores* to create a voice that reimagines woman's power and speaks woman's language as it has never been spoken before.

Ami's Genealogy

With the Wife's "arts," Chaucer establishes a new vision of love within the context of the "genealogies of Ovidianism" offered by both Ovid and Jean de Meun. Throughout her *Prologue*, the Wife battles not just the texts of Jankyn's book but also the role that sacred history has assigned to her, based on the actions of her other mother, Eve, who, significantly, heads the catalog of "wicked wives." Jankyn reads to her:

Of Eva first, that for hir wikkednesse
Was al mankynde broght to wrecchednesse,
For which that Jhesu Crist hymself was slayn,
That boghte us with his herte blood agayn.
Lo, heere expres of womman may ye fynde
That womman was the los of al mankynde.

(ll. 715–20)

Here we have a brief, but entirely typical, view of women's role in sacred
history. Redemption itself is subordinated to woman's "wickedness" which
brings on all humankind's "wretchedness." Chaucer does not try to rewrite
that history, nor does he offer a heterodox revision of Scripture. Rather, he
uses the pagan Golden Age mythology from Jean (who borrows from Ovid)
to set forth an analysis of woman's "wickedness" different from and more
complex than that in Jankyn's book.

In the *Roman de la Rose*, Ami explicitly bases his history of gender conflict on Ovid's story of the decline of the Golden Age and the origins of
"Ovidian" love doctrines, as the Roman poet describes them in the *Ars
Amatoria* and the *Amores*. Ovid makes clear in *Ars* II that his art is for the
poor and not the rich, whose wealth makes "art" unnecessary:

Non ego diuitibus uenio praeceptor amandi;
nil opus est illi, qui dabit, arte mea.
secum habet ingenium qui, cum libet, "accipe" dicit;
cedimus, inuentis plus placet ille meis.
pauperibus uates ego sum, quia pauper amaui;
cum dare non possem munera, uerba dabam.

(*Ars* II, 161–66)

[I have not come as the teacher of love for the rich.
My art is nothing to anyone who can "give."
Whoever can say, when he wants, "Please accept
this gift," has his own arts. I concede; he pleases
more than my techniques. I am the prophet of the
poor, because, poor myself, I loved. I couldn't give
gifts, so I gave words.]

Later he continues the theme of feminine greed, saying that women do not
now value poems as gifts:

Carmina laudantur sed munera magna petuntur:
dummodo sit diues, barbarus ipse placet.
aurea sunt uere nunc saecula: plurimus auro
uenit honos, auro conciliatur amor.

(II, 275–78)

[Songs are praised, but great gifts are sought. As
long as he is rich, the barbarian can please. We are
certainly living in a "golden age." With gold comes
great honor, with gold comes love.]

We find a related discussion in *Amores* III, viii, where Ovid gives a tour de force exposé on girls, gifts, and the Golden Age. Ovid makes no pun on "golden" here, but laments that in the real Golden Age, before the economic expansion of the empire, there was no moneyed military class able to win women's hearts by spreading wealth around. Now women scorn poetry and want only gifts that the nouveaux riches can bring.[33] If we put Ovid's comments from the *Ars* and the *Amores* together into one larger narrative, we see that his love doctrines result directly from this fall from a Golden Age. The fall brings an end to the power of poets, and thus, to "conciliate love," poor men, whose poetry is now scorned, need to give a new gift—a gift of *verba* since the rich and powerful have their own form of *ingenium* in their money. As friend of the poor and friend of the poet, Ovid helpfully supplies the craft that will allow poor men to compete with the wealthy, though artless, lovers who control the market. Ovidian art, then, fits into a grand economic, historical scheme, and, as is customary in Ovid's world of love, *verba* compensate for a lack, creating some kind of Ovidian justice, balancing the economic inequality that prevents crafty but poor poets from fulfilling their desires.

Turning to the *Roman de la Rose*, we see that Ami, borrowing Ovid's phrases, also describes an age in which "honey flowed from the oak and no one furrowed the earth."[34] Love was free, equal, in a pure and simple state—women craved no gifts, and men craved no dominance. Now the world is changing, Ami tells us, and women have become greedy monsters: "If a woman were to see a heavy purse . . . she would run to it with open arms. . . . Everything is going into decline" (ll. 8347ff.). And so Ami, like Ovid, knows that wealth, or, in the allegorical language of the poem, taking the road of "give too much," can get Amant into the castle and win him the rose with ease: "Its walls will shake and the towers waver and the gates will open by themselves" (ll. 7915ff.). One can take this shorter way "without my art or teaching," says Ami, who thus makes clear that he directs his strategy—a long discourse directly from the *Ars Amatoria*—to the poor man, just as Ovid had. The poor man did not have to compete in this way in the Golden Age, when, as Ami says, "loves were loyal and pure, without greed and rapine." So now, in lieu of "gold," men need Ovidian art to soften the gatekeepers, appease Fair Welcoming, and get into the castle. Ami knows that Ovid provides an answer to the question of how to play the game of love, and he describes the fall into a desperate state that demands deceit and, therefore, demands Ovid.[35] This Ovidian ethic dominates much of the poem, since even Reason recommends, or at least condones, deceit: "It is always better . . . to deceive than to be deceived, particularly in this battle when one never knows where to seek the mean" (ll. 4399ff.).[36]

Ami has shown how women's greed forces men to become Ovidian artists. In the Jaloux's speech that follows, Ami shows the other side of the issue, demonstrating how *male* desire for domination forces *women* also to become Ovidians, employing fraud and trickery. Male possessiveness, like female greed for gold and gifts, has helped bring an end to the age of free and simple love. These two crimes explain, we might say, the origins of *Ars Amatoria* I and III. However, we must realize that Jean de Meun does not base the Jealous Husband's speech and the commentary that follows on Ovid. Jean offers them as part of his own contribution to the "art of love."

Ami delivers the Husband's diatribe to expose the evils of male posses-siveness, as had Reason before him in her long discourse on lust and mer-cantile greed. In this portrayal of the Jaloux as a mad boor who should be "fed to wolves," we hear an awareness that antifeminism, as thoroughly represented here as anywhere, is based on an excessive desire for power that "violates the law of love." the Jaloux, Ami says, "makes himself lord over his wife, who, in turn, should not be his lady but his equal and his companion, as the law joins them together." Ami continues, "For his part, he should be her companion without making himself her lord or master" (ll. 9421ff.). The result of such a claim to *maistrie* is that "love" will fail, for "love must die when lovers want lordship; [it] cannot endure or live if it is not free and active in the heart."

Jean de Meun has given the traditional antifeminist texts a voice, em-bodying what in the source texts is disembodied and distanced, as if fallen from heaven as knowledge.[37] He demystifies the texts of Theophrastus et al., so stolid and so "anthologized" in books like Jankyn's, and attributes them to a brute. Jean de Meun knows, as the Wife of Bath does, and as Christine de Pizan will later claim in her *Book of the City of Ladies*, that the accusations against women are arbitrary and unauthoritative. Historically, the antifeminist texts are designed to guide clergy away from marriage, and their effect on "romantic" love is never at issue.[38] Significantly, then, Ami has looked beyond the antifeminist tirades to see what effect they have on love, holding them responsible for poisoning it.

After the Jaloux's raving catalog of female evils, Ami explains that women will certainly respond to men's abusive quest for domination with scorn and trickery in order "to defend and protect themselves" (ll. 9383ff.). Female fraud does not cause men's suspicion and hatred; they are, rather, its source. The "cause and effect" implied here reveals Jean's insight into the workings of authority, power, and love. By seeing antifeminism as a cause of this "fall," Jean de Meun reverses the assumptions at the heart of the antifeminist texts—that the Christian "fall" is the result of female carnality, as the Wife's first excerpt from Jankyn's book makes clear.[39]

Jean de Meun's treatment of the Jaloux and his depiction of woman's deceit as the result of man's violating the law of love constitute a new chapter in the gender/power relations described by Ovid—a chapter that paves the way for the Wife of Bath and her battles with "Foul Mouthed" and "Jealous" husbands. Chaucer saw in the *Roman de la Rose* not just an anthology of Ovidian quotes and images but a genealogy of Ovidian craft—the reasons *why* men and women employ treachery. In view of this genealogy, the Wife of Bath has no choice but to respond to male power with fraud and manipulation. It is a fallen world, and Ovidian art is the lot of fallen (wo)man.

"Like My Mother Taught Me": La Vieille

Using *Ars Amatoria* I and II, Ami arms Amant against Fair Welcoming, Foul Mouth, and the gatekeepers, teaching him how to pursue and win his love. La Vieille, expanding *Ars Amatoria* III, arms the *women*, fulfilling Ami's prediction that women must use fraud to do combat with men. She does not just lift material from Ovid; she synthesizes Ovidian strategy from the *Ars* and from her own literary mother, Dipsas. And though her discourse is heavily indebted to *Ars* III, particularly its dicta on cosmetics and hygiene, La Vieille does not try to make women more appealing to men, as Ovid does. She seeks to make them better equipped to *deceive* men. Accordingly, we find throughout La Vieille's discourse an increased interest in deceit.

As Ovid arms the Amazons he attacks men, like "false Jason" (fallax Iaso), for being treacherous and deceitful to their women. Later (in what he calls a mad rush of insanity) he tells freed female slaves how to deceive their men and guardians (*Ars* III, 29ff., 667ff.). Thus it appears that Ovid fairly balances his aid to the Greeks, but in many ways this third book does not parallel the first two. In Book III, Ovid proposes to teach women "how to love"; men already know how, because they have read his books. At the outset he gives a catalog of deceived women, and then tells us: "Quid uos perdiderit, dicam: nescitis amare: / defuit ars uobis; arte perennat amor" [What destroyed you I say? You did not know how to love. You had no art, and art preserves love] (III, 41–42). Men deceive women, so women must know how to prepare against this deceit and sustain love. Ovid then suggests grooming—a woman should make herself attractive, clean under her fingernails, and avoid bad breath. But he makes no statement that would balance his advice to men in *Ars Amatoria* I to "deceive the deceivers" (the women) who actually inflicted the first wound (l. 645).[40] In *Ars* III, Ovid never says that women, in turn, should deceive men. Instead he tells them to respond to men's deceit with *knowing how to love* so as to avoid rejection.

Ultimately, then, Ovid's guide for women tells them how to remain appealing and be chosen. In the *Roman de la Rose*, La Vieille's "art of love" displays an increased directness and vehemence; she takes Ovid's idea that men are dangerous deceivers and concludes—unlike Ovid—that *women* should now do the deceiving. For example, Ovid says that women should dress so as to accentuate the positive because whenever he sees a snowy shoulder, he would gladly kiss it (III, 307ff.). La Vieille adds emphasis (ll. 13313ff.): a woman with white skin should have her dressmaker design a low-cut outfit, not to invite kisses, but so that she may "deceive more easily." Ovidian counsel takes on a new status when a woman, the new Dipsas, does the teaching, turning *Ars* III into an effective response to the craft and low cunning taught to men in Books I and II.[41]

Not only does La Vieille provide a woman's voice for *Ars* III, she borrows some material from Ovid's enemy (and her own "mother") Dipsas, the old counselor from the *Amores*. Forget poems and get money, says La Vieille (l. 13617) as she sends Homer packing and repeats Dipsas's advice to reject poets and their worthless gifts.[42] Ovid, evidently aware of Dipsas's words, tells his pupils to make their poetry a "type of gift" by cleverly writing verse praising their women (*Ars* II, 281–86). La Vieille is not so easily deceived, for she adds Ovid's own name to Homer's as she banishes the cheap poets—a direct attack on the *magister* himself, implying that his evolving, shifting "gift of words" fools no one.

Ovid playfully confounded himself—a bit—by writing *Ars Amatoria* III. La Vieille confounds him more fully, teaching the scorn and trickery Ami says must erupt from the mistreatment of women in a fallen world. Jean's dramatic reworking of Ovid provides a major step toward the Wife of

Bath. Chaucer saw that Jean, using Ovid, defended the Amazons and "historically" justified their strategies through Ami's genealogy. Chaucer also saw in La Vieille a powerful rewriting of *Ars Amatoria* III. He allows his Wife of Bath to adopt Ami's advice to trick slanderers and also to adapt La Vieille's arts of profit and control. Omitting Ovid's hygienic hints about pimples and bad breath, the Wife represents Chaucer's own dynamic contribution to the tradition of writing an "art" to arm the Amazons. In the Wife's use of her ancestral texts, Chaucer offers his own vision of Ovidian love in a post–Golden Age world of sexual combat and competition. The literary historical evolution behind Chaucer's poem is here primarily pagan. But the Wife's world is, of course, Christian, so we must examine Ovidian language and female behavior in relation to the Christian Fall, a mythology equally pertinent to Chaucer's depiction of human language and society throughout the *Canterbury Tales*.

An Enemy Poised

Ovid's and Jean de Meun's depictions of the fall from the Golden Age both place Ovidian deceit in a large historical scheme. In contrast to these genealogies, some medieval Latin evaluations of Ovid depict his art not as the *solution* to the problems of the fall but as a reflection of the fallen state of men and women, sinners trapped in falseness and carnality. Ovid may have playfully seen himself as the enlightened voice of the disenfranchised, but these authors see him as the sinful enemy of truth.

William of St. Thierry describes the fall away from God and from the natural love of the spirit as just such a fall into the flesh. "Love," he says, "was placed in the human spirit by the author of nature." But "after man let God's law slip," "love had to be taught *by men*" (italics added). It should have been taught as pure and solidified, but carnal love "had its own teachers"—such as the "doctor artis amatoriae" who "wrote of the fire of carnal love." William's attitude toward Ovid wavers; he attempts, as Leclercq puts it, to "excuse Ovid" but cannot avoid condemning him. William grants that Ovid was creating a system to control passion and tried in the *Remedia* to cure the ills he had caused earlier: "Indeed he did not aim to excite the rise of carnal desire that burns with a natural fire, without [maintaining] a proper mixture of reason." Despite Ovid's efforts to rule love, however, he led his disciples "into all kinds of misbehavior and useless foment of desire, pressing on toward some kind of insanity."[43] For William, finally, Ovidian love represents the explosive state of desire in a fallen world, an earthly perversion of God's love. By comparison, in the *Roman de la Rose*, Ami offers Ovidian strategy as the necessary response to the possessiveness and greed that in themselves constitute the initial "violation of the law of love."

The *Antiovidianus*, in its feisty condemnation of Ovid's corpus, provides an equally fascinating version of Ovid and the fall:

> Nasonem mea musa ferit, quia stercora sumens
> Auravit musa tam rutilante sua
> Effecit suis decorosis versibus, vt sit
> Fel mel, nox lux, mors vita laborque quies.
> Inde sathan, draco callidus, hostis iniquus et audax,
> Insidians iuuenum mollia corda capit.
> Subuerterunt mala verba fidem, sanctos quoque mores
> Corrumpunt sepe. Sit michi prima parens
> Hinc testis, sathane pravis seducta loquelis.
> Heu patimur verbis omnia dampna malis!
> Hoc opus oro vide, visum diffundere cura.
> Quondam Nasonis, sis rogo preco dei.
>
> (Kienast, ed., ll. 3–14)

> [My muse strikes Ovid, because taking up dung,
> with his shining muse he made it gold, and in his
> pleasing verses made gall into honey, night into
> light, death into life, and labor into rest. From
> whence comes Satan, the subtle dragon, bold and
> base enemy; poised, he snatches the soft hearts of
> the young. Evil words subvert faith and often
> corrupt sacred mores. Let our first parent be
> witness to me of this, for she was seduced by the
> depraved speech of Satan. Lo! all our sorrows we
> suffer because of evil words. I beg you, behold this
> work, which, having been seen, seek to spread.
> You who were once a herald of Ovid, be, I pray, a
> herald of God.]

These are strong words, but the poet offers nothing maverick or heterodox in his portrayal of Ovid's deceitful rhetoric as the source from which Satan will come to snatch "the soft hearts of the young." The poet, like the theologian William, locates Ovid's poems in a scheme of Christian sacred history by linking Ovid to the Fall. Eve, he tells us, was tricked by the depraved speech of Satan, whom we must imagine to have been quite the

Ovidian. Here and in William's tract, we see that Ovid can be source, result, or symptom of the Fall. In Ami's genealogy, by contrast, he is an expedient tool, and in his own writings, of course, he is benevolent savior.

These theological evaluations of Ovidian love could lead us to see a stern critique of Ovidian rhetoric in the Wife of Bath. After all, if Ovid is a great Satan, then "Ovid" and "woman" are both at the heart of the Christian story of the Fall. As Saint Bernard laconically puts it, "Eve spoke only once and threw the world into disorder."[44] A playful but strident thirteenth-century French *dit* warns its readers that woman's appearance belies the poison within:

> Femme par sa douce parole,
> Atret li home e puis l'afole;
> Femme est dehors religiouse,
> Dedanz poignaunt e venimose.
> (*Le Blasme des Fames,* ll. 47–50)

> [Woman, with her sweet words, attracts man and
> then drives him crazy. Outwardly she is nun-like,
> but inwardly she is prickly and venomous.]

Woman is a "hell mouth," she "shuns fidelity," and is "more artful than the devil."[45] Just as Christian moralists link Ovid to the Fall, this *dit* links "woman" to the deceitful language of carnal, fallen man. An "Ovidian woman," then, would either be redundant or pose a double threat.

As we have seen, Petrarch offers the fascinating complaint that Ovid showed a "womanly spirit" not only about his exile but in his love poetry too. And Boccaccio says that Ovid's love poems show him as "an effeminate and lascivious man." It is easy to look at Ovid's love strategy and think of him as a "sexist" poet, but we must be aware of the morally gendered vocabulary leveled against him by Christian writers. To Ovid's medieval opponents and critics, both "woman," as the first sinner, and Ovid, as the ribald poet of falseness, display foul weakness and depravity.

How, then, should we read the Wife's arts? Which "medieval Ovid" should we use to gloss her? Alison's craft displays much more than simple carnality or Satanic evil. Chaucer gives the Wife an Ovidian power not in order to condemn her but to equip her for an important confrontation. Her actions more closely follow the history of gender conflict described by Ami than they do the moral schemes traced by William of St. Thierry and by the *Antiovidianus* poet. The Wife's *Prologue,* then, not only illustrates Chaucer's "translation" of Ami's Ovidian genealogy but also goes far beyond any simple moralization of Ovid as it attempts to forge a way back to the Golden Age, when love was fair and balanced. As a recent study of medieval tracts on "marital affection" shows, Jean de Meun, in composing Ami's discourse, may have been influenced by contemporary debate on love and fairness between married people.[46] Chaucer's poem also works toward a code of marital affection that is beyond treachery and beyond claims to inherited power. As we will now see, the Wife attempts to overcome these conventions most dramatically when she teaches Jankyn that he does not need that book of wicked wives. If he burns it, she will drop all the fearsome qualities it attributes to her and will leave off her practice of Ovidian craft. In this way the Wife's "art of love," ultimately, will look toward a marriage and a romantic world that are free of art and game.

The Book

Jankyn's book defines the Wife as a "wicked" source of human "wrecchednesse," and so it must be surrendered before the couple can attempt to restore any kind of Golden Age. Unlike the old rich stooges the Wife has controlled before, Jankyn seems immune to her Ovidiana, creating a dire emotional situation that leaves the Ovidian mistress craving what she cannot have. Part of Jankyn's power must derive from the texts in his book of wicked wives, including "Ovides Art," where he may have read that women seek new lovers at their husbands' funerals. Jankyn's control over the Wife comes from his careful hesitancy—he is "daungerous" with his love, making the Wife desire him more:

> We wommen han, if that I shal nat lye,
> In this matere a queynte fantasye:
> Wayte what thyng we may nat lightly have,
> Therafter wol we crie al day and crave.
> Forbede us thyng, and that desiren we;
> Preesse on us faste, and thanne wol we fle.
> With daunger oute we al oure chaffare;
> Greet prees at market maketh deere ware,
> And to greet cheep is holde at litel prys.
>
> (III, 515–23)

She loves a man who needs to be bought, despising one who is a bargain.

"Every wise woman knows this," says the Wife, and the advice comes from no less an authority than La Vieille herself. La Vieille explains that since men scorn what they can get for nothing, a woman should not give a man her love without first making him deliver some goods (*Roman*, ll. 13695ff.). The Wife works just such a scheme on husbands one through four. But Jankyn flips the gender roles; though the *Roman de la Rose* is not in his book, unless it is one of the "many others mo," Chaucer has it in his library, and he uses it to make Jankyn a good match for the Wife.[47] Jankyn has read and appropriated one of her texts—indeed, her "mother's" advice—and thus has almost neutralized her power. In this conflict we see that Jankyn and the Wife wage a literary battle that eventually drives them into physical conflict.

As they reach an accord, the Wife takes the "bridel" so that she can have "governance of hous and lond" and of Jankyn's "tonge" and "hond" (ll. 812ff.). To solidify this *maistrie*, the Wife must act the censor: "[I] made hym brenne his book anon right tho" (l. 816). This forced destruction burns away not only Jankyn's power but also the very details of the Wife's own identity and art. What is possibly left of the Wife when the book is gone, and what could be left of Jankyn the clerk when his fathers' text is lost? The irony, as Pratt long ago pointed out, is that he has never actually followed the main thrust of the book—to avoid marriage.[48] His bitterness must come from this tension: he reads the tales and thinks them "swete"; he tries, too, to inflict them on the Wife, but he himself cannot obey them. In burning the book, the Wife liberates them both from this tension, from the literary imperatives that define them. The book's the thing, she knows, that prevents love.

The Wife's exposure of the antifeminist tradition finds powerful support, just a few years after Chaucer created her, in the work of an actual woman writer, Christine de Pizan. As she builds the City of Ladies, an extended refutation of antifeminist "authority," Christine has the character Reason explain why men write about the evils of women. The causes include the men's own vices and the defects of their bodies; jealousy or the pleasure they get from committing slander; and "to show they have read many authors." Those in this last group "base their own writings on what they have found in books and repeat what others have said and cite different authors."[49] "They believe they cannot go wrong," Reason continues, "since others have written in books what they take the situation to be, or rather, *mis*-take the situation" (I, 8, 10).[50] Later in discussing antimatrimonial literature, Reason's sister Righteousness makes a similar point: "Without my having to say any more to you, you can easily see that such foolishness spoken and written against women was and is an arbitrary fabrication which flies in the face of truth" (II, 13, 1).[51]

The very existence of Christine's work arises from her desire to de-mystify this magical, male creation of authority. At the outset of her story, Christine is near despair, finding herself believing everything she has heard about the evils of women. After thinking about the antifeminist corpus, including Mathéolus and, we must assume, the *Roman de la Rose*, Christine reports: "I finally decided that God formed a vile creature when He made woman. . . . As I was thinking this, a great unhappiness and sadness welled up in my heart, for I detested myself and the entire feminine sex, as though we were monstrosities in nature" (I, 1, 1).[52] Both Christine and the Wife know the power of books of wicked wives, in any manifestation, and they try in their own ways to discredit them.[53]

Strangely enough, Walter Map, Valerius in Jankyn's collection, provides some insight into this problem of authority. In his *De Nugis Curialium*, which includes the previously circulated antimatrimonial tract *Ad Rufinum* (his contribution to Jankyn's book), Map wonders why the epistle has been "greedily seized upon, eagerly copied, and read with vast amusement" (313). He complains that many have tried to deny that he wrote the work, attrib-uting it to the ancient Valerius, a name Map invented. "My fault," he says, "is in this only—that I live. I am not inclined, however, to amend this by dying" (312). Map knows that he has created authority by giving his text apparently classical origins. He fears that when he, a living man, is fully acknowledged as the author, the excitement will end and his work will "fall out of the blanket into the mud." Therefore, he can only look forward to his death and bodily decay, for then, he predicts, the "book will begin to receive favor," and "for the remotest posterity, antiquity will make me an authority" (212).[54] Map knows that authorities are made, not born, and though he never challenges antifeminist doctrines, he exposes the whole process by which a text becomes an authority, just as Christine does in her attack on authors who blindly rehearse bits of antifeminist jargon and lore.

Jankyn's book, then, full of works by white males who were dead even in Chaucer's time, carries this same sort of pseudo-authority and pretends to give its owner wisdom and power. Jankyn has something the Wife does not have, and possession of this text provides the clout that creates a sexual and marital hierarchy. This power comes not from "truth," but from the weight of ancient doctrine built up in the anthology, doctrine that Christine de Pizan calls "arbitrary and false." "Men" are those empowered by such a tradition of texts, and "women" are not only the object of these texts but are those who *lack* such texts of their own. "By God," the Wife cries, if only "wommen hadde writen stories, / As clerkes han withinne hire oratories," then we would hear of more male "wikkednesse / Than al the mark of Adam may redresse" (ll. 693–96).

The Wife of Bath does all she can to arm herself against the power that the male tradition has amassed. By reviving *Ars Amatoria* III and importing the French theorist La Vieille, she seeks both to topple male authority and to show that she herself has a textual history—a history that knows something of male "wikkednesse" and male violations of the law of love. In the process she creates herself as a "text," that of woman as trickery, garrulousness, and greed. These fabricated identities, both the Wife's and Jankyn's, arise from the same literary conventions, and both ultimately must fail. But the Greeks are more powerful than the Amazons, traditionally better armed and able to supplement their power with physical dominance, as we see when Jankyn hits the Wife. And so, before the couple can find peace, and before the Wife will deliver kindness and fidelity, the book has to go. Giving up the book is easier said than done, and Jankyn's aggressive reaction to having a few pages torn out reflects a distinct anxiety over the potential loss of privilege and power.

Is Jankyn still a "man" without the book? And what is left of the Wife if her genealogy, as men have imagined it, is burned up? The Wife offers us a glimpse of at least one version of this post-Ovidian, post-antifeminist world. Liberated from their conventional identities, Alison and Jankyn cease their respective pursuit of domination, and a "golden age" ensues. We may suspect that their unity, wrought by deceit and violence, is no real unity at all. But the text only tells us that they lived together happily and faithfully. If they faltered before Jankyn's untimely death, the poem tells us nothing about it.

We might also object that the "golden age" the Wife forges includes her own *maistrie* and control. We cannot determine just how much "maistrie" the Wife maintains after Jankyn submits to her will. But perhaps the power she wields does not represent an unfair swing, since Ovid's Golden Age simply meant that one could seduce a woman without digging into his pocket. And since Jankyn is not rich, by loving him the Wife tacitly surrenders the materialistic desire that guided her in the past. Right after their marriage, she gave him her own "lond and fee" (l. 630), and now, at the end of the battle of authorities, as the Wife finally receives *maistrie*, she continues to give, pledging to Jankyn her kindness and fidelity. This giving, this putting off the "old woman," leaving the strategy of Dipsas, *Ars* III, and La

Vieille, balances Jankyn's surrender of his elders' book of wisdom. We may be witnessing not so much a mythic Golden Age, but the best relations possible in a world of conflicting authorities and inherited demands on identity.[55]

But after the qualified resolutions of her *Prologue*, the Wife reimagines her experiences in fictive form, creating a text in place of the one she just burned. To do this she trades the role of Ovidian *magister* for that of Ovidian narrator. The Wife's *Tale* includes her self-indicting version of Ovid's tale of Midas. As storyteller, the Wife transforms the account into a criticism of women, making a basically neutral Ovidian text into an antifeminist depiction of women as hopeless gossips, as overflowing mouths in search of an audience. The Wife revises the tale intentionally, not to tease bad male listeners, but to illustrate the co-opting and glossing behind the creation of texts like those in Jankyn's book.[56] She writes a new chapter in this abusive volume to flaunt power over the production of truth. Men gloss up and down, and this is how they do it.

A surge of the same rhetorical power allows Socrates to argue any given side of an argument in Plato's *Phaedrus* and allows Ovid to make utterly contradictory statements in arming all sides in the arts of love. The Wife shows what rhetoric can do, shows how an author can manipulate words to create a new version of history and truth. But she does not let the narrative rest here, for she applies her art to another old but more local story. In her Arthurian tale, she again plays with the women's roles, not, this time, parodying the inanities of antifeminist lore but depicting a feminine wisdom and power that go beyond Ovidian deceit. The story of the Old Hag and her young pupil, the knight-rapist, redefines, or indeed abolishes, the gender/power struggles the Wife found in Ovid's love poems, in the *artes* of love in the *Roman de la Rose*, and in her own *Prologue*.

The central "metamorphosis" rejuvenates the Old Hag, whose control over the hapless knight reflects the Wife's own power and constitutes a cameo appearance by Ovid's Dipsas or La Vieille. Through the Old Hag, the Wife implicitly acknowledges and honors her own literary heritage. Without them, she would not have made it. Yet the Old Hag differs from her elders and from the others in the *Tale's* analogues who are trying to overcome enchantment.[57] Her unique speech on true "gentilesse" exposes the same type of arbitrary assignments of value that inform the antifeminist tradition. In no analogue to the story would such a distinction be meaningful, for it refers back to the textual battle fought in the *Prologue*. The Old Hag does in miniature what the Wife does in her assault on her husbands—reveals the conventionality of social and sexual hierarchies and the corresponding myths of male superiority.

It seems that the Wife and the Old Hag have both achieved ultimate success by transforming their respective men into humble, gentle, obedient husbands. And so the Hag herself, like the Wife at the end of the *Prologue*, "puts off the old woman" and becomes young and beautiful. Chaucer gives the Wife the power of imaginative creation, which seems to have worked in what one critic, in another context, calls "the 'wish-world' of metamorphosis."[58] She has reversed the "great [Ovidian] inconstancy of things" in the triumph of art over experience.

She has also transferred her chaotic marital experiences into the authority of art, offering in her *Tale* a "literary" version of the story of Jankyn concluding that his wife should rule him. The knight-rapist's final submission recalls Jankyn's pledge of obedience. Jankyn tells Alison, "Myn owene trewe wyf, / Do as thee lust the terme of al thy lyf" (ll. 819–20); the knight's words to his new wife sound the same gracious note of affectionate marital calm: "My lady and my love, and wyf so deere, / I put me in youre wise governance . . . For as yow liketh, it suffiseth me" (ll. 1230–31, 1235). In this parallel, the rape itself corresponds to the objectification of women inherent in the production and use of antifeminist texts. Although rape of a virgin and disdain for marriage seem separate methods of dominance, both express the male power that is central to the universe of the poem.[59]

The Wife knows that the story in her *Prologue* is not enough, that it has no authority. Like Walter Map, she knows that antiquity creates authority, and so she tells a story from the "days of old." As Map creates an ancient Roman aura around his epistle, so the Wife reaches back to old Briton. Both know that authority must come from a distance, either fictive or chronological. Map's authority was weak because he was alive, the Wife's because she is a woman, a situation that she, like Map, no doubt, has no desire to remedy. She will not become a man, but she will assume the role of storyteller—she will write a story of rape and the powerful women of authority who have the knight at their mercy. Implied here is a little bit of the "wikkednesse" that women would tell of if they had literary position and power, which for this moment the Wife has. Her old tale, she hopes, will provide some corrective to the equally and indeed more ancient tradition against her.

Ovid plays many roles in the *Wife of Bath's Prologue and Tale*, throwing many complicated voices into the narratives and love languages that Chaucer weaves together in this, his most ambitious study of love and power. The Ovidian Wife, though herself a created voice, becomes an expert in these Ovidian voices, this rhetoric of craft and control, as she combats the antifeminist rhetoric of fear and scorn. In the *Troilus* we traced the opposition between Ovidian words and the divine Word. Why does Chaucer here provide no comparable anti-Ovidian critique, allowing Ovid to serve, rather, as the triumphant doctor who supplies arms to the disempowered?

The *Troilus* critiques a worldview that restricts itself to game and to secret, lusty rapture. Troilus, an innocent, puts his faith in this world, one of manifest Ovidian game, and makes it into "ernest." The Ovidian boundaries reflect those of the pagan world—to be pagan is to read Ovid literally, to invoke his doctrines as the only source of identity and discourse. The Wife's *Prologue and Tale* also looks to a world beyond Ovidian craft. Ovid serves the Wife well in the fallen world, the world of the Jaloux and the book of wicked wives. As Ami's genealogy makes clear, Ovidian fraud and trickery are her only recourse against the gendered hierarchies constructed by antifeminism. Women are not born Ovidians; they have Ovidianism thrust upon them.

The question the *Prologue and Tale* raises, then, is this: How can men and women both get beyond inherited, bookish identity and get out of the fallen world of Ovidian language, games, and strategy? The Wife's *Prologue and Tale*, like the end of the *Troilus*, looks beyond this imprisoning cycle of Ovidian words. The Wife will drop all her Ovidian arts if Jankyn will surrender the pseudo-Ovidian antifeminist power he has marshaled. The Old Hag will be faithful and beautiful if the knight-rapist surrenders his claims to authority and shows that he has wisdom enough to follow his wife's will.

I earlier proposed that the skepticism surrounding Ovidian art in the *Troilus* becomes celebration in the Wife's *Prologue and Tale*. We see now that this celebration is not an end in itself; it brings about another kind of celebration, that of marital affection and unity. Surprisingly, then, Chaucer's view of Ovidian art here is not so drastically opposed to what he offered in the *Troilus*. Rather, the Wife represents an evolution in his treatment of Ovid. The issues are more complex, the Ovidian voices more varied and intertwined, and mastery over them so much more empowering and crucial to one's identity and fate. Chaucer has worked hard in the story of the Wife to express the literary, textual, and social conflicts in terms of Ovid, just as he had in the *Troilus*. But in this second art of love we see a more intricate account of Ovidian game, as a character struggles for her own identity and for a share of marital affection in a world of gritty human experience and abstract clerkish authority.

As she addresses modern women writers, Hélène Cixous, a more recent French theorist than La Vieille, exhorts her readers to "kill the false woman who is preventing the live one from breathing."[60] Looking back at the Wife's *Prologue and Tale*, we are tempted to report that the Wife kills the false woman by incarnating herself according to antifeminist tradition and then by exposing the arbitrary origins of her identity and burning the book of accumulated misreadings that prevents the real woman from living. This would be quite a neat coda to our study of the Wife's Ovidian power and poise. But to what extent has the Wife done this? To what degree has she overcome her identity as "text," that is, the false text written by and for men? To what degree does celebration of Ovidian art actually give way to a "golden age" beyond convention and beyond game?

Our study of Ovid has shown several features of the Wife's struggles and art: she takes on and routs the antifeminist tradition; she parodically retells the tale of Midas; and she reinvents the education of the knight-rapist. In all cases she reimagines the discourses and identities she has inherited. Through her creative power, Chaucer himself reimagines the works of his clerkly fathers, Ovid and Jean de Meun. But the Wife's ultimate "liberation" as a woman is hard, indeed impossible, to gauge. Tracing the Wife's movement toward freedom from the conventions of identity, I have neglected to address that what we know of the Wife comes, obviously, from her current report—what she tells the pilgrims, in the only moment in which we hear her voice. Does she show any signs of liberation, of having preserved any of the "golden age" luster she enjoyed with Jankyn? Or is she hopelessly bound to a series of inescapable conventions and voices? In a word, what would she do with the sixth? Would she court him in textbook Ovidian fashion, as Diomede does Criseyde, using her "tonge large" to lay out hook and line?

Ultimately, the Wife has given us a glimpse of marital affection, of the peace and equality she once worked toward and achieved. But the "golden age" is over; she is there no longer. Nor is she up in the eighth sphere, looking down on the wretched world as Troilus does. She is on horseback, an ageless Ovid, still teaching the "olde daunce" and ready for a whirl or two if the price is right. Still a "wife," she must live in language and artistry in an eternal Ovidian "gift of words."

5
Exile and Retraction

N THE *Troilus* and the *Wife of Bath's Prologue and Tale*, Chaucer's role as the servant of the servants of love evolves, as does the function of Ovidian game. Throughout both works, Chaucer demonstrates that Ovid's art offers great power. In the *Troilus*, characters turn time and again to the *Ars*, the *Remedia*, and the *Heroides* as a way to create themselves and to realize their desires. To some extent they succeed: Pandarus, as the "art of love" incarnate, wins Criseyde for Troilus. Criseyde manages to sustain the loss of one lover and move on to another in a textbook Ovidian recovery. Diomede, finally, uses his Ovidian "tonge large" to help him win Criseyde. Medieval commentaries maintain that Ovid offers a "complete art of loving," and in these local cases, Ovid's *artes* do succeed—easing mutability, shackling accidents, and bolting up change.

But in testing these arts, Chaucer unbolts change and frees the wheel of Fortune. He summons a flood of images from the *Metamorphoses* and from the "history" of the Trojan War to raze the fragile structures of Ovid's games. And he invokes the sadness of "old" exiled Ovid to spoil the arts of the brash young doctor of love. Some characters survive through Ovidian wit, but no one is immune to pain. Criseyde, for her part, gives Ovidian words not because she has an innate love of fiction or because she wants to make a fool of Troilus, but because she has to.

In the Wife's *Prologue* we meet at least two Ovids different from the one in the *Troilus*. Ovid appears here not as the *magister* of *Ars Amatoria* I and II, but as father both of the antifeminist tradition and of female power. The Wife's Ovid is the armer of the Amazons, the creator of Dipsas, who begot La Vieille, who begot the Wife herself. According to the history of gender conflict in Chaucer's sources, the Wife must summon Ovidian art as her only weapon against the antifeminist tradition, according to which women are lustful, overbearing, vindictive, conniving, and in general the source of all human wretchedness, marital or otherwise. The Wife's use of Ovid restores the female function of *Ars Amatoria* III and allows her to liberate herself boldly, and bodily, from the caricatures offered in Jankyn's book of wicked wives.

In both these arts of love, Chaucer has done much more than merely tell stories from the *Metamorphoses*, invoke myths, or playfully update one of Ovid's guides to love. Rather, as a storyteller, and as a student of the complex interrelation of authority, language, and truth, he has embraced Ovid fully and profoundly, studying not only the power of love but the power *in* love. Chaucer both becomes an Ovidian, a playful servant of lovers, and also creates Ovidian characters who display both the craft and the limits of Ovid's arts. In Western literary history, his works must stand along with Ovid's as attempts to examine the range of human responses to change and to desire.

Ovid served Chaucer well, providing him images, characters, dramas, and doctrines with which to shape his own arts of love. But has Chaucer, in turn, served Ovid too faithfully? Does his use of Ovid, however sophisticated, dynamic, and circumspect it may be, still constitute a danger for Chaucer? Ovid renewed is still Ovid, the poet branded by some medieval authorities as weak, effeminate, depraved, deceitful, and even Satanic. Chaucer confronted Ovid thoroughly and intensely and depicted himself as a Naso novus. As we turn to Chaucer's final assessment of all he has done, we wonder what further role Ovid plays in Chaucer's vita, his story of the trials and the fate of a Christian poet who loved fiction and fictionalized lovers.

In his own time, Ovid, author of the *Ars Amatoria*, could not escape punishment, as Chaucer well knew from Ovid's poems and from his medieval biography. Chaucer, the poet of neo-Ovidian arts of love in a Christian world, plays a part in a similar struggle with audience and authority. Ovid had to bear responsibility for the voices he created in his love poems, the voices of play, sensuality, and desire. Chaucer, too, eventually, is compelled to atone for the Ovidian voices he crafted. The creator of Pandarus, Troilus, Criseyde, and Alison must share in their conflicts with history and with "trouthe." Chaucer cannot simply stand distant, behind the veil of fiction, a veil he knew had not protected Ovid from censor and exile.

Chaucer, or at least the voice he creates to deliver the *Parson's Tale* and the *Retraction*, offers his readers the stark image of a love poet confronting his work and his own death.[1] Ovid, in exile, also faces death and reviews his own life and works. Both poets contemplate their poetic doctrines and their literary ambitions, aware of the implications of their having decided to write the sort of poetry they did. Chaucer makes clear in his *Retraction* that saints' lives and translations of Boethius are worthy of being remembered, and Ovid tells the God of Love he wishes he had composed epic instead of amatory verse.[2] A self-confessed verse addict, Ovid extends his lament over thousands of elegiac couplets in the *Tristia* and the *Ex Ponto*.[3] Chaucer concludes his career with a long prose tract on penance and the brief, prose retraction, leading to simple silence and constituting the rejection of poetry. Ovid's and Chaucer's final works seem incomparable, yet the gross differences reveal the distinct way in which a Christian Ovidian love poet, perceiving the dangers of his work, must end his career.

Chaucer, on his rhetorical or actual deathbed, probably did not have Ovid's exile poetry in mind or strive to depict himself as the banished poet he knew from scholastic commentary. But Chaucer's final decisions about his life and work are deeply rooted in his Ovidianism and in the ethical poetics surrounding his experience of Ovid. For this reason, Ovid's poems of exile from the hellish "death" by the Black Sea provide a fascinating context in which to examine how makers of books in pagan and Christian cultures go about taking their leave.

The *Ars Exilii*

In discussing the *Troilus*, we saw that throughout the exile elegies Ovid self-consciously writes his own chapter in the *Metamorphoses*. As Ovid spins a tale of exile and death brought on by his transgressions in the "art of love," he finds a vocabulary to express his sorrow in the images of his recent "book of bodies changed."[4] As he does so, he offers, particularly in *Tristia* II, an elaborate theory of authorial intention and reader response. Misunderstanding and exile force the ever-protean Ovid to play the unfamiliar role of literary historian and critical theorist.

As we have seen, Caesar Augustus regarded the *Ars Amatoria* as antithetical to Roman moral laws because it encouraged adultery. So the emperor banished Ovid and banned his poetry from public libraries. Ovid's additional crime, his "error," is a matter of historical conjecture, and diverse scholars have said diverse things.[5] Whatever else Ovid may have done or seen, the *Tristia* clearly indicates that Augustus was angered at the behavior recommended in the poem and that Ovid saw his exile, at least in part, as the result of this displeasure. In his own defense, Ovid claims that despite appearances his work was just game and could never have become reality. His detractors misunderstood the relation between fiction and truth, and made earnest out of game.

After stressing fiction's special status, its insulation from reality, Ovid offers a related but more complex defense. Whatever one may say about the text, the author should not be punished, because he is not his text. His poem, no matter what it seems to be saying, does not reflect his character and intentions, and readers (including emperors) should not conflate the two. "Believe me," he says, "my life is not like my song. It is modest, but my muse is playful" (*Tristia* II, 353–54).[6] Earlier, Ovid addresses a friend: "You know that the *mores* of the author are unrelated to these arts" [Scis artibus illis / auctoris mores abstinuisse sui] (*Tristia* I, ix, 59–60). Ovid is arguing for a complete separation of art and personal morality because "the book is no indication of the spirit of the author" [Nec liber indicium est animi] (*Tristia* II, 357), and "he who knows so little cannot teach" [quodque parum novit nemo docere potest] (l. 348).[7] In every defense Ovid maintains that he intended only "for to pleye," as the Wife of Bath says, and that his poem, his famous *carmen*, is neither dangerous nor evil. This purity of purpose, this innocence, unifies all Ovid's claims.

Through these defenses Ovid defines the role of the author. He did not intend the text to inspire adultery, and thus he maintains that no one could have learned it from him. For Ovid, "authorial intention" determines the meaning of the text. To let the work itself determine meaning would be disastrous, and so, he warns, believe the poet and not the poem. Ovid's own morality notwithstanding, Augustus still judged the text dangerous and potentially corrupting.[8] An author cannot control the effect of a text once it enters public life.

But Ovid is never beaten, even in exile, and he has an appropriate counter to this type of argument. The readers themselves, he argues, should see that there is nothing harmful in his song—if they read with an "upright mind" [recta mente] (*Tristia* II, 275–76). Ovid now holds the audience responsible for interpretation. "Every type of poem can be harmful to the spirit," he reasons, "but this does not mean that every poem is guilty" (II, 264–65).[9] Thus even Homer and Virgil can corrupt since their works contain instances of deceit and lechery.[10]

Through this theory and strategy, Ovid shifts the responsibility for the corruptive power of his verse from himself to his readers, cleverly indicting the readers' own morals. The moral content is static until actualized by human will. To accuse Ovid, one would have to admit that he or she could not read "with an upright mind." Who would be willing to admit this? To condemn Ovid's text is to condemn oneself. We cannot help thinking of Chaucer's great artist, the Pardoner, who employs a similar strategy when he says that only those with clean spirits can come to offer to his relics. Who would publicly admit sin by lingering behind?

Despite the wit and energy of his various defenses, Ovid was never recalled from exile. Neither his patriotic writings, his reader-response theory, nor his claims about his own character could help him. His work's unintended effect—the charges of teaching adultery and the subsequent wrath of Augustus—stood prominent and unchanging, and Ovid, the metamorphosed man of sorrows, was left alone in exile. Cut off from wife and family, he knocks with his letters at the gates of Rome, beseeching his "god" to let him return home.[11]

This dramatic author-text conflict persists in the work of some of Ovid's many medieval followers, including Baudry. Late in life, as he reflects on his corpus, he must write an apologia: "But whatever I say, let my deeds maintain a sense of honor, let my heart thrive on purity, and my mind on shame" [Sed quicquid dicam, teneant mea facta pudorem / cor mundum vigeat mensque pudica mihi]. As Wilkinson tells us, "Like Catullus and Ovid before him, [Baudry] warns his readers against deducing his morals from his verse."[12] Baudry's words display the dangers of Ovidian game; writers must always defend themselves by claiming that their work does not reflect their character. Jean de Meun too offers a retraction/apology in the *Roman de la Rose:* His bawdy speech only reports what others have said, and the apparent antifeminism comes from *past auctores* (ll. 15159ff.).

Chaucer repeatedly does something similar by apologizing, disclaiming, and, of course, putting stories into other characters' mouths. All writers, poets, and narrators fall into the danger of being associated with what they write, of being one with their texts, and thus being targets for attack. Many medieval commentators on the *Ars Amatoria*, assuming a "real" connection between text and author, report that Ovid was writing about his own youthful, lascivious behavior.[13] Classical and medieval notions of "authorship" may not be identical, but fear and a self-conscious responsibility link Ovid to his medieval followers. Medieval poets are not venerable anonymous glossators whose labors are free of ego and identity; they are poets, fiction makers with no supreme authority to protect their works from attack—as the famous quarrel about the *Roman de la Rose* clearly proves. Jean de Meun anticipated controversy and misunderstanding and tried, unsuccessfully, to prevent it.[14]

Ovid himself did not ward off controversy very well, and in the wake of misinterpretation and punishment his only hope comes through "intercession." Unlike Chaucer, Ovid cannot ask anyone to "pray" for him, but he can, and incessantly does, beg his friends to intercede with Augustus on his behalf, however fruitless this may be.[15] It may seem odd for us to see Ovid, a playful skeptic, as a true "believer" in the mythic deity of emperors, and yet that saturates almost every elegy he writes. He knows he has angered the emperor but still believes that mercy is possible: "The violator of a temple can seek refuge at the altar and does not dread to seek the aid of the angered god" (*Ex Ponto* II, ii, 27–28). Ovid depicts Augustus as Jove and calls him a "prince, slow to anger, quick to reward, and sorry whenever he is forced to play the disciplinary father." He calls the emperor "indulgent" and is confident that Augustus "prefers to frighten many with fear and punish only a few with the powerful thunderbolt" (*Ex Ponto* I, ii, 121ff.).[16] Ovid hopes that someone can make the great Jove rethink his anger and reprieve the poet from this death in exile.[17]

Ovid paints his exile on the Black Sea as a type of hell. He tells Severus that he has been "thrust down to the shores of the Styx" [Stygias detrusus in oras] (*Ex Ponto* I, viii, 27), and complains to Maximus that the land of Pontus is "hard by the Styx" [a Styge nec longe Pontica distat humus] (III, v, 56). Earlier he asks Maximus to give him the same postmortem respect that Achilles gave to Patroklos and Theseus gave to his friend Pirithous, whom he accompanied to the Styx. "How far is my death from Stygian water?" asks the exile (see II, iii, 41ff.), who refers to his new world as a cold, dangerous arena haunted by shaggy, monstrous, Getish natives.[18]

Hell and death naturally lend themselves to Ovid's use of the *Metamorphoses*, as he becomes the first in a long line of Western authors to plunder this rich mythological handbook. At *Ex Ponto* I, ii, he compares his sorrows to those of Niobe, envying her the transformation that puts an end to her tears. But Ovid, whose sorrow ever increases, finds a more accurate parallel in Tityus:

> Vivimus ut numquam sensu careamus amaro,
> et gravior longa fit mea poena mora.
> sic incomsumptum Tityi semperque renascens
> non perit, ut possit saepe perire, iecur.
>
> (*Ex Ponto* I, ii, 37–40)

[I live; I never lack sharp sense, and my punishment becomes more grave as time passes. Thus
Tityus's liver, unconsumed and ever reborn, does
not die, so that it can die often.]

The Trojan War also dominates Ovid's depiction of his banishment and
exile. We have seen his comparison in the *Tristia* of his night of exile and
the fall of Troy (see *Tristia* IV, iii, 71ff.). He later compares his sorrows to
those of Hector and compares his wife's sorrow to that of Andromache when
she "saw bloody Hector dragged by Achilles' chariot" (*Tristia* IV, iii, 27ff.).
Together, these several dramatic patterns of imagery reveal that Ovid, author of the "art of love," is now writing an "art of exile."[19] He reimagines
parts of his past poetry, both elegy and epic, and casts himself as the central
figure.

Throughout this mythopoetic drama, Ovid addresses the question,
"Why do I still write?" On the practical level, he has a specific goal—to
return to Rome. But ultimately he is celebrating the imagination, doing
what he does best with the raw materials around him. He has no Roman
nightlife or urbane love-games to sing of, so he poetically renders barbarian
weaponry, bitter weather, and the intense longing of separation. He allevi-
ates his sorrow by imagining himself in Rome again. "Grateful that minds
can go wherever they please," Ovid talks with friends and travels to "the
celestial realms" to dwell with the "joyous gods" before returning to his
hellish abode, near the Styx (*Ex Ponto* III, v, 48ff.). This vision, this poetical
re-vision of his life indicates Ovid's allegiance to the powers of imagination.
Ingenium may have gotten him into this state, but *ingenium* can also get him
out.

Through these acts of imagination, Ovid's exile writings constitute his
bid to live on in the memory of his fellows and of posterity.[20] Ovid ends the
Metamorphoses with a bold plea to be remembered, and despite his teasing
talk in the *Tristia* about burning the epic and killing himself, Ovid would
never do either, loving both himself and his poetry too much. *Tristia* IV, for
example, ends with Ovid's humble, hopeful thanks to the "candide lector"
whose reading of Ovid assures the poet's eternal life (IV, x, 125ff.). "Although I soon die," he concludes, "I will not, O earth, be thine." Ovid
sometimes even plays confidently with the idea of his future fame. Telling
his wife that his exile and his letters to her have guaranteed her a place in
history, Ovid cautions her to be loyal and to supplicate Caesar because
women of future generations are watching and will scrutinize her behavior

(see *Ex Ponto* III, i). All in all, Ovid's pleas, his attacks on treacherous friends, his imagery of Troy, of the Styx, and of cold, comfortless "death," all take their part in an *ars exilii*—Ovid's grand plan for poetic immortality.

Fame, gotten by any means, defeats a dignified and legitimately achieved anonymity. So when Ovid hears that his amatory verses have been debased in Roman theatrical performances—something Ovid had never intended, since his "muse was not ambitious for applause"—he stoops to the occasion and says he is "not ungrateful for anything that would hinder [his] oblivion and bring the name of the exile back to men's lips" (*Tristia* V, vii, 25ff.). Ovid also knows that even though his amatory verse brought him exile, it will also bring him immortality. As he definitively and laconically puts it: "I curse the poems whose injury I recall, yet I cannot live without them" (see ll. 30–33).

As a Roman poet in exile, Ovid could only pursue immortality in this way.[21] He knew all about "change," writing his great epic about it, and so he sought to overcome the mutability that could render him unknown to posterity:

> Iamque opus exegi, quod nec Iovis ira nec ignes
> nec poterit ferrum nec edax abolere vetustas.
> cum volet, illa dies, quae nil nisi corporis huius
> ius habet, incerti spatium mihi finiat aevi:
> parte tamen meliore mei super alta perennis
> astra ferar, nomenque erit indelebile nostrum,
> quaque patet domitis Romana potentia terris,
> ora legar populi, perque omnia saecula fama,
> siquid habent veri vatum praesagia, vivam.
>
> (*Metamorphoses* XV, 871–79)

> [Now I have done my work, which neither Jove's
> ire nor flames, nor sword, nor hungry time can ever
> destroy. Let that day come when it wishes—that
> day which has rights over my body only—to finish
> my uncertain span. Nevertheless, the better part of
> me will be borne, immortal, on high, and my name
> will be indelible. And wherever Roman power
> stretches out over conquered lands, I will be read,
> and through all time in fame, if the prophecies of
> the seers have any truth, I will live.]

Ovid could not do what Chaucer does, and what Spenser does at the end of his "mutability" cantos. In a pre-Christian world, the poet can only hope to be remembered. Looking at these final words of the *Metamorphoses* and at the quest for immortality throughout the exile writings, we can now only wonder if Ovid knew how right he was.

But poetry gives Ovid even more than a chance to enter history; it also provides him great personal nourishment and comfort. Medieval commentators discerned a therapeutic motive as they explain the *intentio* and the *utilitas* of the exile poems. Ovid wrote, they tell us, to beg for reinstatement, to incite pity and aid from his friends, to teach others how to bear up against adversity, and to alleviate his own misery and weariness.[22] Schoolmasters base these last assessments on some of Ovid's own comments, including the following passage from the *Ex Ponto:*

> Cur igitur scribam, miraris? miror et ipse,
> et tecum quaero saepe quid inde petam.
> an populus vere sanos negat esse poetas,
> sumque fides huius maxima vocis ego,
> qui, sterili totiens cum sim deceptus ab arvo,
> damnosa persto condere semen humo?
> scilicet est cupidus studiorum quisque suorum,
> tempus et adsueta ponere in arte iuvat.
> saucius eiurat pugnam gladiator, et idem
> inmemor antiqui vulneris arma capit.
> nil sibi cum pelagi dicit fore naufragus undis,
> et ducit remos qua modo navit aqua.
> sic ego constanter studium non utile servo,
> et repeto, nollem quas coluisse, deas.
> quid potius faciam? non sum, qui segnia ducam
> otia: mors nobis tempus habetur iners.
> nec iuvat in lucem nimio marcescere vino,
> nec tenet incertas alea blanda manus.
> cum dedimus somno quas corpus postulat horas,
> quo ponam vigilans tempora longa modo?
> moris an oblitus patrii contendere discam
> Sarmaticos arcus, et trahar arte loci?
> hoc quoque me studium prohibent adsumere vires,
> mensque magis gracili corpore nostra valet.
> cum bene quaesieris quid agam, magis utile nil est
> artibus his, quae nil utilitatis habent.
> consequor ex illis casus oblivia nostri:
> hanc messem satis est si mea reddit humus.

(I, v, 29–56)

[Why indeed should I write? you wonder. I myself
have wondered what I can possibly get out of this.
Don't people think poets insane and that I am a
good example, since, though I have been deceived
by sterile ground, I insist on sowing seed in cursed
soil? Certainly, each man is eager for his own
studies and is pleased to dedicate time to the arts
he is accustomed to. The wounded gladiator
swears off battle, and yet the same man, forgetful
of his old wound, seizes his arms. The sunken
sailor says he will have nothing to do with the sea,
but still he plunges oars into the water in which he
but lately swam. Thus I serve constantly a useless
pursuit, and I return to the gods I wish I had never
worshiped. What, rather, should I do? I am not a
man of slothful leisure. For me, empty time is a
type of death. Nor does it please me to fall weary
with too much wine till dawn. Dice do not attract
my unsteady hands. When I have given to sleep
the time the body requires, how should I spend
the long waking hours? Forgetting my own
customs, should I learn to string the Sarmatian
bow and be drawn in by local arts? Strength
prevents me from taking up such pursuits, for my
mind is more hearty than my fragile body. Although you do well to wonder what I think I am
achieving, there is nothing to me more useful than
these useless arts. They bring me oblivion from
my sorrows: these fruits are harvest enough for
me.]

Ovid does a great deal with these lines as he forges a powerful poetic mani-
festo. No other human pursuit—if we take his catalog of vices and distrac-
tions as representative—offers him lasting fulfillment. Excessive drink,
gambling, sleep, athletics (elsewhere he tells us he does not overeat or visit
prostitutes), all provide only limited escape from the sorrow of his exile of
death. What he seeks is *oblivia*, a sweet antidote to the written troubles of
the brain. He finds this oblivion, he tells us, in poetry. Strangely, this personal, narcotic escape will save him from historical anonymity. Ovid wants
to forget his sufferings, but he does not want anyone else to.

Ovid sees his early love poetry as a risky agricultural investment, in his own terms, "sterile," "deceptive," and "damning," and yet he persists in sowing seed in "damnosa humo" (l. 34). Recreating his sorrows in new fables, depicting himself as Hector, Niobe, Tityus, Diomedes, and Actaeon frees him from misery and wards off poetic death. For Ovid, these moments of escape are "harvest enough." Like the sunken sailor and the wounded gladiator, he returns to the source of his sorrow, continues in the pursuit that can destroy him but can also yield his only remaining joy.

Ars poetica christiana

Ovid assesses his own art and life because exile forces him to become introspective. But how did medieval Christian poets view their own commitments to poetry? Did they seek any of the therapeutic benefits that Ovid so cherished? Boccaccio, who was, as we have seen, a medieval Ovidian, endured a Christian poetic crisis and was, luckily, comforted by Petrarch: "Why forsake letters? . . . All history is full of examples of good men who have loved learning, and though many unlettered men have attained to holiness, no man was ever debarred from holiness by letters."[23] During his career, Boccaccio was sensitive to the power fictions had in healing. In the proem of his *Decameron*, he gives thanks for the "pleasing discourses" [*piacevoli ragionamenti*] that saved him from the misery of unrequited love. This unnamed text, Milicent Joy Marcus argues, is the *Consolation of Philosophy*, and through the implied parallel Boccaccio's own poem "will thus take its place in the cumulative tradition of consolation through fiction."[24]

Boccaccio was saved by fictions, and now he will compose a work that offers consolation to his readers. As Marcus observes, Boccaccio puts himself into a tradition that uses stories to "stave off death" (*An Allegory of Form*, 114), for his storytellers in the *Decameron* themselves turn to fiction while in flight from the plague.[25] Poetry, if used rightly, can be therapy, comfort—in essence, a kind of remedy.

How may we compare Boccaccio's doctrine of therapy to Ovid's? All poetry and all "therapy" are not the same. Boccaccio specifically strives, as Marcus argues, to "exempt himself, as the author of the *Decameron*, from the category of bad poets" who follow the harlot muses that Lady Philosophy chastises at the opening of the *Consolatio*. In his *Esposizioni sopra la Comedia di Dante*, Boccaccio argues that at the opening of the *Consolatio*, Lady Philosophy does not condemn all poetry but only "dismisses the false muses so that she may usher in her own" (Marcus, *An Allegory of Form*, 118). *Inferior* muses inspire Boethius to "write verses which, failing to free him from pain, instead dramatize his suffering in order to elicit a predictable response from the public" (ibid., 119).[26] A poet must know the hierarchy among the muses and the relative merits of different types of poetry. Boccaccio was aware of these distinctions. He writes no personal elegy but crafts a poem to provide true comfort for his readers, just as he was comforted by the *Consolatio*.

Significantly, in these opening elegiac couplets of the *Consolatio*, Boethius appears, as Anna Crabbe argues, "in the guise of a despairing Ovid."[27] Boethius wants his readers at this point to recall the *Tristia*, the five books of which mirror the *Consolatio* itself, and he wants to establish a "hierarchy of responses to adversity" (Crabbe, "Literary Design," 245).[28] In this hierarchy, Boethius has given Ovid low rank, and has summoned the "disreputable love elegy" only to mark its immediate dismissal. As Crabbe says, Ovid's muses can offer no real consolation "apart from rather maudlin sympathy" and an "incitement to self-pity" (ibid., 248). Boethius is saved from this overindulgence by Philosophy, by her wisdom and by her higher, *healing* poetry. Ovid's *Tristia* could provide Boethius a vehicle for complaint but could offer him no liberation—no real "remedy" for his anguish.

One of Boethius's descendants, the narrator of the *Plaint of Nature*, undergoes a comparable progression. As Alexandre Leupin explains, "After having flirted with the phantasmal seductions of narcissistic falsigraphy," the narrator is "brought out of the stupor of his ecstatic vision by the soothing remedy of natural reason." Reason works much like Lady Philosophy and "illuminates and dissipates the dark vapors paralyzing his mind."[29] In just such a brooding elegiac state, Ovid himself, unlike Boethius and the *Plaint*'s narrator, produces thousands of lines of static lament. He endures his exile unclaimed and unsaved by any transcendent philosophical intervention. The contrast that Boethius forges between himself and Ovid in the *Consolatio* did not go unnoticed in the Middle Ages. The *Antiovidianus* poet, in the course of his attack on the idle groaning in the *Tristia*, sharply contrasts the two and tells Ovid: "No friend worked to reverse your exile, nor were you able to find in yourself some means of relief, as did the beloved exile Boethius, shining with the highest honor of praise."[30]

Chaucer, as a reader of Ovid and a translator of Boethius, may have recognized the inferiority of Ovid's response to adversity. He was certainly aware of wise and foolish ways to confront exile and death, and so chose a very different option, pulling up far short of the abyss of despair and loquacious self-indulgence. In addition, though, unlike Boccaccio, he cut himself off from all muses, from all wit and creation.

The humorless, though not colorless, catalog of sins in the *Parson's Tale* and the rejection of poetry in the *Retraction* have caused readers of Chaucer much concern, and critics have sought the perfect formula with which to understand the poet's final gesture. In the *Retraction*, one critic writes, "for once we see Chaucer as a writer who holds himself morally responsible for his writings." Here, says another, he "escapes from the narrative frame and now refers to the larger context of biography."[31] Ovid, Boethius, and Boccaccio—each is a precedent for becoming biographical. But why and how does Chaucer do it?

One of the earliest critical comments on Chaucer's life bears an important relation to the *Retraction* and reveals an interesting paradigm. Thomas Gascoigne, fifteenth-century chancellor of Oxford University, under the topic "Poenitentia" in his *Dictionarium theologicum*, testifies to Chaucer's repentance. He says the poet regretted having written of base loves and was upset that he could not destroy his works. And Chaucer, at the point of death, cried out: "Ah me, ah me, I cannot now revoke or destroy those base writings of mine about the foul and vile love of men for women, for already these works have passed from man to man" [Vae mihi, vae mihi quia revocare nec destruere iam potero illa quae male scripsi de malo et turpimmimo amore hominum ad mulieres sed iam de homine in hominem continuabuntur].[32] We recall that Venus's words to Chaucer in Gower's *Confessio Amantis* also depict Chaucer as a love poet who must come to reckoning and confession. Gascoigne's comments also sound a good deal like those of the commentators on Ovid's *Remedia*, or on any other of Ovid's works that was seen as a remedy, balance, or compensation for the harm done by the *Ars Amatoria*. Chaucer wrote ribald poetry, and now he, and perhaps posterity, will suffer the consequences.

In Gascoigne's comments, Chaucer the love poet thus continues, after death, to fit paradigms applied to Ovid for centuries in the medieval schoolroom. Gascoigne's reduction of Chaucer to an immoral bard who wrote a lubricious art of love should not surprise us because the ethical poetics associated with the "medieval Ovid" formed a central part of Chaucer's culture's understanding of poets and poetry.[33] But the reduction must still seem facile to us, since we know that Chaucer did not just translate or imitate Ovid, but rather constantly revised and recreated him, giving him new voices and locales. Chaucer does not use Ovid unself-consciously, and though it is easy to see how Ovid's *ars* might "sownen into synne," it is not clear how Chaucer's arts of love might harm or corrupt his readers. Did Chaucer's contemporaries fear that readers would learn something dangerous from Pandarus or from the Wife of Bath?

In the *Troilus*, Ovid comes under fire as a maker of illusions that falsify reality and feed deadly desire. In the *Wife of Bath's Prologue and Tale*, a woman marshals Ovidian forces to make peace and establish long overdue marital justice. We would imagine that such sophisticated, critical use of Ovid would bring the Christian Chaucer merit. But in the grossest terms, Chaucer *wrote love poems* and would be called to account for them, as we see from Gower, from Gascoigne, and from the scenario we traced for the *Legend of Good Women*. However much Chaucer worked to create a new poetic vision of love, some contemporaries could see only the "gross" link to Ovid, the conspiracy between these artists of love.

Chaucer knew these ethical paradigms, and so at the end, he indicates that he fears God's wrath. He, like Ovid, dreads the "death of exile," and, accordingly, he begs his readers to intercede with prayers that beseech *his* God to bring him to eternal life in the heavenly city. Ironically, or quite fittingly, Chaucer wants what Ovid wants—immortality. At the end of his last work, Chaucer knows that he can "immortalize" himself more easily by, to borrow Langland's phrase, "piercing" heaven "with a paternoster" than by writing a new fiction, another *ars* of some kind, as Ovid does from exile.[34]

In the *Troilus* and in the *Wife of Bath's Prologue and Tale*, Chaucer renews Ovid, confronts him as complexly and as sensitively as we modern critics could ever imagine. But Chaucer somehow knew that this was not enough, that Ovid was always a dangerous model and mentor. In the *Retraction* Chaucer admits not that he "wrote about base and scabrous love" but that all poetry, particularly poetry that embraces craft and desire, brings danger to its creator. Does responding to this danger mean that Chaucer has somehow failed or betrayed himself? David Aers maintains that with the *Retraction* Chaucer, evidently in a moment of weakness at the end of his life, "asserts a model of the individual and his one dimensional psychological simplicity which has no grounding in the poetic totality, the bulk of which is simply rejected."[35] In this view, Chaucer got scared at the last minute, just when he had completely obliterated his biographical identity in a lively, sprawling story of human desire and power.

But is the *Retraction* so at odds with the bulk of Chaucer's corpus or with his conception of the function of poetry? Aers assumes a biographical moment that severely separates Chaucer's words from their rhetorical and literary historical context. Penance makes a great deal of sense for a Christian poet, just as self-immortalization does for a pagan one. "Penance," as a recent critic of Langland has put it, "is the means by which Christians overcome the reign of mutability in their spiritual lives." Working from the model of Solomon, whose biblical writings serve as penance for his past misdeeds, Eric Eliason argues that Langland saw his own constant revisions of *Piers Plowman* as penance that provides "nourishment for the spiritual life."[36]

Chaucer's "revision" does not come in rewriting the *Tales* but in re-envisioning the concept of "pilgrimage" through penance.

Before the final curtain of silence falls in the *Retraction*, the poet formally concludes the Canterbury pilgrimage and tale-telling contest with the *Parson's Tale*, essentially a handbook for the penitent. Before he speaks, the Parson makes clear that, unlike Ovid, he will sow no seed in *damnosa humo*. He rejects poetry as sterile and claims religious doctrine as the only truly fruitful verbal pursuit:

> Thou getest fable noon ytoold for me,
> For Paul, that writeth unto Thymothee,[37]
> Repreveth hem that weyven soothfastnesse
> And tellen fables and swich wrecchednesse.
> Why sholde I sowen draf out of my fest,
> Whan I may sowen whete, if that me lest?
>
> (X, 31–36)

The Parson's dampening words here help Chaucer reverse the fictive thrust, the imaginative ingenuity, that had been driving the *Canterbury Tales* from the very start. By contrast, a fictive thrust is, as we have seen, all Ovid has to sustain himself. Verse, image, "fable"—any exercise of his poetic faculty—offer him his only hope for succor and, ultimately, for life itself. To "reject" fable would mean to reject all hope, and Ovid was too resourceful an artist for that.

The *Parson's Tale* displays a different type of resourcefulness. Chaucer's final "tale" is about as "un-fabulous"—and certainly as un-Ovidian—as any work can be. Ovid strives for immortality through fiction, but the Parson shows another way to the "blisful lif that is perdurable" (l. 74). Before Chaucer commits his final act for his own soul's nourishment, this prose tract tells how his readers can escape "exile" from the heavenly kingdom and find salvation, the true goal of pilgrimage. The *Parson's Tale* offers, then, a new kind of "art," an "art of penance." It gives the journeying soul a forum not for private lament, but for public, ecclesiastical aid—not a narcotic oblivion from exile and sorrow, but a concrete path to salvation. Heartfelt, Christian "Confessioun of Mouth" will do much more than thousands of lines of artful, sorrowful elegy.

The Parson becomes the new and, indeed, rather *severus praeceptor;* unlike Ovid, of course, he uses no art, and unlike Lady Philosophy, he will not even blend a little poetry with his doctrine. The hierarchy of muses does not concern him, for he summons no muse at all. Chaucer, as the author behind the Parson's voice, becomes a new kind of servant for his audience—a Christian writer who serves "trouthe" and the divine Word. His art offers no succor for lovers, no "gift of words," and provides no arms of any kind to either sex. Rather, it gives the faithful the means to arm themselves against sin, so that "hooly chirche [will] holdeth hem siker of hire savacioun" (l. 92).

The *Parson's Tale,* in its detailed, doctrinal instruction, provides an ultimate sort of remedy for the Canterbury pilgrims and their audience. Chaucer speaks through a non-fictive, non-amorous doctor of the soul. The Parson rejects fable so that no art or game can delude his listeners. This final tale signals a dramatic point in Chaucer's *vita* too, as he chose to reveal it to us. Chaucer knows that his own hopes for salvation are deeply tied to his literary career, and so by writing the Parson's tract and the *Retraction,* he formally and specifically distances himself from his poetry.

We have to specify from his *poetry,* because some of his work, as he sees it, has the merit and the power to stir divine intercession:

> But of the translacion of Boece de Consolacione,
> and othere bookes of legendes of seintes, and
> omelies, and moralitee, and devocioun, / that
> thanke I oure Lord Jhesu Crist and his blisful
> Mooder, and alle the seintes of hevene, /
> bisekynge hem that they from hennes forth unto
> my lyves ende sende me grace to biwayle my
> giltes, and to studie to the salvacioun of my soule,
> and graunte me grace of verray penitence,
> confessioun and satisfaccioun to doon in this
> present lyf, / thurgh the benigne grace of hym that
> is kyng of kynges and preest over alle preestes,
> that boghte us with the precious blood of his herte;
> / so that I may be oon of hem at the day of doom
> that shulle be saved. *Qui cum patre et Spiritu Sancto
> vivit et regnat Deus per omnia secula. Amen.*
>
> (ll. 1087–91)

Unlike Ovid, who seeks poetic medication for his sorrows, Chaucer wants to free himself from the threat of death and exile and "bewail his guilts," personally adopting the lessons the Parson has set forth. Instead of sustaining the power of verse and fable, he wants to "study for the salvation of his soul." He hopes his penitence and his holy writings will allow him to receive the grace of the "king of kings" who holds the poet's fate in his hands. Ovid tries to escape from death through fiction; for Chaucer, escape from death must come through an escape from fiction.

Ovid never wrote saints' lives or translated Boethius, but he does refer Augustus to those of his works that, like Chaucer's religious writings, display him at his humble best.[38] He tells Augustus to read the *Fasti* (dedicated to the emperor), the *Medea* (now lost, but it must have spoken well of Augustus), and those sections of the *Metamorphoses* that praise Julius and Augustus and show, as Ovid tells Augustus, "how warmly I have written of you and yours" (*Tristia* II, 562). Ovid, like Chaucer, claims to have written works that should bring him some divine capital.

Ovid was no Boethius, but he does conduct a fascinating war on several fronts. He seeks oblivion and succor in the act of writing, seeks mercy from his "god," and seeks immortality through his art. All these can provide some sort of liberation from and transcendence of the sorrow he suffers, and he weaves these personal, political and historical concerns together to form a dynamic and dramatic art of exile. Ovid, like Chaucer, thinks "somewhat on his soul" as he worries that his horrid state will continue to plague him beyond the grave. He beseeches his friend Maximus to intercede for him and allow him eventually to return from exile, but if not, Ovid has another favor to ask:

> Denique, si moriar, subeam pacatius arvum,
> ossa nec a Scythia nostra premantur humo,
> nec male compositos, ut scilicet exule dignum,
> Bistonii cineres ungula pulset equi:
> et ne, si superest aliquis post funera sensus,
> terreat et Manes Sarmatis umbra meos.
>
> (*Ex Ponto* I, ii, 107–12)

> [If I die, let me be buried peacefully, and do not
> let my bones feel the weight of Scythian soil. Nor
> let the hoof of Bistonian horses pound my ashes,
> poorly buried, as would fit an exile. And, if any
> sense exists beyond death, let not some Sarmatian
> shade frighten my departed spirit.]

Ovid cannot say that he wants to be "one of hem" that shall be saved on Judgment Day, but he does want peace, and he fears the ghostly torments that would preserve this death in exile even after his body's demise. The personal fates of Ovid and Chaucer form part of either a karmic or super-natural *pryvetee* beyond the scope of all critical inquiry. And the concerns of the poets here, the psychic constitution of imaginative, creative minds facing death—and writing about it in a larger poetic context—set perhaps a good stage on which to leave Chaucer and Ovid.

Chaucer, as a Christian poet rewriting and re-envisioning Ovid for much of his career, does much that Ovid simply cannot do. As a reader of the *Tristia*, he must have seen how Ovid was trapped in art, in a frenzy of images of "metamorphosis," and in fear of death, hopelessly invoking an emperor who would not listen and who thus would do nothing to help the exile. In the *Retraction*, Chaucer wants his record clear so that he can avoid, not Ovid's political banishment, but the "exile" suffered, we might say, by his most treacherous surrogate artist, the Pardoner—banishment from his "true home," the divine kingdom. After Chaucer's many celebrations of fiction, in the *Tales* themselves and in his entire poetic career, the Parson clears a path back from exile. Chaucer's last act is to take this path.

Ovid argues that his life was spotless but his "muse was playful," and for his playful muse he paid a high price. Chaucer knows the dangers of having such a muse, of being a love poet and a maker of "fables." He must finally retract his *fictional* works because he fears being associated with them, fears that posterity will read the author, and indeed the author's soul, according to his playful and imaginative performance. This leaves us at the final paradoxical point: Chaucer's *Retraction* represents a personal, spiritual decision, yet also his last rhetorical act, part of both his elaborate *ars poetica christiana* and his *ars clerici Veneris*.[39] Chaucer's unique place in literary history demanded that he write both "arts," be both an Ovidian servant of love and a Christian servant of the Word. Posterity can be grateful that Chaucer announces his fears about poetry after having spent his life as the great medieval Ovid, producing the dangerous fables and fictions that teach and entertain servants of love.

Notes

Introduction:
Chaucer's Ovidian Arts of Love

1. Eustache Deschamps, "Autre Balade"; quoted and translated in Derek Brewer, *Chaucer*, 39–40.

2. For a concise discussion of the many faces of Ovid in the Middle Ages, see Leclercq, *Love of Learning*, 64; see also his *Monks and Love*, 113ff., on Ovid and medieval literary culture.

3. As Peter Allen puts it in discussing medieval "arts of love," poets must in some way become a "Naso novus" or a new Ovid (*Art of Love*, 3). See his index for other references to medieval poets as the "Naso novus," which indicate that Chaucer takes his place in a larger literary tradition. Allen has written one of the most vital and cogent studies of Ovid's fiction-making arts of love, which he then brings to bear on Andreas Capellanus and Jean de Meun. Allen's premise is that the conflicts and contradictions in these medieval arts of love are rooted in the conflict between the *Ars Amatoria* and the *Remedia Amoris* of Ovid. By reading the medieval poems through Ovid, we see that "love and fiction are intertwined to such a degree that they can be seen as aspects of one another" (1). I thank Professor Allen for sharing his manuscript with me before publication. On the reception and study of Ovid's love poetry in medieval literary culture, see his richly annotated second chapter, "From Rome to France: Under the Sign of Ovid" (38–58).

4. I am thinking here of Wack, *Lovesickness,* which often discusses Ovid's various "remedies" for love as they were used by medieval medical authorities. I refer the reader to a very partial list of recent scholarly works that address Ovid's influence: Jacquart and Thomasset, *Sexuality and Medicine;* Boswell, *Christianity, Social Tolerance, and Homosexuality;* Barkan, *Gods Made Flesh,* on the history of poetic and artistic metamorphosis; Martindale, ed., *Ovid Renewed;* Jacoff and Schnapp, eds., *Poetry of Allusion,* on Dante's use of Virgil and Ovid; Sowell, ed., *Dante and Ovid;* Perry, *Another Reality,* on Ovid, Petrarch, and Ronsard; and Brownlee, *The Severed Word,* on the *Heroides* and the novela sentimental.

5. The phrase comes from Carolyn Dinshaw's *Chaucer's Sexual Poetics.* See also Hansen, *Chaucer and the Fictions of Gender.* Dinshaw analyzes gender in both Chaucer's poetry and in Chaucer scholarship, and Hansen confronts the relationship between feminist criticism and Chaucer studies.

6. *Metamorphoses* 15.879. This is to say nothing of the critical interest, manifested by both studies and editions, in Ovid himself. Through the chapters that follow I will refer to texts I have consulted and found useful. Myerowitz's *Ovid's Games of Love* offers a detailed and serious attempt to interpret Ovid's art and ambitions in the love poems and contains an extensive bibliographic apparatus on Ovid scholarship. Sara Mack's *Ovid,* is a clear and lively introduction, not for the specialist, but for the student of the humanities seeking a dialogue with the classical poet.

7. See Fyler, "Auctoritee and Allusion," 73. Allen and Moritz argue that "in historical terms, the only Ovid that matters to Chaucer is the medieval Ovid, and for that one, given the passage of time, we must perforce trust the medieval commentators even more than our own reading of the book they glossed" (*A Distinction of Stories,* 16). In this work the authors argue that we must read the *Canterbury Tales* according to the categories assigned by medieval scholastics to the "changes" featured in the stories in Ovid's *Metamorphoses:* natural, moral, magical, and spiritual. Allen and Moritz are aware of the importance of the "medieval Ovid" (see p. 15 for their criticism of Fyler).

8. For convenient and detailed accounts, see Alton, "Ovid in the Medieval Schoolroom"; Ghisalberti, "Medieval Biographies of Ovid"; and Hexter, *Ovid and Medieval Schooling.*

9. See also Quain, "The Medieval Accessus ad Auctores," 215–28.

10. See John Fleming, *Classical Imitation and Interpretation,* a detailed study of Chaucer's "deep classicism," as Fleming calls it. Fleming is sensitive to Chaucer's use of Ovid as it comes to him through the *Roman de la Rose.* Fleming, in the context of his discussion of the word *queynt,* comments that the "Latin or 'Ur-Ovid' points us in the right direction," but that Chaucer's poem "is likewise richly informed by anterior vernacular Ovidianism, particularly that of the *Roman de la Rose* and of Boccaccio" (28).

11. See the selections from Dryden in Derek Brewer, *Chaucer;* on Chaucer and Ovid see Hoffman, "Wife of Bath" and *Ovid;* Fyler, "Auctoritie and Allusion," "Fab-

rications," and *Chaucer and Ovid;* Wetherbee, *Chaucer and the Poets;* Hanning, "Chaucer's First Ovid"; and Cooper, "Chaucer and Ovid." See also Morris, *Chaucer Source and Analogue Criticism.*

12. Robert Durling, *Figure of the Poet,* has written of Ovid's view of language and reality, his awareness of game, and his fearless welcome of contradiction. Ovid, he tells us, is the master of "pure technique, which is dis-interested in the sense that it remains above and uncommitted to any of the possible . . . moral positions one can take toward them" (37). Durling sees these poems as part of an "elaborate literary game," designed "to arouse the reader's awareness of the artificiality of conventions, the contrivance, the pretense, the virtuosity of bold manipulation" (43).

13. Lanham, *Motives of Eloquence,* notices this rhetorically based identity of the characters, and I agree that "the Canterbury pilgrims are not just pilgrims. Each is a poet." But I am not adopting his larger argument about the function of game and seriousness in Chaucer and in Ovid too. He states, for instance, that "society must remain a game. Harmony depends on it" (70). See his entire chapter, "Games and High Seriousness in Chaucer" (65–81).

14. I am here echoing Ralph Hexter's comment that the story of Ovid's exile "has the appeal of fiction" (*Ovid and Medieval Schooling,* 83).

15. Although C. S. Lewis, "What Chaucer Really Did"; Windeatt, "Chaucer"; and Fleming, *Classical Imitation and Interpretation,* have studied Chaucer's changes to Boccaccio's text, Chaucer's comprehensive "Ovidianization" of the *Filostrato* has not been argued. Eugene Vance offers a study of the characters' rhetoricity, illustrating that "rhetoricity itself" is a problem; he focuses partly on Pandarus, for whom "truth can have no verbal ground." Chaucer's aim, he says rightly, is "to instigate in his readers a moral consciousness of language that his narrator and characters do not share" (*Mervelous Signals,* 282). An outstanding study of Chaucer and his vernacular sources is Barbara Nolan, *Chaucer and the Roman Antique,* a book acutely sensitive to the role of Ovid in medieval poetics. See esp. chap. 4, "From History into Fiction: Boccaccio's *Filostrato* and the Question of Foolish Love" (119–54), and chap. 6, "Saving the Poetry: Authors, Translators, Texts, and Readers in Chaucer's *Book of Troilus and Criseyde*" (198–246).

16. At *Ars Amatoria* I, 25–30, Ovid claims the authority of *usus* [experience].

17. Ovid, like the wife, takes pride in his own authority. He treats his *Ars Amatoria* in a similar way, referring his readers to it in the *Remedia Amoris,* ll. 485–88. Note too the suggestions to read Ovid in Boccaccio's *Filostrato* (I, 45) and in Gower's *Confessio Amantis* where Amans points out Ovid's limitations. In response to Genius's advice to read Ovid's doctrines of love, the lover claims that "if thei techen to restreigne / Mi love, it were an ydel peine / To lerne a thing which mai noght be" (IV, 2677–79).

18. See Huygens, *Accessus ad Auctores,* 35.

19. Peter Allen studies the *De Amore* and the *Roman de la Rose* as amatory fiction, medieval arts of love in the Ovidian tradition, in *Arts of Love,* 59–110.

20. See Wilkinson, *Ovid Recalled,* 384.

21. Petrarch, *De Vita Solitaria*, quoted in Stroh, *Ovid im Urteil der Nachwelt:* "nisi his moribus et hoc animo fuisset, et clarius nomen haberet apud graves viros" (30).

22. Foucault, "What Is an Author," in *The Foucault Reader,* 108.

Chapter 1: Clerks of Venus

1. On medieval ethical poetics, see especially J. B. Allen, *Ethical Poetics;* Minnis, *Medieval Theory of Authorship;* and Minnis and Scott, eds., *Medieval Literary Theory.*

2. On Servius and the vitae, see Rosa, "Due Biografie."

3. "The need of a comprehensive synthesis of the poet's own revelations or reservations, concerning himself, and of traditional accretions to his biography, was felt with particular intensity from the twelfth to the fourteenth centuries, at the height of the vogue for Ovid" (Ghisalberti, "Medieval Biographies of Ovid," 10).

4. Ibid.

5. See Ghisalberti, "Giovani del Virgilio," 16.

6. See Alton, "Ovid in the Medieval Schoolroom," 74.

7. See also Coulson, "Hitherto Unedited Medieval and Renaissance Lives of Ovid." He traces the developing humanist tendencies of the vitae, particularly in the fifteenth century; see esp. p. 170 and his edition of the vita composed by Bernardo Moretti (191–200). As Coulson notes, Bernardo definitively states that the *Ars Amatoria* was the cause of Ovid's exile and seems to dismiss as speculation other theories about Ovid's famous "error."

8. To date, the *Tristia* has barely been discussed in relation to any poem by Chaucer, except as the locus classicus for his "go min book" (V, 1786), at the end of the *Troilus,* a phrase Chaucer probably got, not from Ovid, but from Boccaccio. See Tatlock, "Epilogue," particularly on the literary evolution of the phrase.

9. See *Tristia* I, i, 117–22.

10. Ovid's "error," the second part of his dual crime (*carmen et error*), remains a mystery, though scholars, both modern and medieval, have speculated thoroughly.

11. Petrarch, *De Vita Solitaria*, quoted in Stroh, *Ovid im Urteil der Nachwelt,* 29–30. Stroh refers to the Basel, 1581, edition of the *Opera,* 279 (with altered punctuation).

12. "Ipse vero in iuvenili estate constitutus, telumque Cupidinis septissime lacessitus, effiminate lascivie sue relaxens, librum de Arte Amatoria composuit in quo quam plurimos contraxit in errorem per amoris varia documenta" (Ghisalberti, "Medieval Biographies of Ovid," 45).

13. See Ghisalberti, "Medieval Biographies of Ovid," 32–33 and appendix N; Huygens, *Accessus ad Auctores,* 34; and Hexter, *Ovid and Medieval Schooling,* 102ff. Hexter discusses the three main "causes" of Ovid's exile, the third of which is invariably "quia librum fecerat de Arte Amatoria, in quo iuvenes doceret matronas decipiendo sibi allicere, et ideo offensis Romanis dicitur missus in exilium" (102).

14. See Alton, "Ovid in the Medieval Schoolroom": "Quidam enim dicunt quod missus est propter o. de arte, in qua docuit non docenda" (75).

15. Hexter, *Ovid and Medieval Schooling,* 95.

16. Alton edits a commentary that says Ovid wrote the *Fasti*, a morally neutral calendar of rituals, because he "recognized the error" he had committed in composing the lascivious verses of the *Ars Amatoria* and because his damnation was a topic of discussion in Rome. See Alton, "Ovid in the Medieval Schoolroom," 75.

17. Baird and Kane, trans., *La Querelle*, 83. For the original French, see Hicks, ed., *Le Débat sur le Roman de la Rose*.

18. Commenting on the availability of the *Tristia* and the *Ex Ponto*, Hexter tells us that they had "no lack of readers, even in the early middle ages" (*Ovid and Medieval Schooling*, 86). Harbert, in Derek Brewer, *Geoffrey Chaucer*, 137–53, provides a look at the type of manuscripts that Chaucer would have had access to and offers a sample catalog that includes the exile poems and other works of Ovid. See also Dillon, *A Chaucer Dictionary*, for a list of allusions to the *Tristia* and the *Ex Ponto*. Shannon, *Chaucer and the Roman Poets*, mentions Chaucer's frequent rendering of lines from these poems.

19. See Hollander, *Boccaccio's Two Venuses*, 112ff.

20. Boccaccio, *Esposizioni sopra la Comedia di Dante*, vol. 6 of *Tutte le operi*, p. 371. Hollander, *Boccaccio's Two Venuses*, refers to this passage in a note (235n85.). He also reproduces some parallels that Boccaccio has engineered as he links the details of his own childhood to that of his ancient, fellow Italian *auctor.*

21. See Baudry's poems in Hilbert, ed., *Baldricus Burgulianus Carmina*, nos. 7 and 8; and see Hexter, *Ovid and Medieval Schooling*, 94–95, 101, 136; and Boswell, *Christianity, Social Tolerance, and Homosexuality*, for brief commentary.

22. Wilkinson, *Ovid Recalled*, 383; Hilbert, ed., *Baldricus Burgulianus Carmina*, no. 200; *Tristia* II, 353–54. On Baudry and the evolution of Ovidian amatory fiction, see Peter Allen, *Art of Love*, chap. 2.

23. See J. B. Allen's long discussion of the commentaries on the *Heroides* and the ethical implications for vernacular poetry, in *Ethical Poetic*, 10ff.

24. See Ghisalberti, "Medieval Biographies of Ovid," 38: "Ovid, who spent a long time in exile, wrote this book of letters out of a desire to regain the benevolence of Roman women" (my translation) [{Ovid} qui positus in excilo vitam in longo tempore ducens, Romanarum mulierum benevolentiam sibi recuperare cupiens, epistolarum librum composuit]. Ghisalberti's appendix B contains Cod. Laur. 91 supp. 23 (fifteenth century) which tells how Roman wives plotted Ovid's exile, leading him to try to appease them by writing the *Heroides*. See also Quain, "The Medieval Accessus ad Auctores," 219 (*Monac. lat.* 19475), which says that Ovid wrote the *Heroides* to give proper examples of love to be followed and to be avoided, since he had previously taught only "illicit loves" to the Roman matrons in his *Ars Amatoria.*

25. Lydgate, *Fall of Princes*, ll. 330ff., quoted in Derek Brewer, *Chaucer*, 24. On the medieval tradition of writing an "apology to women" after having written a potentially antifeminist text, see Jill Mann, *Apologies to Women*. She discusses Chaucer's apologies and those offered by other vernacular authors, including Lydgate, Jehan le Fèvre, and Guillaume de Machaut. Mann argues that "writing against women and then apologizing for it is as often as not just a convenient way of manu-

facturing a literary subject" (25). She distinguishes Chaucer from other male apologists and concludes that he indirectly displays that he alone "has an idea of what a *real* apology to a woman would look like" (30; italics in original).

26. See Ghisalberti, "Medieval Biographies of Ovid," 38n.

27. See David, "Man of Law," 220ff. David argues that the Man of Law overinterprets Chaucer's love poems as "sermons" and therefore that it is Chaucer himself who knows the actual frivolity of his love poems and perceives the need for a palinode.

28. Kolve, *Chaucer and the Imagery of Narrative*, 293–94.

29. This famous passage from the first version of the *Confessio Amantis* was omitted, for unclear reasons, from later versions. Quoted in Derek Brewer, *Chaucer*, 43–44.

30. John Fisher, *John Gower*, 286ff., quoted in David, "Man of Law," 220.

31. *Tristia* I, ix, 61–62.

32. Quain, "The Medieval Accessus ad Auctores," 222–23. He cites MS *Vat. lat.* 1479.

33. J. B. Allen makes a number of important comparisons. He points out the "contrast between the linguistic autonomy of modern literature and the very practical usefulness" of literature as received by medieval critics (*Ethical Poetics*, 288). And as he succinctly says, "For the most part, texts we would call poems were . . . classified as ethics" (11). Likewise, commenting on the *accessus ad auctores*, Hexter reminds us that "most of the works we consider literature were classified as ethics" (*Ovid and Medieval Schooling*, 100). The classification of and comment on Ovid's poems, like Ovid's works themselves, are not without contradiction. As Quain explains, "The *auctor* was cited but his words were interpreted to suit the purpose of the writer. . . . This attempt to maintain the *auctoritas* as a revered figure of the past, even when twisting his words into an opposite meaning, is a sure index of the admiration in which he was held" ("The Medieval Accessus ad Auctores," 225).

34. See Ghisalberti, "Medieval Biographies of Ovid," 43n5.

35. Ibid., 13.

36. Some authors outside the scholastic commentary tradition tell us the carnality of the *Ars* demanded a healing remedy, as William of St. Thierry describes in his tract "De natura et dignitate amoris." See *PL* 184, cols. 381ff. In a rather extreme analysis, one cleric translated this "remedy," the *Remedia Amoris,* till dawn in honor of the Virgin (see Wilkinson, *Ovid Recalled,* 383).

37. Bush, quoted in Quain, "The Medieval Accessus ad Auctores," 225. Quain has an insightful, even Ovidian, reading of the art of the medieval schoolmaster; he argues that "it is impossible to suppose that the medieval writer really believed that Ovid, for instance, had a high moral purpose for writing the *Ars Amatoria*." Quain continues: "Ovid, as an *auctor,* was the possession of the teacher of the Middle Ages and he could be used for whatever purpose the teacher wished. . . . The medieval teacher would doubtless be amused at our suspicions of his intelligence" (226). J. B. Allen seems to follow Quain but places less emphasis on the element of play. He discusses a commentary on the *Heroides* that maintains that the text will, in Allen's

paraphrase, "help us love our girlfriends." Allen adds: "We must not, of course, presume that the medieval reader of the *Heroides* was ridiculous and did not know it; rather we must presume that the medieval reader's quality of life, his set of moral axioms, was such as to make it both plausible and effective that he relate his amorous behavior to Ovid" (*Ethical Poetic*, 32–33).

38. Petrarch, *De vita solitaria:* "Ille mihi quidem magni vir ingenii videtur, sed lascivi et lubri ci et prorsus mulierosi animi fuisse," quoted by Hexter, *Ovid and Medieval Schooling*, 96.

39. Benton, *Self and Society in Medieval France*, 87n1.

40. Kienast, ed., *Antiovidianus*, ll. 3–6, 21–22.

41. "Stercoris et putridi semper pascarjs odore / Aer te recreet posteriore crepans." The contrasts the poem makes between truth, piety, and "gold" on the one hand, and falseness, depravity, and *stercora* on the other, are central to the way we read the Ovidian doctrine spouted by Chaucerian rhetoricians. The process of "aurification" described here calls to mind Chaucer's Canon and the "piss and dung" that he seeks alchemically to transform. See Calabrese, "Meretricious Mixtures."

42. See Huygens, *Accessus ad Auctores*, 35–36.

43. Hexter, *Ovid and Medieval Schooling*, 98–99.

44. Ghisalberti, "Medieval Biographies of Ovid," 15.

45. "Quibus modis retineri valeant." See Huygens, *Accessus as Auctores*, 33.

46. The various materials that I have briefly surveyed, and indeed much more that is beyond my scope here, helped shape Chaucer's Ovid and can help us avoid what Minnis calls the "Loeb Library syndrome," whereby we read a medieval author with modern editions of classical works handy but ignore the contemporaneous textual and cultural presentation of these texts. Minnis refers, for example, to a modern editor's failure to recognize the form and meaning of Andreas Capellanus's *De Amore* III because of an ignorance of medieval commentaries on the *Remedia Amoris*. See Minnis, *Medieval Theory of Authorship*, xiv.

47. Fyler, *Chaucer and Ovid*, 2–17 passim.

48. Ovid's love poems are not just a frivolous prelude to tragedy; in themselves they have a serious side. Ovid opposes Virgil by trivializing mythic Roman grandeur and undermining monadic systems of describing human history, identity, and experience. See the discussion in Fyler, *Chaucer and Ovid*, 3ff.

49. Durling rightly points out that despite the implied failings of the doctor of love, the "posture of lack of control . . . is one of the important subsidiary devices by which the absolute technical control of the poem is suggested" (*Figure of the Poet*, 39). On the function and intent of Ovid's amatory project, see Myerowitz, *Ovid's Games of Love*.

50. My phrase is based on Rolfe Humphries's translation of this line: "Get the names right if you can; anyway have them ring true" (*The Art of Love* [Bloomington: Indiana University Press, 1957], 112).

51. "Ille uel ille, duces, et erunt quae nomina dicas, / si poteris, uere, si minus, apta tamen" (*Ars* I, 227–28). This advice survives in French medieval "arts" such as the *Key to Love*. See Shapiro, ed. and trans., *Comedy of Eros*, 21–22.

52. Lanham's "rhetorical," in *Motives of Eloquence,* may be a synonymous explanation. A related issue is philosophical nominalism—see Taylor, "Peynted Confessions," esp. 120, 123–24.

53. "Intret amicitiae nomine tectus amor. / hoc aditu uidi tetricae data uerba puellae: / qui fuerat cultor, factus amator erat" (*Ars* I, 720–22).

54. In another example, what seems to Fyler, in *Chaucer and Ovid,* 13, a lack of control forms part of a larger strategy of "good timing." The "'*ars*' fails precisely when it is most needed," says Fyler, citing the *Remedia,* ll. 119–20: "When passion streams, give in to the raging stream: approaching any frenzy has its difficulties" [Dum furor in cursu est, currenti cede furori: / difficiles aditus impetus omnis habet]. But again we must look further, because Ovid does not admit defeat in the face of strong, fresh grief. Rather, he goes on to celebrate the art of timely healing: "temporis ars medicina fere est" [the art of timing is also a type of medicine] (l. 131).

55. Hollis, "The *Ars* and *Remedia,*" 93ff., discusses Ovid's "master stroke" in Latin literary history: he takes love, which had been treated as "an overwhelming force, even a disease or madness," and depicts it as controllable by casting his work in the didactic tradition.

56. Fyler, *Chaucer and Ovid,* quotes only the first four lines of this discussion (529–32).

57. See Wack, *Lovesickness,* 70, 280n69.

58. Durling, *The Figure of the Poet,* 37; see Fyler's response to Durling in *Chaucer and Ovid,* 15.

59. Peter Allen argues that the poems about love are really poems about art. The preceptor's own frequent lies "vitiate the reader's belief that the work of art is an accurate and trustworthy representation of anyone's experience . . . and . . . create an understanding that another world can exist outside of that experience—the world of art. . . . This world is limited." Allen continues, "Indeed it is dependent on its limitations which form its borders. Without these limits, readers of the *Ars* find, encounters with fiction and fantasy are dangerous and destructive. Within them, however, art has meaning and gives pleasure. Thus the artist's first job . . . is to create those limits, to set aside a space for the work, a space like that of fantasy, in which—since rules, belief, mutual emotion, and complete emotional involvement are not necessary—it is possible to play" (*Art of Love,* 28–29). See his entire first chapter, "The *Ars amatoria* and *Remedia amoris:* The Illusion of Love, the Love of Illusion."

Chapter 2:
Love, Change, and Ovidian "Game" in the Troilus

1. "Si qvis in hoc artem populo non novit amandi, / hoc legat et lecto carmine doctus amet."

2. "Ad mea, decepti iuvenes, praecepta uenite, / quos suus ex omni parte fefellit amor."

3. Scholars have amended and developed ideas put forth by C. S. Lewis in a classic essay in which he explains how Chaucer "medievalized" Boccaccio. Chaucer does this mainly by adding the colorings of courtly love while, according to Lewis, never forgetting his "erotically didactic purpose" ("What Chaucer Really Did," 32). Ida Gordon's *The Double Sorrow of Troilus,* a study of ambiguity and irony in the poem, explains how Chaucer endows the characters with limited versions of Boethian wisdom: "The irony insures that our pity is not just the ready pity that suffering evokes: by opening our eyes to the nature of their love, it helps us to see the suffering as a consequence of the lovers' blindness or 'sickness' of soul, and as such to be pitied in all charity" (138). For a survey and bibliography on these issues, see Barney, *Chaucer's Troilus.*

4. See Windeatt, "Italian to English" and "Chaucer." See also Windeatt's edition of the *Troilus,* which closely annotates Chaucer's changes and intensifications.

5. Wetherbee, *Chaucer and the Poets,* 93, likewise describes the characters' world as Ovidian, but I am not paraphrasing him here.

6. The absence of a classical/Ovidian point of reference distinguishes the *Filostrato* from the *Teseida,* whose massive authorial glosses, though perhaps not specifically Ovidian, do offer a mythic dimension to the characters' actions.

7. In a comprehensive study of the *Troilus* in the context of Chaucer's awareness of history, Barbara Nolan argues that "Chaucer makes Ovidian *fine amor* . . . a moral fulcrum in his *Troilus*" ("Chaucer and the Roman Antiques," 200). Nolan traces the relations of *fine* and *fole amor,* as Chaucer inherited the concepts from Ovid, from Ovid's medieval commentators, and, most particularly, from the authors of the *roman antique* who supplied Chaucer with the *matere* for his own version of the Troy story. See pp. 198-246.

8. Wetherbee, *Chaucer and the Poets,* 100; Windeatt, "Italian to English," 98.

9. See Lewis, "What Chaucer Really Did," 27, and see *Troilus* I, 155 ff. and *Filostrato* I, 19-32, esp. 23–24, on Troilo's past experience: "Io provai giá per la mia gran follia / qual fosse questo maladetto foco" [I have found before now by my own great folly what this cursed fire is].

10. Translations of extended passages from the *Filostrato* are from Robert Kay Gordon, *The Story of Troilus,* with page number given—in this case, p. 33. Translations of single lines and phrases are my own.

11. See *Troilus* I, 659ff.; *Heroides* V; and *Remedia,* ll. 313ff. On Pandarus, see Fyler, "Fabrications."

12. The line has an ominous parallel in the *Merchant's Tale,* l. 1577, which describes January's final decision to choose May after his "Heigh fantasye and curious bisynesse."

13. If Chaucer's understanding of Ovid comes at all from the academic tradition, he would not view the *Ars* as a poem about the failure of ineffective systems, as Fyler alleges. The *accessus* tradition substantiates my reading: "utilitas est artificiosa amoris peritia [its utility is the skillful art of love], ut patet in primis duobus versis 'si quis in hoc artem populo etc.'" See Ghisalberti, "Medieval Biographies of Ovid," 45, appendix C.

14. Nolan, *Chaucer and the Roman Antique*, 198–237 passim, examines Chaucer's manipulation of the textual history of the poem and traces a similar dynamic tension in the *Troilus*, analyzing how Pandarus's *matere*, pleasure, comes into conflict with the narrator's *matere*, the tragic, ancient story.

15. "Forma bonum fragile est, quantumque accedit ad annos, / fit minor et spatio carpitur ipsa suo."

16. An alternate or parallel source for this advice is *Ars* III, 59ff., where the master prepares the way for his precepts by inciting women to love men, opening up a discussion of health care and the cosmetic arts that enhance beauty.

17. As Windeatt notes, Chaucer also eliminates Crisida's own use of a similar "Carpe diem" argument to convince herself to accept Troilo's love (see *Filostrato* II, 70–71).

18. Here I have used Peter Green's clever translation "don't look too eloquently highbrow"; see *The Erotic Poems*, 180.

19. On the connection between man and city, see McCall, *Chaucer among the Gods*, 94.

20. Quite in contrast to my argument here about Criseyde's literary power, Hansen argues that Criseyde, as a reader, struggles with male texts. Criseyde, Hansen says, is an "unknowing, necessarily persistent but ineffectual reader of deliberately obscure texts, authored by men with intentions that they cannot admit" (*Chaucer and the Fictions of Gender*, 167). See also her discussion of Criseyde's relationship to more powerful, mythic women who appear in the poem and in Chaucer's allusions (159ff).

21. See Huygens, *Accessus as Auctores*, 31; on scholastic reception of the *Heroides*, see J. B. Allen, *Ethical Poetic*, 10–27.

22. Paris knows this, and knows that Helen has been stolen before, using it to his advantage in seducing her, promising that his love will be stronger and more enduring than Theseus's: "That he took you, I praise, but I marvel that he ever could have returned you" [Quod rapuit, laudo; miror, quod reddidit umquam] (see *Heroides* XVII, 149–64).

23. See *Heroides* XVII, 13ff.; 39–40; 143–44. Arn, "Three Ovidian Women," 4–6, adds also that Criseyde's fear of the Greeks (II, 124) recalls Helen's fear of the Trojans (XVII, 227–28).

24. *Filostrato* II, 121–22; II, 76.

25. See Arn, "Three Ovidian Women," 6.

26. "[Helen] more amantis loquitur quia modo vult modo non vult" (Hexter, *Ovid and Medieval Schooling*, 200).

27. See the commentaries edited by Huygens, *Accessus ad Auctores*, 29–33.

28. Criseyde omits one conspicuous feature of Helen's letter—her teasing Paris: "Can you hope that I will be faithful, and not anxious to follow your example?" [Tu quoque, qui poteris fore me sperare fidelem, / et non exemplis anxius esse tuis?] (*Heroides* XVII, 213–14). Paris is killed before Helen gets the chance to make good on this taunt, and her return to Menelaus comes after "Troy and Trojan" pass out of existence.

29. See *Heroides* XVII, 75–90; and *Amores* I, iv.

Chapter 3: Change and Remedy

1. "Qui sapit, innumeris moribus aptus erit."

2. "Nec securus amet nullo riuale caueto: / non bene, si tollas proelia, duret amor." See also *Ars* III, 593–94, for the parallel.

3. Wetherbee, *Chaucer and the Poets*, 93. He also says Chaucer offers his characters "no release into the 'wish-world' of metamorphoses" (ibid.).

4. Windeatt says this passage adds deep pathos and a sense of eternal pity for the lovers ("Italian to English," 101).

5. For instance, when discussing the rape of Europa, Barkan says that the story "defines metamorphosis as an experience that breaks all previously accepted rules. Myths of magical change will be stories celebrating the unfamiliar forms of the sexual impulse, with all their terror and allure" (*Gods Made Flesh*, 13). Barkan surveys these various manifestations, offering a series of close readings of Ovid's poem. Barkan's study expands our conception of "metamorphosis" beyond the mythic and fantastic: "Magical change is always closely tied to a transforming spirit in the real world of cosmos, society, and human personality" (19).

6. Wetherbee, commenting on this allusion, also notices a number of parallels between the lovers and the personal history of Myrrha and illustrates the similarities between Pandarus and the old nurse, both of whom help young, sorrowing lovers and pledge to aid their quests (*Chaucer and the Poets*, 98–99). The tears the lovers weep together, Wetherbee concludes, are a reminder that they each "survive their betrayal," and their "very constancy in the face of betrayal argues the integrity of feeling they have in common" (100). Wetherbee's study is sensitive to the context of the Ovidian story, but he seems unwilling to have the integrity of the lovers' union undermined and desires to see them solely as victims of Pandarus's exploitation. Accordingly, he deemphasizes Myrrha's independent will and the repetition of her crime. For the Ovidian scene, see *Metamorphoses* X, 471: "Postera nox facinus geminat, nec finis in illa est" [the next night the act was duplicated, and it did not end there]. Wilmon Brewer points out what Ovid has done here: "Tradition had recorded the idea that Myrrha repeated her offence during many later nights. Ovid had implied that the total number could have been at most nine, the period of the mother's absence; but he gave the impression that Myrrha offended repeatedly. Byblis had not been deterred by failure; Myrrha was not deterred by success" (*Ovid's Metemorphoses*, 355).

7. "Fugit aurea caelo / luna, tegunt nigrae latitantia sidera nubes, / nox caret igne suo."

8. As Ovid's comment in the *Remedia* shows, Myrrha's transformation is no liberation, but punishment. Myrrha herself clearly states, "Merui nec triste recuso / supplicium" [I do not refuse the dire punishment I have deserved] (*Metamorphoses* X, 484–85).

9. Fyler states that clustered references to Dante, Virgil, Boccaccio, and Ovid, in that they are "complicated and pointing to several texts, are suited to the increasingly claustrophobic atmosphere of Book 4. As the Trojan war becomes hemmed in

by its approaching doom, so Chaucer's narrative comes to seem more and more book-determined" ("Auctorites and Allusion," 83).

10. Perhaps only the *Cleanness* poet's celebration of heterosexual sex can begin to match Chaucer's description of the lovers' mutual joy.

11. Hansen discusses this mythic reference in *Chaucer and the Fictions of Gender,* 157ff.

12. Many of these allusions have been studied, as scholars have begun to understand the force of these additions to the *Filostrato.* See Wetherbee, *Chaucer and the Poets;* Minnis, *Chaucer and Pagan Antiquity;* Windeatt, "Italian to English"; and Fyler, *Chaucer and Ovid.* McCall explores the many uses of classical, but not necessarily Ovidian, allusion and reference to characters, gods, furies and muses. Some references, he argues, develop the theme of love's suffering as "a psychological and moral hell" as part of a contrast to "another cluster of joyous mythic allusions which suggest that earthly love is like paradise" (*Chaucer among the Gods,* 30).

13. Ghisalberti, "Medieval Biographies of Ovid," 45.

14. See the *Consolation* II, Prose viii, and *Roman de la Rose,* ll. 4837ff.

15. See *Filostrato* IV, 14.

16. See Ghisalberti, "Medieval Biographies of Ovid," 40nn 1–2, and appendixes D and E. A characteristic explanation is found in appendix D: "Librum de Arte Amatoria composuit in quo quam plurimos contraxit in errorem per amoris varia documenta" [{Ovid} composed the book concerning the art of love, in which he drew many into error through the various documents of love]. And so, the commentary continues, "compelled by this cause, Ovid undertook the task of writing this work so as to provide them a remedy."

17. See *PL* 184, 381a.

18. At *Troilus* I, 561, the narrator tells us Pandarus speaks just "for the nones," but does not attack his words as "unthrift."

19. Hollander, *Boccaccio's Two Venuses,* discusses how Boccaccio's narrator—not Boccaccio himself—never really betrays the romantic, erotic aspirations of his hero: "Our 'author' will not give over *his* religion of love merely because it ends bad for Troilo. He wants to have his cake and eat it too. That this view is Boccaccio's own is a notion which, for all its currency, seems dubious" (51). Hollander speculates that "in reading Boccaccio's text, Chaucer may have well believed that Boccaccio, while having told an edifying story, had mistakenly sided with the wrong forces" (52). See also James Dean's more recent discussion of the endings of the poems: "Chaucer alters the force and tenor of Boccaccio's rhetoric of closure to emphasize his own concern: the world's mutability rather than Criseyde's or women's ethical or spiritual culpabilities" ("Chaucer's *Troilus,*" 175).

20. See *Metamorphoses* I, 187ff., where Jove pledges in the high style to destroy creation.

21. Nolan comments on Troilus's persistent allegiance to "trouthe": "To the very end of Chaucer's *litel book* . . . Troilus remains true to his faith in *trouthe* and love,

though he also knows from experience that he has misplaced his trust in loving and believing Criseyde" (*Chaucer and the Roman Antique*, 227).

22. The phrase, by no means unique to Chaucer, was still common in Shakespeare's day—for example, Iago's "there's no remedy" (*Othello* I, i, 35). However, the preponderance of allusions to the *Remedia* here in Book V suggests that Chaucer may be playing with the title of Ovid's poem. Hoffman, "The Wife of Bath as a Student of Ovid," 287–88, argues that the phrase "remedies of love" in the Wife's portrait in the *General Prologue* (I, 475), refers directly to Ovid's *Remedia Amoris*.

23. On Pandarus's reaction to Criseyde's final behavior in the poem, see Dinshaw, *Chaucer's Sexual Poetics*, 62ff. She argues that Pandarus understands Criseyde's "slydinge" and, unlike Troilus, does not read her behavior "like a man," or rather that when he does read her like a man, that is, totalizes her and condemns her as a dangerous and evil "female," he is only paying lip service to Troilus.

24. See Vance, *Mervelous Signals*, 301ff., on Diomede and the problem of rhetoric. Vance does not discuss Ovid.

25. Andreas Capellanus (*De Amore*, Book I) relates *amo* to *hamo*.

26. It is interesting to compare what I am calling Ovidian to what Dinshaw identifies as the feminine, for they both are rejected in the poem as the narrator summons authoritative doctrine to finally harness chaotic experience. The male characters in the poem, including the narrator, says Dinshaw, "invoke structures of authority in order to order the disorder" (*Chaucer's Sexual Poetics*, 51). This disorder, she argues, is associated with the feminine. To read like a man is to "constrain, control, or outright eliminate the feminine—carnal love, the letter of the text—in order to provide a single, solid, univalent meaning firmly fixed in a hierarchical moral structure." It is to constitute the feminine as "disruptive Other, constraining and finally turning away from it" (ibid.).

27. See Hexter, *Ovid and Medieval Schooling*, 83ff., on the availability of the *Tristia* throughout the Middle Ages; he cites a series of commentaries including that of Petrarch.

28. See Ghisalberti, "Medieval Biographies of Ovid," esp. 26–45.

29. In discussing the issue, Hollis rightly assesses the degree of realism we should expect from the *Ars*. He says that to attack Ovid's claims of targeting an exclusively courtesan audience (*hetaerae*) and say that married women still might learn from the instruction "takes the *Ars* too seriously. It was not really intended as a practical guide to ensnaring the opposite sex, any more than Virgil intended his *Georgics* to be a practical handbook of farming." Hollis explains that the work's didactic form was "something of a facade" and that the content itself derives from the Greek epigram and the Roman love elegy. "So on two counts the *Ars* had only a tenuous and intermittent connection with real life. Ovid makes both these points in *Tristia* II, but Augustus either failed to understand, or, more probably, pretended not to understand" ("The *Ars* and the *Remedia*," 85). For the story of Ovid's banishment, see Dickinson, "The *Tristia*"; and see Wilkinson, *Ovid Recalled*, 285ff.

30. Wack points out that the thirteenth-century William of Saliceto, in the context of examining travel as a cure for lovesickness, characterizes love for one's homeland, like love for a woman, as a type of *amor heros*. While seeking a cure for their love obsession, Wack explains, "patients languish for their countries and the only cure is to return" (*Lovesickness*, 103).

31. Dillon, *A Chaucer Dictionary*, 171, cross-references these passages.

32. See also Hexter, *Ovid and Medieval Schooling*, 96n55.

33. See Dickinson, "The *Tristia*": "At the time of his banishment he was the most popular living poet in Rome, a public figure" (55).

34. See *Tristia* I, i, 117–22.

35. See also *Troilus* I, 416; III, 910, 1291.

36. McCall discusses the intensification of references to Troy's fall, including the death of Hector, military setbacks for the Trojans, the eventual treachery of Antenor (not mentioned by Boccaccio), and the predicted massacre of the Trojan people (*Chaucer among the Gods*, 98ff.).

37. Ovid also glosses his own experience with allusions to the *Heroides*. Wilkinson hears in the powerful words of Ovid's wife, "I will be but a small burden on the ship of exile" [Accedam profugae sarcina parva rati] (I, iii, 84), an echo of Briseis's lament to Achilles at *Heroides* III, 68 (Wilkinson, *Ovid Recalled*, 314–15). The central tragic event in Chaucer's poem and in Ovid's biography is separation: Criseyde, a political commodity, must leave Troilus and her homeland, and Ovid, a political victim, must leave his beloved wife and Rome. He thus dedicates some very moving passages of the *Tristia* to the horrors and pathos of their separation.

38. In his edition of the *Tristia*, Owen (191–93) argues that Ovid is here referring not to the *Ars* but to the *Amores*. But since Ovid is discussing what he should not have written, the reference seems to be general enough to include his collected love poetry. So Chaucer could have seen this as meaning the *Ars Amatoria*, which is the focus of Ovid's reflection at this point in the text.

39. *MED* 3, pt. 2, *feinen*, sect. 5d. Elsewhere Chaucer uses "feyned" in this neutral sense—*General Prologue*, l. 736; *Legend of Good Women*, Prologue (2), l. 327; *House of Fame*, l. 1478.

40. "Sic igitur carmen, recte si mente legatur / constabit nulli posse nocere meum" (*Tristia* II, 275–76).

41. Owen argues that Ovid admits the "moral" error of his poetry but not the illegality; Owen (p. 12) cites *Tristia* II, 243, 315; and III, ii, 5. However, as Ovid's defense indicates, the immorality must come from the reader who refuses to read with an "upright mind." The work itself, in that it is art and not life, cannot corrupt. At *Tristia* II, 348–49, Ovid offers another refutation.

42. See *Ars* II, 9; *Remedia*, 41ff. The commentary tradition often refers to Ovid's audience as *iuvenes;* see Huygens, *Accessus ad Auctores*, 33; and Ghisalberti, "Medieval Biographies of Ovid," 45, appendix C.

43. See the full passage at *Remedia*, ll. 315 ff., esp. ll. 347ff. On contemplating the lover's flaws, see ll. 411–18. Evidently the lovers' physical separation prevents

Pandarus from making any of these suggestions. On actual medieval remedies for lovesickness, some going back to Ovid, see Wack, *Lovesickness, passim.*

Chapter 4: New Armor for the Amazons

1. "Quod sumus, est crimen, si crimen sit, quod amamus / Qui dedit esse, deus prestat amare michi" (Hilbert, ed., *Baldricus Burgulianus Carmina*, no. 97, ll. 55–56.

2. Critical discourse on the Wife has always been vital, and her relations to Ovid have by no means been neglected. Her debt to Dipsas, for instance, is noted by Robertson, who links the two in the course of framing his famous definition of the Wife as "a literary personification of rampant 'femininity'" (*A Preface to Chaucer,* 321). These connections were most firmly made by Richard Hoffman, who sees the Wife's use of Ovidian doctrine from the *Ars* as powerful evidence of her carnality. Concerning her use of Ovid's comparison between the vagina and a light-giving lantern, Hoffman concludes: "The Wife's defense of adultery on the grounds that her 'lantern' will not be diminished . . . illustrates her lecherous and literal-minded devotion to the precepts of the *Ars Amatoria.*" The Wife's "carnal appreciation of the Ovidian image accords well with her reliance upon the letter of the Old Law rather than the spirit of the New" (*Ovid,* 129, 130). Beyond this, unfortunately, the work done on Ovid's "arts of love" and the Wife of Bath is rather sparse. Part of the reason for this neglect is that when critics refer to the Wife's Ovidianism, they are usually discussing, not her role as doctor of love, but her mistelling of Ovid's tale of Midas. For example, see Patterson, "'For the Wyves Love of Bath,'" who surveys several critical views of the Wife's Ovidian narrative.

3. She is the only character, save Chaucer, actually referred to in the Tales as an authority. See the *Merchant's Tale* IV, 1685ff., where her text has become codified as a handbook on love.

4. On the issue of female power in medieval texts, see Sheila Fisher and Janet E. Haley, *Seeking the Woman,* who rightly point out, in part quoting Marshall Leicester, that "there is no Wife of Bath, no 'she' no 'her,'" for characters like the Wife and Milton's Eve "do not refer to real women" (5). On the issue of the Wife's referentiality, see Leicester, "Of a Fire in the Dark"; and Hansen, *Chaucer and the Fictions of Gender* and "The Wife of Bath." For a more "referential" reading see Amsler, who argues that the Wife's *Prologue* offers a "bourgeois, urban critique of woman's sexual, textual, and political economy in the fourteenth century" ("The Wife of Bath," 68).

5. On the Wife and La Vieille, see Muscatine, *Chaucer and the French Tradition,* 204ff. P. M. Kean, who, like Muscatine, does not address Ovid, offers a detailed study of the Wife, La Vieille, and female dominance (*Chaucer and the Making of English Poetry,* 148ff.). Patterson, "'For the Wyves Love of Bath,'" offers an elaborate comparison, tracing their respective arts of sexual "delay" and even charting and diagraming their rhetorical rhythms.

6. In discussing marriage relations in several of the Tales, Kean cites this passage as a locus classicus on the issue of dominance, but she does not link it to Ovid or apply it directly to the Wife and her husbands. See Kean, *Chaucer and the Making of English Poetry*, 140–42.

7. The exegetical readings of the Wife by Hoffman and Robertson have been powerfully challenged as Chaucerians seek to illuminate various ideological aspects of the Wife's struggle with the texts and institutions of male authority. The new awareness of the Wife's status is evident, for example, in that Derek Pearsall, in his handbook overview of the *Prologue,* can now say casually that the Wife uses her powers "to win a measure of independence in a world that is unfair to her sex" (*The Canterbury Tales*, 73). In an important essay, "The Wife of Bath," Mary Carruthers explains the Wife's quest for *maistrie* in terms of her socioeconomic status, responsibility, and good sense, which provide her the independence and the freedom to love that "auctoritee" deny her.

A number of critics (including Sheila Delany, Peggy Knapp, and Carolyn Dinshaw) have furthered the cause of the Wife by addressing her "sexual poetics." In "Strategies of Silence," Delany redefines the question "what do women want most" as "what do men think women want most," which translates, she says, into "what do men want women to want" and "what do men want" or "what do I want." It does not matter that "in the tale the original question is both set and answered by women, because only a man could ask this question, and it can only be asked on behalf of men" (65). Knapp, examining the complex "fabric" of the Wife's discourse and identity, explores the Wife not only as "exegete and commentator" on Scripture but as "entrepreneur, feminist, temptress, and sociopath" (*Chaucer and the Social Contest*, 114). In *Chaucer's Sexual Poetics*, Dinshaw approaches an area in which the Wife has traditionally suffered attack, her glossing of texts, which is as unjustified and opportunistic as that done by men. Dinshaw is most interested in how the Wife, "as the literal text," the "devalorized feminine letter in the discourses of patriarchal hermeneutics," insists on "the positive, significant value of the carnal letter as opposed to the spiritual gloss" (120). Reading the Wife's Ovid is essential to our apprehension of these textual/sexual issues.

8. Ovid tells men to use tears (*Ars* I, 659), Ami tells Amant the same, and we also find this advice in medieval versions of the *Ars*, such as the *Key to Love*. Use a wet hand to apply fake tears, says Ovid, for "they do not always come in time"; the author of the *Key* says use an onion (see Shapiro, ed. and trans., *Comedy of Eros*, 35–36).

9. There is no specific study of Ovid and the antifeminist tradition. Wilson and Makowski, *Wykked Wyves*, make occasional references to the debt owed Ovid by various scholastic writers, such as Andreas and Walter Map, who draw from Ovidian poems in the course of their larger projects. Manuscript evidence suggests that Ovid did appear in collections like Jankyn's. British Lib. Add. MS 34749, for example, contains the tracts of Map and of Theophrastus, along with part of the *Ars Amatoria.* Pratt (who unfortunately gives no bibliographic details) testifies to Ovid's appear-

ance in such collections in "Jankyn's Book of Wikked Wives"; his is the best, though limited, study of the topic.

10. For an excellent survey of Roman legislation concerning marriage and sexual relations, see Brundage, *Law, Sex, and Christian Society*, 22. Brundage does not discuss Ovid but does examine the Lex Julia de adulteriis of 18 B.C., providing a clear context in which to see Ovid's supposedly corruptive influence.

11. See Huygens, *Accessus ad Auctores*, 35. The text is an *accessus* to the *Ex Ponto*.

12. *Ars* I, 31ff., and *Ars* III, 57–58, contain these audience specifications.

13. Wilkinson, *Ovid Recalled*, 121.

14. As Brundage notes, "Roman marriage, at least among the upper classes, was concerned with property, politics, and power. . . . *Paterfamiliae* (male heads of households) had intercourse with their wives in order to produce heirs for their property who would continue the existence of their families" (*Law, Sex, and Christian Society*, 22). According to the Lex Julia, then, "upper-class women were forbidden to have sexual intercourse with anyone at all, save for their husbands" (30).

15. Medieval commentaries on the *Remedia*, working from the opening of the text itself, repeat that youths were suicidal or overwhelmed by passion. See Ghisalberti, "Medieval Biographies of Ovid," 45, appendix D.

16. "Sed, quaecumque uiris, uobis quoque dicta, puella, / credite: diuersis partibus arma damus" (ll. 49–50).

17. In Ovid's letter to his stepdaughter, a young woman poet whom he calls Perilla (*Tristia* III, vii), we find a sensitivity, encouragement, respect, and recognition for the woman artist whom he compares to Sappho.

18. Chapter references are to the translation by Earl Jeffrey Richards. For the French, see the edition done by Maureen Curnow, 647–49.

19. See Christine de Pizan, "Le Livre de la Cité de Dames," ed. Curnow, 926ff., esp. 928–29.

20. See Pratt, "Jankyn's Book of Wikked Wives"; and the annotations in the *Riverside Chaucer*, ed. Benson (871), for fuller descriptions of the contents of Jankyn's book. Here I have identified the three major works of the tradition that figure most significantly in the Wife's *Prologue*. On the Wife's play with authority, see Leicester, *The Disenchanted Self*, 114–39. Dinshaw notes that the gynecological treatises attributed to the woman Trotula (mentioned as part of Jankyn's book) were actually written by men, which testifies to the "correlation between the masculine silencing of women's writing . . . and the masculine control of their bodies" (*Chaucer's Sexual Poetics*, 20).

21. It is sometimes difficult to specify medieval sources, especially if stories are included in both the *Metamorphoses* and the love poems. For example, when Walter Map discusses the modesty of Penelope and the Sabine women and the vice of Scylla and Myrrha, he may be working from the *Ars Amatoria* or from the "book of bodies changed." See *De Nugis Curialium*, 295. The *Ars* fits well into Jankyn's book because it focuses on "female lust" and offers examples, some, such as the story of Pasiphaë, recounted in greater detail than in the *Metamorphoses*.

22. Jerome, *Epistola Adversus Jovinianum* 1, 48, quoted in *Riverside Chaucer*, 872. The editors indicate that quoted Latin glosses are taken from "the Ellesmere and related manuscripts" (865). See Silvia, "Glosses on the *Canterbury Tales*."

23. For a lively, recent discussion of the Wife's struggles with texts, authority, and "glossing," see Hanning, "'I Shal Finde It in a Mener Glose,'" who explores glossing as a "metaphor for all kinds of language manipulation, even what might be called textual harassment" (27).

24. Hélène Cixous, "The Laugh of the Medusa," 284. In saying that the Wife is both text and body I mean to indicate that she is both a compilation of scholastic antifeminist features and an expressive figure aware of her distinctly female sexuality as she pursues her own sexual politics. Dinshaw explores the medieval metaphorical relations between the physical body and the "body" of a text, arguing that in the Wife's assertion of the carnal, she depicts herself as "the truth of the text." Dinshaw combines various medieval interpretive theories to explore the Wife's assertion of the bodily as it stands in opposition to the Pauline interpretive model that would "discard the female when the male spirit has been uncovered." See *Chaucer's Sexual Poetics*, 113–31.

25. The *Riverside Chaucer* edits out Robinson's correct citation of *Ars* III, giving the impression that the Wife is just manipulating proverbs.

26. Bryan and Dempster, eds., *Sources and Analogues*, 217.

27. Ibid., 211.

28. See *Riverside Chaucer*, 869. This glosse cannot be taken as an "authoritative, historical" interpretation of Chaucer's meaning; rather, it is accidental evidence of what the Wife is up against.

29. See Huygens, *Accessus ad Auctores*, 33. This comment is to be distinguished from the common evaluation of *Ars* II as a book about how to *retain* the woman who has been sought and seduced, for the schoolmaster here is clearly referring to the guide to the women themselves, *Ars* III.

30. Deschamps, *Miroir*, rubric to chapter XVIII. Deschamps at this point discusses the dangers of allowing a woman to venture about freely, particularly at church, where she may flirt with other men. See *Miroir* XLIII, ll. 4102ff.

31. Christine de Pizan warns women against exercising this type of freedom: "Neither should she use pilgrimages as an excuse to get away from town in order to go somewhere to play about or kick up her heels in some merry company. This is merely sin and wickedness in whoever does it, for it is offensive to God and a sad shame" (*Treasure*, 152). The Wife, who says quite explicitly that she seeks to "pleye" in the company of "lusty folk," is thus in many ways alone in her assertion of freedom if even a soul mate like Christine, the author of stories of great women and a combatant in the war with male authority, issues restrictions.

32. Also quoted in Bryan and Dempster, eds., *Sources and Analogues*, 220.

33. See *Amores* III, viii, 1–4, 9–10.

34. *Roman*, 8355ff.; and compare *Amores* III, viii, 39–40.

35. See *Roman*, ll. 7231ff., and Langlois's notes for the many Ovidian borrowings in Ami's discourse—including the famous advice to brush dust from your lover's dress. If there is no dust, "brush off what's not there."

36. "Car adès vient il meauz, beau maistre, / Deceveir que deceüz estre; / Meïsmement en cete guerre, / Quant le meien n'i sevent querre."

37. See Leicester, *The Disenchanted Self*, 114ff, where the author discusses the assumed authority of the antifeminist texts.

38. On the antifeminist textual tradition, particularly the uses and abuses it was put to, see Wilson and Makowski, *Wykked Wyves*, 1–11.

39. Dinshaw, *Chaucer's Sexual Poetics*, gives a convenient survey of this medieval reading of "woman" and cites scriptural commentaries on Genesis. See her introduction and its notes. On early patristic views of women (esp. Origen and Tertullian), see Brundage, *Law, Sex, and Christian Society*, 64ff.; on views from the High Middle Ages, including comments by Nicholas of Lyra, Aquinas, and Hortiensis, ibid., 425ff. On medieval conceptions of women's nature, see Bloch, "Early Christianity and the Estheticization of Gender," in his *Medieval Misogyny*, 37–63.

40. Later, from exile, Ovid will give his "straight" evaluation of marriage: "wives" should respect and obey husbands according to right and law. Brundage notes that "the amused tone of Roman authors faded . . . when they talked about marriage" (*Law, Sex, and Christian Society*, 22).

41. La Vieille not only balances Ovid's call for men to deceive women but combats the generalized notion that the *Ars Amatoria* is all about the evils of women. Even 200 years later, Christine de Pizan lamented in the *Book of the City of Ladies* that Ovid wrote that women were deceptive and false, expressing no awareness, strangely, that Ovid was a double agent and later armed the Amazons. It is unclear why Christine does not mention the third book; she was likely responding to the generalized reputation of the *Ars Amatoria* as an antifeminist text. Perhaps our best evidence for this reputation is its inclusion in Jankyn's book. Lucia Rosa mentions a copy of Arnulf's commentary on the *Ars* that stops somewhere in Book II for no apparent reason (see Rosa, "Su alcuni commenti inedite," 202), indicating perhaps that the neglect of Book III was part of actual practice. As we have seen, *Ars* III was glossed as ethics, focusing on the cosmetic, not the combative, strategy.

42. *Ars* II similarly advises women to accumulate, in the section on the Golden Age (discussed above), and also reports that without gold, Homer himself is scorned.

43. *PL* 184, 381aff. See also Huygens, *Accessus as Auctores*, 17–18. I have consulted the French translation in Jean Dechanét, *Oeuvres Choisie de Guillaume de St. Thierry*, 151–73. See also Minnis's mention of the passage (*Medieval Theory of Authorship*, 51); and Leclercq's translation and discussion in *Monks and Love in Twelfth-Century France*, 66–69.

44. Vance, surveying some of the relations between language and social order, quotes Saint Bernard and also John of Garland's assessment that "in death's eternal kingdom Woman is enthroned forever; from her mouth flows gall that is taken for

nectar and kills [*necat*] body and soul" (Vance, *Mervelous Signals,* 259). The image is strikingly similar to the description in the *Antiovidianus* of the form/content rift in Ovid that creates, among other paradoxes, gall/honey [fel mel] (Kienast, ed., l. 6).

45. "Femme est enfer qe tut receit, / Tut tens ad seif e tuit tens beit. / Femme ne set estre fel. . . . Femme ad un art plus qu deable" (*Le Blasme des Fames,* ll. 95–97, 101, in Fiero, Pfeffer, and Allain, eds., *Three Medieval Views of Women,* 127). For help with the Old French throughout this chapter, I thank Robyn Holman. Translations from the *Book of the City of Ladies* are those of Earl Jeffery Richards.

46. See Kooper, "Loving the Unequal Equal," where the author discusses the theological texts on marital affection that may be behind Ami's call for equality at *Roman,* ll. 9391–9400.

47. Although Chaucer does not name the *Roman de la Rose* or Deschamps's *Miroir* in Jankyn's book, these poems provide the Wife a pool of antifeminist doctrine to embody as well as refute. Chaucer only omits them because they do not have classical, "auctorial" status and because Chaucer at times does not like to be too explicit about his sources. Consider, for example, his refusal to mention Boccaccio as the source of the *Troilus.*

48. Pratt, "Jankyn's Book of Wikked Wives," 27.

49. "Autres, pour monstrer que ilz ont biaucoup veu / d'escriptures, se fondent sur ce qu'ilz ont trouvé en livres et dient après les autres et aleguent les autteurs" (Curnow, 643).

50. "Et leur semble que ilz ne pueent mesprendre, puisque autres ont dit en livres ce que ilz veullent dire, et come ce medire" (ibid., 646–47).

51. "Et sans que plus t'en dye, tu puez bien sçavoir que ces babuises dittes et escriptes contre les femmes furent et sont choses trouvees et dittes a voulenté et contre verité" (ibid., 818–19).

52. "Et in conclusion de tout, je determinoye que ville chose fist Dieux quant il fourma femme. . . . Adonc moy estant en ceste penssee, me sourdi une grant desplaisance et tristesce de couraige en desprisant moy meismes et tout le sexe feminin, si somme ce ce fust monstre en nature" (ibid., 619–20).

53. Priscilla Martin quotes a longer version of this passage, commenting that "Christine's *persona* has internalized the material which Jankyn uses against the Wife." Her argument is that "through Jankyn and Chaunticleer Chaucer mocks the pompous and prejudiced uses men can make of books" (13) and that "Chaucer is well aware of the effects of man-made language" (12). See pp. 231–33, for citations on reading and women. See also her discussion of the Wife (90–102).

54. "In remotissima posteritate michi faciet auctoritatem antiquitas."

55. Hanning, "'I Shal Finde It in a Maner Glose,'" toward the end of his discussion of how Alison "has been fighting books more than people" (46), concludes by emphasizing the Wife's complex and seemingly inevitable entrapment by acts of "textual harassment": "The Wife is thus an ironic representation of Chaucer's awareness of how, by imposing identity on others by means of transmitted authorities, we let them choose only between conforming to stereotypes and being attacked—and

in the latter case, conforming to counterstereotypes" (49). Hansen has argued that the Wife represents "not the full and remarkable presence we have normally invested her with, but a dramatic and important instance of women's silence and suppression in history and in language" ("The Wife of Bath," 400). "The Wife," she says, "turns out to be a reflection of 'categorizing principles' rather than a speaking subject" (413) and "ineffectively and only superficially rebels against the patriarchal authority that has produced her" (407). See also Hansen's longer discussion of the Wife, in *Chaucer and the Fictions of Gender,* 26–57.

56. Patterson, "'For the Wyves Love of Bath,'" is right that the retelling involves the "self-gratification" of antifeminism, but I do not agree with his convoluted argument about the Wife's rhetorical art of "delay," which intentionally lures the male audience away from the "full story." There is a parallel, Patterson says, between Midas (a bad, carnal listener who prefers the song of Pan to Apollo), and the male antifeminist audience of the Wife's *Tale*—both neglect the reading that leads to "self-knowledge" (658).

57. The others thus have more tangible "self-interest" than the Old Hag of the Wife's *Tale.* See Bryan and Dempster, eds., *Sources and Analogues,* 223ff.

58. Wetherbee, *Chaucer and the Poets,* 93.

59. We may even see the rape as an extreme type of patristic "glossing." Dinshaw, *Chaucer's Sexual Poetics,* 127ff.

60. Cixous, "The Laugh of the Medusa," 284.

Chapter 5: Exile and Retraction

1. On the *Retraction,* see Tatlock, "The Epilogue"; Sayce, "Chaucer's 'Retractions'"; J. D. Gordon, "Chaucer's Retraction"; and Wurtle, "Penitence."

2. See *Ex Ponto* III, iii, esp. 29–46.

3. "The lover is oft aware of his own ruin yet clings to it, pursuing that which sustains his own fault. I also find pleasure in my books though they have injured me, and I love the very weapon that made my wounds" (*Tristia* IV, i, 33–36).

4. See Nagle, "The Poetics of Exile."

5. See Owen, ed., *Tristia* II, 1–47. See Williams, *Change and Decline;* Hollerman, "Ovid and Politics"; Rogers, "Emperor's Displeasure"; Goold, "Cause of Ovid's Exile"; Thibault, *Mystery of Ovid's Exile;* and Syme, *History in Ovid.*

6. "Crede mihi, distant mores a carmine nostro / (vita veracunda est, Musa iocosa mea)."

7. See also *Ars* I, 31–34; and Hollis, "The *Ars* and *Remedia,*" 84ff.

8. On the banning of Ovid's poems, see *Tristia* III, i, 59–82; and xiv, 5–18.

9. "Posse nocere animis carminis omne genus. / non tamen idcirco crimen liber omnis habebit."

10. On Homer, see *Tristia* II, 371ff.; on Virgil, II, 533ff.

11. Ovid often refers to Augustus as his "god." See, for example, "Destinat in veritas quaeso contendere terras, / et mecum magno pareat aura deo" (*Tristia* I, iv, 21–22). On Ovid as old man and the "Old Man" of the *Pardoner's Tale*, see Calabrese, "Make a Mark That Shows."

12. Hilbert, ed., *Baldricus Burgulianus Carmina*, no. 200, ll. 147ff.; Wilkinson, *Ovid Recalled*, 383.

13. See, for example, Ghisalberti, "Medieval Biographies of Ovid," 45, appendix C.

14. See Hicks, ed., *Le Débat sur le Roman de la Rose;* and Baird and Kane, trans., *La Querelle de la Rose.*

15. Many elegies exhort others to intercede for him; see, for example, *Ex Ponto* I, ii, "To Maximus"; II, ii, "To Messalinus"; III, i, "To His Wife." He tells Maximus: "Tears run down our face as we beg you to beg Caesar. You can soften his heart, let him imagine the tomb in which I rot, and let him let it be less remote." Medieval commentary noted that the *intentio* is to encourage his friends to beg for his reinstatement; see Ghisalberti, "Medieval Biographies of Ovid," appendix N.

16. For examples, see, *Tristia* IV, iv, 89, where Ovid looks for the favor of a "god appeased"; and *Tristia* II, 33ff., where Ovid asks Augustus to be a benevolent merciful Jove, with whom he shares the titles, "father and ruler." In *Ex Ponto* III, vi, he tells his friends not to fear writing to him because the gods do not necessarily punish one who has received a god's wrath. Ovid gives examples of divine mercy, saying that "no god is milder than our prince, for justice tempers his strength." We have seen how the *Antiovidianus* poet criticized Ovid for reproaching the "god" who intended this punishment as a curative measure.

17. Nagle, *The Poetics of Exile*, 22–32, conveniently groups most of the relevant passages concerning exile as death.

18. See *Tristia* III, x; *Ex Ponto* III, iv, "To Rufinus."

19. As Nagle notes, concerning the generic choices Ovid faced: "Searching for an appropriate medium, he realized the similarity of the *poeta relegatus* and the *exclusus amator*, and hit upon erotic elegy as providing the closest approximation to his new situation" (*The Poetics of Exile*, 70). Nagle puts side by side a host of echoes and parallels between the erotic and the exile poems. She says, for instance, that Ovid's advice to his wife to weep theatrically when approaching Augustus would fit well in, and indeed comes from, the *Ars Amatoria.*

20. See Nagle, *The Poetics of Exile*, 79–80.

21. On poetic immortality in the Latin tradition, see Curtius, *European Literature and the Latin Middle Ages*, 476–77.

22. See Ghisalberti, "Medieval Biographies of Ovid," 14–15 and appendix N.

23. J. D. Gordon, "Chaucer's Retraction," 93–94, quoting Hutton, *Giovanni Boccaccio*, 250. Gordon tells us how Chaucer, perhaps sensitized by criticism of his "vivid, realistic, and sometimes coarse presentation of the physical aspects of love," was led to a reappraisal of his work and "renunciation of all worldly achievements." Although Chaucer "lacked a theory to sustain him" and lacked the "philosophical

independence of Petrarch," he nonetheless had a "far-sighted intimation of new and greatly enlarged possibilities for the literary artist" (93).

24. Marcus, *An Allegory of Form*, 114.

25. Marcus continues: "That Boccaccio was literally saved from the clutches of death by a storytelling friend must therefore not be read as a hyperbole, but as a credible statement of the healing power of fictions" (*An Allegory of Form*, 114). On a related issue, Olson, *Literature as Recreation*, emphasizes the role of "delight" in medieval literary theory and also traces poetry's medical and psychological effects.

26. These unproductive exercises in self-pity give us, Marcus says, "parenthetical insights into the operations of [the muses'] better sisters—the handmaidens of Lady Philosophy who adorn her teachings with verse" and whose task is "healing sick minds, rather than pandering to them" (*An Allegory of Form*, 119).

27. Crabbe, "Literary Design," 244.

28. Crabbe reads Boethius's opening soliloquy in light of the *Tristia*, tracing the common themes of old age, a death wish, and an appeal to friends who have not helped. Concerning the hierarchy, she writes that "if Socrates stands at the top, Ovid can scarcely be said to qualify at all" ("Literary Design," 245).

29. Leupin, *Barbarolexis*, 76–78.

30. "Non nullus amicus / Te revocare studet, nec reperire vales / In te, quo releueris, vt ille Boecius almus / Exul agit, summe, laudis honore nitens" (Kienast, ed., ll. 123–26).

31. Minnis, *Medieval Theory of Authorship*, 208; Patterson, "The 'Parson's Tale.'" See also J. B. Allen, "The Old Way and the Parson's Way."

32. Gascoigne, *Dictionarium theologicum*, quoted in Wurtle, "Penitence," 358. Wurtle shows that Gascoigne's despair over Chaucer does not take the *Retraction* and the *Parson's Tale* into account and renders Chaucer as a type of Judas, one who comes to regret past deeds too late. Less effective is Wurtle's textual explanation of the *Retraction*, part of which he sees as Chaucer's own interpolation of the preexisting end of the *Parson's Tale*. For the inventive diagram of the interpolation, see appendix 1.

33. Minnis offers a definitive example. Tracing Romans 15:4 in literary works, in particular Ovid's *Metamorphoses*, he looks at Chaucer's use of the doctrine in the *Nun's Priest's Tale* and concludes: "It is only fitting that Chaucer should end his tale by echoing the justification of *moralisatio* found in one of the greatest compilations of moralized *fabulae*, the *Ovide moralisé*" (*Medieval Theory of Authorship*, 206).

34. Whether or not Chaucer had read Ovid's complaint about friends suddenly silent and useless (*Ex Ponto* II, vii), he did know the limits of earthly aid—just how much, or how little, friends can help. We think immediately of Jean de Meun's Ovidian Ami and Chaucer's own incarnation of "friend" in the ever helpful but severely limited Pandarus.

35. Aers, *Chaucer*, 116.

36. Eliason, "Vanitas Vanitatum," 241. Eliason compares Langland's ambition to Ovid's, saying that "in relying on penance rather than fame to counter the effects of

vanitas, Langland commits himself to a poetic based on humility rather than pride" (253).

37. The Parson's use of 1 Timothy 1:4 and 4:7 and 2 Timothy 4 here is telling; he invokes them to justify his rejection of fable, whereas the humanist Peter Bersuire, in his commentary on Ovid's *Metamorphoses*, uses the same verses as evidence that fiction can indeed serve God's truth. See Minnis and Scott, eds., *Medieval Literary Theory*, 366. The Parson's comments here, while not a direct reference to Ovidian commentary, are undoubtedly a self-conscious statement playing off of medieval literary theory on the value of fiction and poetry to Christian readers.

38. See *Tristia* II, 547ff.

39. Howard, *Chaucer*, 499–502, discusses how the *Retraction* represents a medieval "art of dying."

Works Cited

Aers, David. *Chaucer, Langland, and the Creative Imagination.* London: Routledge, 1980.

——. *Community, Gender, and Individual Identity.* London: Routledge, 1988.

Alan of Lille. *The Plaint of Nature.* Trans. James Sheridan. Toronto: Pontifical Institute of Mediaeval Studies, 1980.

Allen, Judson Boyce. *The Ethical Poetic of the Latter Middle Ages.* Toronto: University of Toronto Press, 1982.

——. *The Friar as Critic: Literary Attitudes in the Latter Middle Ages.* Nashville: Vanderbilt University Press, 1971.

——. "The Old Way and the Parson's Way: An Ironic Reading of the Parson's Tale." *JMRS* 3 (1973): 255–71.

——, and Theresa Anne Moritz. *A Distinction of Stories.* Columbus: Ohio State University Press, 1981.

Allen, Peter. *The Art of Love: Amatory Fiction from Ovid to the Romance of the Rose.* Philadelphia: University of Pennsylvania Press, 1992.

Alton, E. H. "Ovid in the Medieval Schoolroom." *Hermathena* 94 (1960): 21–38; 95 (1961): 67–82.

Amsler, Mark. "The Wife of Bath and Women's Power." *Assays* 4 (1987): 67–83.

Andreas Capellanus. *On Love.* Trans. P. G. Walsh. London: Duckworth, 1982.

Andrew, Malcolm, and Ronald Waldron, eds. *The Poems of the Pearl Manuscript.* Berkeley and Los Angeles: University of California Press, 1978.

Arn, Mary-Jo. "Three Ovidian Women in Chaucer's Troilus: Medea, Helen, Oenone." *Chaucer Review* 15, no. 1 (1980): 1–10.

Baird, Joseph L., and John R. Kane, trans. *La Querelle de la Rose: Letters and Documents.* Chapel Hill: University of North Carolina Press, 1978.

Barkan, Leonard. *The Gods Made Flesh: Metamorphoses and the Pursuit of Paganism.* New Haven: Yale University Press, 1986.

Barney, Stephen. *Chaucer's* Troilus. Hamden, Conn.: Shoestring Press, 1980.

Battaglia, Salvatore. "La tradizione di Ovidio nel medioevo." *Filologia Romanza* 6 (1959): 185–224.

Bennett, Judith M., Elizabeth A. Clark, Jean F. O'Barr, B. Anne Vilen, and Sarah Wesphal-Wihl, eds. *Sisters and Workers in the Middle Ages.* Chicago: University of Chicago Press, 1989.

Benton, John F. *Self and Society in Medieval France: The Memoirs of Abbot Guibert of Nogent.* Toronto: University of Toronto Press, 1984.

Berchorius, Petrus. *Reductorium morale, liber XV: Ovidius moralizatus.* Ed. Jean Engels. Utrecht, 1966.

Binns, J. W. *Ovid.* London: Routledge and Kegan Paul, 1973.

Bloch, Howard R. *Medieval Misogyny and the Invention of Western Romantic Love.* Chicago: University of Chicago Press, 1991.

Boccaccio, Giovanni. *Tutte le operi di Giovanni Boccaccio.* Verona: Mondadori, 1964.

Boethius. *The Consolation of Philosophy.* Ed. and trans. Richard Green. Indianapolis: Bobbs-Merrill, 1962.

Boswell, John. *Christianity, Social Tolerance, and Homosexuality: Gay People in Western Europe from the Beginning of the Christian Era to the Fourteenth Century.* Chicago: University of Chicago Press, 1980.

Brewer, Derek. *Chaucer: The Critical Heritage.* Vol 1: 1385–1837. London: Routledge and Kegan Paul, 1978.

———. *Geoffrey Chaucer.* London: Bell, 1974.

Brewer, Wilmon. *Ovid's Metamorphoses in European Culture.* 2 vols. Boston: Marshall Jones, 1941.

Brownlee, Marina Scordilis. *The Severed Word: Ovid's Heroides and the Novela Sentimental.* Princeton: Princeton University Press, 1990.

Brundage, James. *Law, Sex, and Christian Society in Medieval Europe.* Chicago: University of Chicago Press, 1987.

Bryan, W. F., and Germaine Dempster, eds. *Sources and Analogues of Chaucer's Canterbury Tales.* Atlantic Highlands, N.J.: Humanities Press, 1941.

Calabrese, Michael A. "'Make a Mark that Shows': Orphean Song, Orphean Sexuality, and the Exile of Chaucer's Pardoner." *Viator* 24 (1993): 269–86.

———. "'Meretricious Mixtures': Gold, Dung, and the Canon's Yeoman's Prologue and Tale." *Chaucer Review* 27, no. 3 (1993): 277–92.

Carruthers, Mary. "The Wife of Bath and the Painting of Lions." *PMLA* 94 (1979): 209–22.

Chaucer, Geoffrey. *The Riverside Chaucer.* Ed. Larry Benson. Boston: Houghton Mifflin, 1987.

———. *Troilus and Criseyde: A New Edition of The Book of Troilus.* Ed. Barry Windeatt. London and New York: Longman, 1984.

Christine de Pizan. *The Book of the City of Ladies.* Trans. Earl Jeffrey Richards. New York: Persea Books, 1982.

——. "Le Livre de la Cité de Dames." Ed. Maureen Curnow. 3 vols. Ph.D. diss., Vanderbilt University, 1975.

——. *The Treasure of the City of Ladies.* Trans. Sarah Lawson. Harmondsworth: Penguin, 1985.

Cixous, Hélène. "The Laugh of the Medusa." In *The Signs Reader: Women, Gender, and Authorship,* ed. Elizabeth Abel and Emily K. Abel, pp. 279–97. Chicago and London: University of Chicago Press, 1983.

Cooper, Helen. "Chaucer and Ovid: A Question of Authority." In Martindale, 71–81.

Coulson, Frank T. "Hitherto Unedited Medieval and Renaissance Lives of Ovid (I)." *Mediaeval Studies* 49 (1987): 152–207.

Crabbe, Anna. "Literary Design in De Consolatio." In *Boethius: His Life, Thought and Influence,* ed. Margret Gibson, pp. 237–77. Oxford: Blackwell, 1981.

Curtius, Ernst Robert. *European Literature and the Latin Middle Ages.* Trans. Willard R. Trask. Princeton: Princeton University Press, 1973.

Dante. *La Divina Commedia: Inferno.* Ed. Aldo Vallone and Luigi Scoranno. Naples: Ferraro, 1985.

David, Alfred. "The Man of Law vs. Chaucer: A Case in Poetics." *PMLA* 82 (1967): 217–25.

Dean, James. "Chaucer's Troilus, Boccaccio's Filostrato, and the Poetics of Closure." *Philological Quarterly* 64 (Spring 1985): 175–84.

Dean, Nancy. "Chaucer's Complaint: A Genre Descended from the Heroides." *CL* 19 (1967): 1–27.

Dechanét, Jean. *Oeuvres Choisie de Guillaume de St. Thierry.* Paris: Aubier, 1944.

Delany, Sheila. "Strategies of Silence in the Wife of Bath's Recital." *Exemplaria* 2, no. 1 (1990): 49–69.

Deschamps, Eustache. *Oeuvres Complètes.* Vol. 9. Paris: Librairie de Firmin Didot et cie, 1878–1903.

Dickinson, R.J. "The Tristia: Poetry in Exile." In Binns, 154–90.

Dillon, Bert. *A Chaucer Dictionary: Proper Names and Allusions.* Boston: G. K. Hall, 1974.

Dinshaw, Carolyn. *Chaucer's Sexual Poetics.* Madison: University of Wisconsin Press, 1989.

Durling, Robert. *The Figure of the Poet in Renaissance Epic.* Cambridge, Mass.: Harvard University Press, 1965.

Economou, George D., ed. *Geoffrey Chaucer.* New York: McGraw-Hill, 1975.

Eliason, Eric Jon. "Vanitas Vanitatum: Piers Plowman, Eclesiastes, and Contempt of the World." Ph.D. diss., University of Virginia, 1989.

Fiero, Gloria, Wendy Pfeffer, and Mathé Allain, eds. *Three Medieval Views of Women.* New Haven: Yale University Press, 1990.

Fisher, Sheila, and Janet E. Haley. *Seeking the Woman in Late Medieval and Renaissance Writings.* Knoxville: University of Tennessee Press, 1989.

Fleming, John V. *Classical Imitation and Interpretation in Chaucer's "Troilus and Criseyde."* Lincoln: University of Nebraska Press, 1990.

Foucault, Michel. *The Foucault Reader.* Ed. Paul Rabinow. New York: Pantheon, 1984.

Fyler, John M. "Auctoritee and Allusion in Troilus and Criseyde." *Res Publica Litterarum* 7 (1984): 73–92.

———. *Chaucer and Ovid.* New Haven: Yale University Press, 1979.

———. "The Fabrications of Pandarus." *Modern Language Quarterly* 41 (1980): 115–30.

Ganim, John. "Consciousness and Time in Troilus and Criseyde." In his *Style and Consciousness in Middle English Narrative,* pp. 79–102. Princeton: Princeton University Press, 1983.

Ghisalberti, Fausto. "Giovanni del Virgilio espositore delle Metamorfosi." *Il Giornale Dantesque* 34 (1933): 3–110.

———. "Medieval Biographies of Ovid." *JWCI* 9 (1946): 10–59.

Gibson, Margret, ed. *Boethius: His Life, Thought, and Influence.* Oxford: Blackwell, 1981.

Goold, G. P. "The Cause of Ovid's Exile." *Illinois Classical Studies* 8 (1983): 94–107.

Gordon, Ida. *The Double Sorrow of Troilus: A Study of Ambiguities in* Troilus and Criseyde. Oxford: Clarendon Press, 1970.

Gordon, James D. "Chaucer's Retraction: A Review of Opinion." In *Studies in Medieval Literature in Honor of Albert Croll Baugh,* ed. MacEdward Leach, pp. 81–96. Philadelphia: University of Pennsysvania Press, 1961.

Gordon, Robert Kay. *The Story of Troilus.* New York: Dutton, 1964.

Gower, John. *The English Works of John Gower.* Vol. 1. Ed. G. C. Macaulay. Early English Text Society, 1900 (Reprinted 1957).

Guillaume de Lorris and Jean de Meun. *Roman de la Rose.* Ed. Ernest Langlois. Paris: SATF, 1914–24.

———. *The Romance of the Rose.* Trans. Charles Dahlberg. Hanover, N.H., and London: University Press of New England, 1983.

Hanning, Robert W. "Chaucer's First Ovid: Metamorphoses and Poetic Tradition in the Book of the Duchess and the House of Fame." In *Chaucer and the Craft of Fiction,* ed. Leigh A. Arnathoon, pp. 121–63. Rochester, Mich.: Solaris Press, 1986.

———. "'I Shal Finde It in a Maner Glose': Versions of Textual Harassment in Medieval Literature." In *Medieval Texts and Contemporary Readers,* ed. Laurie A. Finke and Martin B. Shichtman, pp. 27–50. Ithaca and London: Cornell University Press, 1987.

Hansen, Elaine Tuttle. *Chaucer and the Fictions of Gender.* Berkeley and Los Angeles: University of California Press, 1992.

———. "The Wife of Bath and the Mark of Adam." *Women's Studies* 15 (1988): 399–416.

Hexter, Ralph J. *Ovid and Medieval Schooling.* Munich: Bei der Arbeo-Gesellschaft, 1986.

Hicks, Eric, ed. *Le Débat sur le Roman de la Rose.* Paris: Champion, 1977.

Hilbert, Karlheinz, ed. *Baldricus Burgulianus Carmina.* Editiones Heidelbergenses, 1979.

Hoffman, Richard, L. *Ovid and the Canterbury Tales.* Oxford: Oxford University Press, 1966.

———. "The Wife of Bath as Student of Ovid." *NQ* 209 (1964): 49–50.

Hollander, Robert. *Boccaccio's Two Venuses.* New York: Columbia University Press, 1977.

Hollerman, A. W. J. "Ovid and Politics." *Historia* 20 (1971): 458–66.

Hollis, A. J. "The Ars Amatoria and Remedia Amoris." In Binns, 84–115.

Howard, Donald. *Chaucer: His Life, His Works, His World.* New York: Dutton, 1987.

———. *The Idea of the Canterbury Tales.* Berkeley and Los Angeles: University of California Press, 1976.

Hutton, Edward. *Giovanni Boccaccio: A Bibliographical Study.* London, 1910.

Huygens, R. B. C. *Accessus ad Auctores, Bernard d'Utrect, Conrad d'Hirsau, "Dialogus Super Auctores."* Leiden, 1970.

Jacobson, Howard. *Ovid's Heroides.* Princeton: Princeton University Press, 1974.

Jacoff, Rachel, and Jeffrey T. Schnapp, eds. *The Poetry of Allusion: Virgil and Ovid in Dante's "Commedia."* Stanford: Stanford University Press, 1991.

Jacquart, Danielle, and Claud Thomasset. *Sexuality and Medicine in the Middle Ages.* Trans. Matthew Adamson. Princeton: Princeton University Press, 1988.

Kean, P. M. *Chaucer and the Making of English Poetry.* Vol. 2. London: Routledge and Kegan Paul, 1972.

Kienast, K., ed. Antiovidianus. In *Aus Petrarcas ältesten deutschen Schülerkreisen: Vom Mittelalter zur Reformation,* ed. K. Burdach, vol. 4, pp. 81–111. Berlin, 1929.

Knapp, Peggy. *Chaucer and the Social Contest.* New York: Routledge, 1990.

Kolve, V. A. *Chaucer and the Imagery of Narrative.* Stanford: Stanford University Press, 1984.

Kooper, Erik. "Loving the Unequal Equal: Medieval Theologians and Marital Affection." In *The Olde Daunce: Love, Friendship, Sex and Marriage in the Medieval World,* ed. Robert R. Edwards and Stephen Spector, pp. 44–56. Albany: State University of New York Press, 1989.

Lanham, Richard. *The Motives of Eloquence: Literary Rhetoric in the Renaissance.* New Haven: Yale University Press, 1976.

Leclercq, Jean. *The Love of Learning and the Desire for God.* New York: Fordham University Press, 1961.

———. *Monks and Love in Twelfth-Century France.* Oxford: Clarendon Press, 1979.

Leicester, Marshall H. *The Disenchanted Self: Representing the Subject in the Canterbury Tales.* Berkeley and Los Angeles: University of California Press, 1990.

———. "Of a Fire in the Dark: Public and Private Feminism in the Wife of Bath's Tale." *Women's Studies* 11 (1984): 157–78.

———. "Ovid Enclosed: The God of Love as Magister Amoris in the Roman de la Rose of Guillaume de Lorris." *Res Publica Litterarum* 7 (1984): 98–129.

Leupin, Alexandre. *Barbarolexis: Medieval Writing and Sexuality.* Cambridge, Mass.:

Harvard University Press, 1989.

Lewis, C. S. "What Chaucer Really Did to Il Filostrato." In Schoech and Taylor, 16–33.

Lowes, J. L. "Chaucer and the Ovide moralisé." *PMLA* 33 (1918): 305–25.

Lubac, Henri de. *Exégèse médiévale: Les quatre sens de l'Ecriture.* 4 vols. Paris: Aubier, 1959–64.

Mack, Sara. *Ovid.* New Haven: Yale University Press, 1988.

Mann, Jill. *Apologies to Women.* Cambridge: Cambridge University Press, 1991.

Map, Walter. *De Nugis Curialium: Courtiers' Trifles.* Ed. and trans. M. R. James. Revised by C. N. L. Brooke and R. A. B. Mynors. Oxford: Oxford University Press, 1983.

Marcus, Millicent Joy. *An Allegory of Form: Literary Self-Consciousness in the* Decameron. Stanford French and Italian Studies, no. 18. Stanford, 1979.

Martin, Priscilla. *Chaucer's Women: Nuns, Wives, and Amazons.* Iowa City: University of Iowa Press, 1990.

Martindale, Charles, ed. *Ovid Renewed: Ovidian Influences on Literature and Art from the Middle Ages to the Twentieth Century.* New York: Cambridge University Press, 1988.

McCall, John. *Chaucer among the Gods: The Poetics of Classical Myth.* University Park and London: Pennylvania State University Press, 1979.

Miller, Robert P. *Chaucer: Sources and Backgrounds.* New York: Oxford University Press, 1977.

Minnis, A. J. *Chaucer and Pagan Antiquity.* Cambridge: D. S. Brewer; Totowa, N. J.: Rowman and Littlefield, 1982.

———. *Medieval Theory of Authorship.* Philadelphia: University of Pennsylvania Press, 1984.

———, and A. B. Scott, eds. *Medieval Literary Theory and Criticism, c. 1100–c.1375: The Commentary Tradition.* Oxford: Clarendon Press; New York: Oxford University Press, 1988.

Morris, Lynn King. *Chaucer Source and Analogue Criticism: A Cross-Referenced Guide.* New York: Garland, 1985.

Murphy, James. *Rhetoric in the Middle Ages.* Berkeley and Los Angeles: University of California Press, 1976.

Muscatine, Charles. *Chaucer and the French Tradition.* Berkeley and Los Angeles: University of California Press, 1957.

Myerowitz, Molly. *Ovid's Games of Love.* Detroit: Wayne State University Press, 1985.

Nagle, Betty Rose. *The Poetics of Exile.* Brussels: Collections Latomus, 1980.

Nolan, Barbara. *Chaucer and the Roman Antique.* Cambridge: Cambridge University Press, 1992.

Olson, Glending. *Literature as Recreation in the Middle Ages.* Ithaca: Cornell University Press, 1982.

Otis, Brooks. *Ovid as an Epic Poet.* Cambridge: Cambridge University Press, 1970.

Ovid. *Amores, Epistolae, Medicamina Faciei Femineae, Ars Amatoria, Remedia Amoris.* Ed. R. Ehwald. Leipzig: Teubner, 1907.

————. *Amores, Medicamina Faciei Femineae, Ars Amatoria, Remedia Amoris.* Ed. E. J. Kennedy. Oxford: Oxford University Press, 1961.

————. *The Erotic Poems.* Ed. Peter Green. Harmondsworth: Penguin, 1982.

————. *Metamorphoses.* Ed. W. S. Anderson. Leipzig: Teubner, 1977.

————. *Tristia II.* Ed. S. G. Owen. Oxford: Oxford University Press, 1924. Reprint, Amsterdam: A. M. Hakkert, 1967.

————. *Tristivm Libri Qvinqve Ibis Ex Ponto Libri Qvattvor Halievtica Fragmenta.* Ed. S. G. Owen. Oxford: Oxford University Press, 1915.

Patterson, Lee. "'For the Wyves Love of Bath': Feminine Rhetoric and Poetic Resolution in the Roman de la Rose and the Canterbury Tales." *Speculum* 58 (1983): 656–95.

Pearsall, Derek. *The Canterbury Tales.* London: Allen and Unwin, 1985.

Perry, Kathleen Anne. *Another Reality: Metamorphosis and the Imagination in the Poetry of Ovid, Petrarch, and Ronsard.* New York: Lang, 1990.

Pratt, Robert A. "Jankyn's Book of Wikked Wives: Medieval Antimatrimonial Propaganda in the Universities." *AnM* 3 (1962): 5–27.

Quain, Edwin A. "The Medieval Accessus ad Auctores." *Traditio* 3 (1945): 215–64.

Rand, E. K. *Ovid and His Influence.* Boston, 1925.

Robertson, D. W. *A Preface to Chaucer.* Princeton: Princeton University Press, 1962.

Rogers, Robert Samuel. "The Emperor's Displeasure and Ovid's." *Transactions and Proceedings of the American Philological Association* 97 (1966): 373–78.

Rosa, Lucia. "Due Biografie medievale di Ovidio." *La Parola del Passato* 13 (1958): 168–72.

————. "Su alcuni commenti inedite alle opere di Ovidio." *Annali della Facoltà di lettere e filosofia dell'Università di Napoli* 5 (1955): 191–231.

Rowland, Beryl. *Companion to Chaucer Studies.* New York and Oxford: Oxford University Press, 1979.

Sayce, Olive. "Chaucer's 'Retractions': The Conclusion of the Canterbury Tales and Its Place in Literary Tradition." *Medium Aevum* 40 (1971): 230–48.

Schoech, Richard, and Jerome Taylor, eds. *Chaucer Criticism.* 2 vols. Notre Dame: University of Notre Dame Press, 1960.

Shannon, Edgar F. *Chaucer and the Roman Poets.* New York: Russell and Russell, 1957.

Shapiro, N. R., ed. and trans. *The Comedy of Eros: Medieval French Guides to the Art of Love.* Urbana: University of Illinois Press, 1971.

Silvia, Daniel S. "Glosses on the Canterbury Tales from St. Jerome's Epistola Adversus Jovinianum." *Studies in Philology* 6 (1965): 28–39.

Sowell, Madison U., ed. *Dante and Ovid: Essays in Intertextuality.* Binghamton, N.Y.: Medieval and Renaissance Texts and Studies, 1991.

Speirs, John. *Chaucer the Maker.* London: Faber and Faber, 1951.

Stroh, Wilfried. *Ovid im Urteil der Nachwelt: Eine Testimoniensammlung.* Darmstadt, 1969.

Syme, R. *History in Ovid.* Oxford, 1978.

Tatlock, John S. P. "The Epilogue of Chaucer's Troilus." *MP* 18 (1920–21): 625–59.

Taylor, Paul Beekman. "Peynted Confessions: Boccaccio and Chaucer." *Comparative Literature* 34 (1982): 116–29.

Thibault, J. C. *The Mystery of Ovid's Exile*. Berkeley and Los Angeles: University of California Press, 1964.

Vance, Eugene. *Mervelous Signals: Poetics and Sign Theory in the Middle Ages*. Lincoln: University of Nebraska Press, 1986.

Wack, Mary Frances. *Lovesickness in the Middle Ages: The Viaticum and Its Commentaries*. Philadelphia: University of Pennsylvania Press, 1990.

Weissman, Hope Phyllis. "Antifeminism and Chaucer's Characterizations of Women." In *Economou*, 93–110.

Wetherbee, Winthrop. *Chaucer and the Poets: An Essay on Troilus and Criseyde*. Ithaca and London: Cornell University Press, 1984.

Wilkinson, L. P. *Ovid Recalled*. Cambridge: Cambridge University Press, 1955.

William of St. Thierry. De natura et dignitate amoris. In *Patrologia Latina*, ed. J. P. Migne, vol. 184, cols. 379–408.

Williams, Gordon. *Change and Decline: Roman Literature in the Early Empire*. Berkeley and Los Angeles: University of California Press, 1978.

Wilson, Katerina M., and Elizabeth M. Makowski. *Wykked Wyves and the Woes of Marriage*. Albany: State University of New York Press, 1990.

Windeatt, Barry. "Chaucer and the Filostrato." In *Chaucer and the Italian Trecento*, ed. Piero Boitani, pp. 163–83. Cambridge: Cambridge University Press, 1983.

———. "Italian to English in Chaucer's Troilus." *English Miscellany* 26–27 (1977–78): 79–103.

Wurtle, Douglas. "The Penitence of Geoffrey Chaucer." *Viator* 11 (1980): 335–59.

Index

Abelard, Peter, 2, 4

accessus ad auctores: and medieval biographies of
Ovid, 11–14, 72; and the ethical poetics of the
medieval reception of Ovid, 21–23, 72

Achilles, 61–62

Aeneid: and the medieval commentary tradition, 12

Aers, David, 126

Agamemnon: as exemplar in the *Remedia Amoris,*
61–62

Alan of Lille: narrator of *The Plaint of Nature*
compared to Boethius and to Ovid in his poems
of exile, 124

Allen, J. B., 134n.1, 136nn.33, 37, 137n.37,
153n.31; and Moritz on Ovid and Chaucer,
132n.7

Allen, Peter, 31, 131n.3, 133n.19, 138n.59

Alton, E. H., 3

Anchises: character in Ovid's *Metamorphoses,* 53

Andreas Capellanus, 2, 146n.9; *De Amore* as an
Ovidian art of love, 7, 137n.46

Anius: character in Ovid's *Metamorphoses,* 53

antiovidiana (medieval attacks on Ovidian love),
23–27

Antiovidianus (fourteenth–century Latin poem
against Ovid) 24–26; compared to the *accessus ad
auctores,* 25, 137n.41; on Ovid's exile, 26, 74,
124; connecting Ovid to Fall of Adam and Eve,
102–3

163